GCSE

FRENCH

Alasdair McKeane

LONGMAN REVISE GUIDES

Longman

LONGMAN REVISE GUIDES

SERIES EDITORS:
Geoff Black and Stuart Wall

TITLES AVAILABLE:
Art and Design
Biology
Business Studies
C.D.T. – Design and Realisation
Chemistry
Economics
English
English Literature
French
Geography
German
Mathematics
Physics
World History

FORTHCOMING:
British and European History
C.D.T. – Technology
Computer Studies
Commerce
Home Economics
Human Biology
Music
Office Studies and Keyboarding
Religious Studies
Science
Social and Economic History

Longman Group UK Limited,
Longman House, Burnt Mill, Harlow,
Essex CM20 2JE, England
and Associated Companies throughout the world.

© Longman Group UK Limited 1988

First published 1988

British Library Cataloguing in Publication Data

McKeane, Alasdair
   French. — (Longman GCSE revise guides).
   1. French language – For schools
   I. Title
   448

   ISBN 0–582–02506–0

Produced by The Pen and Ink Book Company,
Huntingdon, Cambridgeshire.
Set in 10/12pt Century Old Style.

Printed and bound in Great Britain at
The University Printing House, Oxford.

CONTENTS

		Editors' Preface	iv
		Acknowledgements	iv
CHAPTER	1	Types of assessment	1
	2	Examination preparation and presentation	6
	3	Vocabulary topics and settings	15
	4	Basic Speaking	67
	5	Higher Speaking	82
	6	Basic Listening	94
	7	Higher Listening	112
	8	Basic Reading	126
	9	Higher Reading	147
	10	Basic Writing	168
	11	Higher Writing	185
	12	Grammar	208

EDITORS' PREFACE

Longman GCSE Guides are written by experienced examiners and teachers, and aim to give you the best possible foundation for success in examinations and other modes of assessment. Examiners are well aware that the performance of many candidates falls well short of their true potential, and this series of books aims to remedy this, by encouraging thorough study and a full understanding of the concepts involved. The Revise Guides should be seen as course companions and study aids to be used throughout the year, not just for last minute revision.

Examiners are in no doubt that a structured approach in preparing for examinations and in presenting coursework can, together with hard work and diligent application, substantially improve performance.

The largely self-contained nature of each chapter gives the book a useful degree of flexibility. After starting with the opening general chapters on the background to the GCSE, and the syllabus coverage, all other chapters can be read selectively, in any order appropriate to the stage you have reached in your course.

We believe that this book, and the series as a whole, will help you establish a solid platform of basic knowledge and examination technique on which to build.

Geoff Black and Stuart Wall

ACKNOWLEDGEMENTS

To the Examining Groups for providing liberal quantities of advice, materials and encouragement, and permission to reproduce questions:
London and East Anglian Group for GCSE Examinations (LEAG) (East Anglian Examinations Board, London Regional Examining Board, University of London School Examinations Board)
Midland Examining Group (MEG) (East Midland Regional Examinations Board, Oxford and Cambridge Schools Examinations Board, Southern Universities' Joint Board for School Examinations, West Midlands Examinations Board, University of Cambridge Local Examinations Syndicate)
Northern Examining Association (NEA) (Associated Lancashire Schools Examining Board, Joint Matriculation Board, North Regional Examinations Board, North-West Regional Examinations Board, Yorkshire and Humberside Regional Examinations Board)
Northern Ireland Schools Examination Council (NISEC)
Southern Examining Group (SEG) (The Associated Examining Board, Oxford Delegacy of Local Examinations, Southern Regional Examinations Board, South-East Regional Examinations Board, South-Western Examinations Board)
Welsh Joint Education Committee/Cyd-Bwyllgor Addysg Cymru (WJEC)
Cambridge International Examinations (IGCSE).

To my wife Anne for research, many suggested improvements, and encouragement. To my sons John George and Andrew for their patience. To Peter Davies for thorough and civilized help and advice. To Dave Rogers for help with 'Language tasks' and IGCSE. To Jasper Kay and Geoff Black for assistance with vocabulary. To Stuart Wall for judicious encouragement.

Note: The suggested answers provided in this booklet, while in accordance with the Examining Groups' guidelines, are the author's own and are not 'official answers'. The Examining Groups are unable to enter into any correspondence concerning the suggested answers.

TYPES OF ASSESSMENT

AIMS OF GCSE FRENCH

NOVEL FEATURES OF THE GCSE

ASSESSMENT IN FRENCH

WRITING

GRADES – MINIMUM ENTRY REQUIREMENTS

GRADE DESCRIPTIONS

IGCSE

G E T T I N G   S T A R T E D

This book sets out to help you to do well as a candidate for GCSE French. It will lay out for you the precise requirements of your examination, and will provide you with the necessary tools to give your best performance. No matter which Examining Group's GCSE you are taking, you will find every chapter relevant. You can use the chapters in any order to suit your revision plan and to match your strengths and weaknesses.

After working your way through each chapter, you will have had the chance to see and try the sorts of question set by the GCSE Examining Groups and you will have read the examiner's comments on the student answers.

Buying this book indicates your desire to do well. However, to prove your keenness you must work through it conscientiously. *Bon courage, et bonne chance!*

ESSENTIAL PRINCIPLES

1 > AIMS OF GCSE FRENCH

> The main aim of the GCSE is to help you to use French effectively for purposes of practical communications

The GCSE **National Criteria** for French are a set of rules laid down by the Education Minister that all GCSE Examining Groups must follow. It lists the following seven aims.

1   To develop the ability to use French effectively for purposes of practical communication.
2   To form a sound base of the skills, language and attitudes required for further study, work and leisure.
3   To offer insights into the culture and civilization of French-speaking countries.
4   To develop an awareness of the nature of language and language learning.
5   To provide enjoyment and intellectual stimulation.
6   To encourage positive attitudes to foreign language learning and to speakers of foreign languages and a sympathetic approach to other cultures and civilizations.
7   To promote learning skills of a more general application (e.g. analysis, memorizing, drawing of inferences).

(GCSE National Criteria French)

Relax! Not all of these can be directly tested by the GCSE examination, and the first four are certainly the most important. If, at the end of your GCSE course, you can communicate effectively in French, you need have no worries about the examination.

2 > NOVEL FEATURES OF THE GCSE

> Many traditional examination exercises are *not* allowed

The introduction of the GCSE French Examination in 1988 marked the biggest change in modern languages examinations this century. Anyone who took one of the old-fashioned O Level or CSE examinations might hardly recognize it. Several exercises are banned by the National Criteria, and the following will **not** be found in any GCSE:

- summary
- précis
- dictation
- translation into French
- reading aloud
- reproduction tests
- comprehensions with answers in French*
- listening comprehensions read by your teacher

*except IGCSE French

The absence of these exercises from the examination should mean that you spend very little time doing them in class, although some teachers may still use them as teaching tools.

The principle underlying all the exercises in GCSE is that they should be **based on situations in which you might find yourself in a French-speaking country, or when contacting French speakers by letter or telephone.** This means that those who take GCSE French should find themselves able to understand and speak French at least well enough to 'get by'. Gone will be the days when people said 'I did French at school, but I can't speak it.' The intention is to provide students with the **ability to communicate in French.**

When setting and marking GCSE questions, there is a new **emphasis on success.** Students are given tasks which are well within their grasp. However, they are expected to score very highly on them at all levels of performance. So candidates who eventually gain grade F will have shown that they can perform the more straightforward tasks in the examination well. In GCSE French, **all** candidates, however brilliant, have to attempt the straightforward tasks and show their competence at these.

> The Defined Content contains all you need to know for the exam. There are no hidden surprises

As well as changing the emphasis on how students are examined, for the first time GCSE French Examining Groups have each published a **Defined Content.** This contains:

- a list of the topic areas to be covered
- a list of the tasks students should be able to perform
- a list of all the vocabulary needed for their examinations
- a list of the grammar students are expected to know

I am sure that there is no need to stress its usefulness to candidates. For the first time, GCSE French candidates (and, perhaps more importantly, their teachers and those setting the examinations) can be absolutely sure that no unforeseen vocabulary or grammar will occur in the examination. The Defined Content of the various Examining Groups have been used in preparing the Vocabulary and Grammar chapters of this *Longman Revise Guide*.

Finally, in GCSE French, unlike in O Level and CSE, there is equal weight for performance in each of the four language skills.

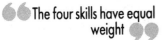The four skills have equal weight

- Speaking   25%
- Listening   25%
- Reading   25%
- Writing   25%

This will allow credit to be given to those who understand and speak French well, but find writing difficult. In some O Level syllabuses, writing accounted for 60%+ of the marks. Consequently, those who found writing hard did badly. Indeed, as the next section will show, writing is not even compulsory for GCSE. This is in line with the National Criteria's statement that GCSE French should 'attract a much greater number of candidates than now enters for GCE and CSE modern languages examinations'. The inclusion of French as a core subject in the National Curriculum is a further measure of official support for the new examination.

3 > ASSESSMENT IN FRENCH

The requirements for GCSE French are very similar for most of the examinations set by the different Examining Groups. This is because they have to fit the 'National Criteria for French', that is the rules laid down for GCSE French Examinations by the Minister of Education.

In nearly all French syllabuses, the examination counts for 100% of the marks. Unlike most GCSE subjects, there is usually **no coursework**. There are one or two exceptions to this rule, for example the MEG French (Mature) syllabus. If you **are** doing an examination with coursework, make sure you know when pieces of work are due to be handed in. It is definitely a bad idea to be late with coursework!

In French there is a part of the examination for each of the **four** language skills. So there are tests in:

- Speaking
- Listening
- Reading
- Writing

These are arranged to take place on different days.

Speaking will be conducted by your own teacher between March and May, at a time which your teacher will choose. In most cases the speaking test will be tape-recorded.

Listening comes early in the full examination period, in late May. This is so that you do not get too much out of practice in this skill, which is more difficult to revise at home.

Reading and **Writing** are examined in very late May or in June.

Most Examination Groups also run a November examination.

The tests in each of the four skills are usually divided into two. So there are in fact 8 tests:

- Basic Speaking
- Basic Listening
- Basic Reading
- Basic Writing
- Higher Speaking
- Higher Listening
- Higher Reading
- Higher Writing

The Basic tests are taken by all candidates. The Higher tests are optional. The more Higher tests you take (and, of course, do well in), the higher the maximum grade you can obtain. Check with the table below. You should consult with your teacher what he or she thinks you should enter for and act on that advice. Take especial note of the results of mock examinations. Please note that you cannot do a Higher paper in a skill without also doing the Basic paper in that same skill.

There are two Examining Groups which have slight variations to the pattern outlined above. The SEG (Southern Examining Group) calls its papers 'General Level' (= Basic) and 'Extended Level' (= Higher). The MEG (Midlands Examining Group) divides its Higher papers into Higher Part 1 and the more difficult Higher Part 2. The idea is to extend further the range of choices the candidate has. You could, for example, do only Higher Part 1 Listening if that was your probable ceiling. However, if candidates have done Higher Part 1 in a skill they would be well advised to attempt Higher Part 2, as they have nothing to lose by doing so.

4 ⟩ WRITING

 You must *choose* to do Writing to get grades A, B or C

There are **special rules about Writing** laid out in the National Criteria for French. It's important to understand these, expecially if you are aiming to gain grade A, B or C.

The first point about Writing is that it is *not compulsory*. You can gain a GCSE grade just by entering for combinations of Basic and Higher Listening, Reading and Speaking. However, if you do **not** do Writing, you cannot get a higher grade than grade D, no matter how well you did on the other papers. **So if you don't do Writing, you cannot be awarded grades A, B or C.**

To get grades A or B, you must choose *Higher* Writing

The second point is that **you cannot be awarded grade A or B if you have not done Higher Writing.** So, if you are aiming at a high grade, you **must** do Higher Writing ('Extended Level' for SEG). If you are taking MEG GCSE, you must do Higher Part 1 **and** Part 2 to be awarded grade A or B.

5 ⟩ GRADES – MINIMUM ENTRY REQUIREMENTS

Check with the table below what the **minimum** entry requirements are for the different grades of GCSE French. **Everyone** has to do the 'core' of Basic Speaking, Basic Listening and Basic Reading. After that you can choose which extra tests to add on.

Highest grade possible	*Minimum* entry required
Grade E	Core (= Basic Speaking + Basic Listening + Basic Reading)
Grade D	Core + any one other test
Grade C	Core + Basic Writing + any one other test
Grade B	Core + Basic Writing + Higher Writing + any one other test
Grade A	Core + Basic Writing + Higher Writing + any two other tests

Notes:
SEG has 'General Level' (= Basic) and 'Extended Level' (= Higher)
MEG divides Higher tests into Part 1 and Part 2. Two Part 1 tests in different skills count the same as one complete Higher test.

Remember that if you enter for **only** the minimum you will have to do very well in all those papers to get the grades shown. It's better to play safe and enter for **as many papers** as you can be reasonably expected to manage.

To summarize: GCSE French usually has 100% of the marks for the final examination. There are four skills; Listening, Reading, Speaking and Writing. Each skill is tested at two levels, Basic and Higher. Everybody has to do at least Basic Listening, Basic Speaking and Basic Reading. You can organise the rest of your entry to suit what you are good at, although the more you try, the better the potential grade. Finally, you must do at least Basic Writing to gain a grade C, and Higher Writing as well to gain a grade A or B.

6 ⟩ GRADE DESCRIPTIONS

The Examining Groups provide descriptions of performance for key grades F and C. These should provide a yardstick by which to judge your own performance. Those gaining grade G will not be as good as those awarded grade F, and those gaining grade A will clearly be better than those described under grade C. You may be somewhat surprised by the reference to 'good' levels of attainment for Grade F. However, the new emphasis on success means that such candidates have indeed performed well in straightforward tasks.

Grade F: Candidates awarded this grade will normally have shown a good level of attainment in Basic Speaking, Basic Listening and Basic Reading. Alternatively they may have shown a good level of attainment in any two Higher tests.

Grade C: Candidates awarded this grade will normally have shown

either a very high general level of competence in Basic Speaking, Basic Listening, Basic Reading and Basic Writing together with a high level of competence in one of the Higher tests;

or a good overall standard in Basic level and in two or more Higher tests.

EXAMINING GROUP	LEAG		MEG			NEA		NISEC		SEG		WJEC	
Speaking													
Time allowed (minutes)	10	20	10	12	15	5–10	10–15	10	15	10	17	10	15
Role-plays	2	3	2	3	3	2/VS	4/VS	2	2	2	3/VS	2	4
Conversation	√	√	√	√	√	√	√	√	√	√	√	√	√
Notes or Picture Stimulus				√							√		
Level	B	H	B	H1	H2	B	H	B	H	GL	EL	B	H
Listening													
Time allowed (minutes)	30	30	20	20	20	30	30	30	30	30	45	30	40
Recorded on tape	√	√	√	√	√	√	√	√	√	√	√	√	√
Questions & answers in E/W	E	E	E	E	E	E	E	E	E	E	E	E/W	E/W
Reading													
Time allowed (minutes)	30	30	25	25	25	25	40	45	40	30	30	30	40
Questions & answers in E/W	E	E	E	E	E	E	E	E	E	E	E	E/W	E/W
Writing													
Time allowed (minutes)	45	60	25	30	35	25	50	45	50	30	60	30	45
Number of words in total		200		100	150		100		200		200		240
Lists/Forms	O		C					*				*	
Messages	O		C			*C		*		*C		*	
Postcards	O		C			*C		*		*C		*	
Letters	CO	O		CO		C	C	*		C		*	C
Visuals/ Pictures		O					*C				*		CO
Narrative/ Topic/Report		O			CO		*C	*	*				CO

Key:

B	= Basic	EL	= Extended Level	C	= Compulsory
H	= Higher	E	= English	CO	= Compulsory but with an Option
H1	= Higher Part One	W	= Welsh	*	= Could appear
H2	= Higher Part Two	VS	= Visual Stimulus		
GL	= General Level	O	= Option		

Table 1.1: Grid to Show GCSE Examining Group Requirements

7 ▷ **IGCSE**

IGCSE French is not normally available to students resident in the UK unless they attend an International School. Candidates entering for the IGCSE are advised to consult their teacher regarding the differences between IGCSE French and the standard GCSE. Note, however, that the aims of the two are identical, with the skills divided into Speaking, Listening, Reading and Writing.

EXAMINATION PREPARATION AND PRESENTATION

APPROACHING THE GCSE

GETTING ORGANIZED

REVISION PLANNING

REVISION TECHNIQUES

EXAMINATION TECHNIQUES

PREPARING SPEAKING

PREPARING LISTENING

PREPARING READING

PREPARING WRITING

GETTING STARTED

This chapter is intended to point out two aspects of preparing for GCSE French. First, **study skills** enabling you to make the best possible use of your valuable time in the run-up to the GCSE examination; this will also be of general use in preparing for other subjects. Second, hints and tips to improve your performance in the four **language skills** tested in GCSE French, namely Speaking, Listening, Reading and Writing. Because performance in French is a skill, it is improved by practice. And any good musician or sporting star will confirm that the best forms of practice contain variety. *Alors, allons-y!*

ESSENTIAL PRINCIPLES

What sort of student are you? Could you improve?

The foundations of success in GCSE French are laid early in your course, not so much by your teacher as by how **you** personally approach your work. Let us compare a good student and a poor student, as seen from the teacher's point of view.

Good student	Poor student
■ Is a regular attender	■ Attends irregularly
■ Catches up with work after absence – usually without prompting	■ Makes no effort to catch up. Needs to be 'chased'
■ Always writes notes in lessons	■ Lets teacher's explanations wash over him/her. Has lost notebook and/or pen
■ Tries his/her best during pairwork	■ Chats in English during pairwork
■ Sits with a good view of board and teacher	■ Sits at the back or in corners
■ Asks when stuck	■ Gives up if stuck. Claims not to understand
■ Does homework on time	■ Does homework late, or not at all
■ Works at a regular time	■ Works when he/she feels like it
■ Presents work – rough or neat – tidily, with dates, page numbers, titles, etc	■ Work is messy
■ Writes legibly, with clear accents. Has obviously done a rough draft of homework	■ Hard to read. Accents ambiguous. Hands in first draft with altered letters, crossings-out, etc. Difficult to mark
■ Re-reads corrected homework, notes errors and resolves to act on comments and corrections	■ Never looks at anything teacher writes except the mark at the bottom of work
■ When no homework is set, finds something extra to do in French	■ When no homework set, does nothing except cheer
■ Is basically interested in most aspects of the subject	■ Only took French because there was no other option
■ Quite enjoys French	■ Hates French

The key to a successful approach is **motivation.** You know your reasons for taking GCSE French. Whatever they are, look for ways to succeed.

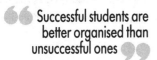

Successful students are better organised than unsuccessful ones

Observation suggests that successful students are organized. Many students fail to reach their full potential because they approach the mechanics of studying the wrong way. Here are some **practical ways** you can get yourself organized.

1 **Have set routines for work.** If you have a fixed time or times in the day or week when you do homework, then you don't have to spend time deciding when to do it. Your school, after all, has a set timetable for lessons for that very reason. Set times save you time.

2 **Have set times when you do not work.** This ensures that you get enough leisure time. 'All work and no play makes Jack a dull boy', as the proverb runs. Again, you save time on decision-making.

3 **Do assignments as they are set.** This is particularly important in French, where one piece of work often builds on the previous one, and where you need detailed, early feedback from your teacher to support your learning. By doing work immediately, you also save the time you might spend worrying about how and when to do the work. Do it NOW!

4 **Have a suitable place for study.** The ideal location is free from distractions. Aim for a table or desk free from clutter, with good lighting, and pens, pencils, paper and reference books within reach (so you don't have to keep getting up).

5 **Do a reasonable amount of study per week.** This might, perhaps, be in the range 35–45 hours weekly, including the 25–27 hours or so spent in lessons in school. (Many adults work about that number of hours.) You may, of course, work longer if you can do so effectively.

6 **Approach topics on the 'before, during and after' principle.**

- **Before** a new topic – read ahead in your textbook to prepare yourself.
- **During** the lesson – take notes or take part, as appropriate.
- **After** the lesson – go over the notes and the textbook material **as soon as possible**.

Being organized doesn't take any more time than being unorganized. In fact, it **saves time**. And most importantly, it makes you a **more efficient learner** who will certainly gain a better grade in GCSE than your unorganized fellow students.

3 > REVISION PLANNING

As has been suggested, being organized produces better results. This applies, of course, to revision as well as to normal study. Here are some tips about efficient revision.

1 **Count the weeks**. Work out how many weeks there are left before the GCSE examination. For GCSE French, the various examinations are spread over several weeks, so time the run-up to each one individually. There is little point in slaving over your Writing the day before your Speaking test, for example.

2 **Use the FREE pull-out revision planner**. This is at the back of this book. Write in the topics you wish to revise, week by week and skill by skill. Allow a week near the end for 'slippage' – time to catch up on what you have missed. Make sure you have sufficient variety, and don't be over-ambitious about what you can get done. You may need to decide what is top priority for you.

3 **Know what the examinations involve**. Check the details for each test given in this book. Knowing what to expect gives direction and urgency to your revision and prevents you wasting time on irrelevant material.

4 **Check that you can do what is required**. The Vocabulary chapter of this book lists all the tasks you are expected to be able to perform, as laid down by the Defined Content of the various Examining Groups. So there's no excuse for not making sure you can do them!

5 **Identify questions**. Although there are only a few sample and past papers available for GCSE French, the Defined Content makes it possible to work out fairly accurately the sort of question that might be asked. For example, there is a limited number of things that could be asked of a petrol-pump attendant using the vocabulary laid down in the Defined Content. If you know them, you have nothing to fear from a role-play exercise on that topic.

6 **Analyse your own performance**. If you have done a mock examination, work out where your weaknesses are and do something about them. If you are uncertain where to begin, consult your teacher who, after all, knows your abilities best. Even if you haven't done a mock examination, you can still give direction to your revision by honestly pinpointing things you don't do well.

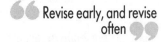 Revise early, and revise often

Directed revision pays off. **Revise early, and revise often!**

4 > REVISION TECHNIQUES

The most difficult thing about revision is overcoming boredom. By definition, you have seen the things you are revising before, so you need to find ways of compensating for the lack of novelty.

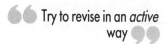 Try to revise in an *active* way

Many students revise ineffectively because they merely read through notes and chapters in the text-book and let the information wash over them. This is almost always a waste of time, certainly after the first half-hour or so. The key is to **do something**. Activity is an aid to concentration. In a skill-based subject like French, where your performance in various skills is being measured, you will improve your performance by practice. Try some or all of the following techniques.

1 **Write notes**. When reading, say, grammar rules, make yourself skeleton notes which are sufficiently detailed to jog your memory. Some students do this on small pieces of card (index cards or chopped up pieces of cereal packet) which they carry about with them and consult at odd moments. The same goes for vocabulary. Writing a word down with its gender and meaning will help to fix it in your memory. Another hint is to write down a phrase which contains the word and its gender. When reading texts, make a note of every word you had to look up. As time goes on, you will have to look up fewer and fewer.

2 **Work with a friend**. This can relieve the boredom. Pick a friend who is about the same standard as you are. Working with someone a lot better can be good for their ego, but not for yours. Similarly, working with someone a lot weaker doesn't teach you anything new. Testing each other is a good idea. Don't forget to include written testing, which is the ultimate proof of whether you know things. There is a danger of being side-tracked when working with someone else, so don't rely on this method of revision alone.

3 **Set yourself tests**. While learning, make a note of things you find hard, and test yourself later – at the end of your session, then the following day, then the following week. You have to be honest with yourself about how you get on! Keep a chart of your marks as a rough guide to progress.

4 **Tick off what you've done**. Using the pull-out revision planner, tick off the topics you have dealt with. Do NOT tick off ones you have missed out! The more you have dealt with, the better you will feel. You can also tick off the various language tasks and grammar topics in the relevant sections of this book.

5 **Set realistic targets**. Don't try to do too much in one session – you'll end up frustrated and become more and more depressed. Far better to learn, say, 10 irregular verbs and succeed than to try to learn 56 and fail miserably.

6 **Reward yourself**. If you have done a reasonable stint of revision, or done well in a test, give yourself a treat – a sweet, or a coffee break, or the chance to watch a favourite soap opera. Having something to look forward to is a great incentive.

7 **Don't go too long without a break**. 45–50 minutes is probably the longest most people can concentrate without a break – even if it's only to stretch your legs for five minutes.

8 **Give yourself variety**. Vary what you look at – revise different skills in French. Also, vary the subjects you do in any one session – three spells of 45–50 minutes on three different subjects will be more productive than a 3-hour 'slog' on one area.

9 **Don't be fooled by other students**. During the examination season, some fellow students will be loudly proclaiming either that they 'never do any revision' or that they are 'up till 2 a.m. every morning working'. Ignore them. They are being hysterical, and may well not be telling the truth anyway. What matters to you is not how much or how little revision your friends do, but how much **you** do.

Most important of all, don't kid yourself that you are working when you aren't. You can't revise at all while watching TV, chatting to friends, washing your hair or eating a meal. So don't even attempt it. Instead, use these activities to reward yourself **after** a revision session.

5 ▷ EXAMINATION TECHNIQUES

❝ Put these hints into practice ❞

The best cure for examination nerves is the knowledge that you have done all reasonable preparation. There are also various practical things you can do to make sure you can concentrate on the examination paper.

THE EVENING BEFORE AN EXAMINATION

- Put everything you need the following morning, ready packed, by the front door to eliminate last-minute panic. Include spare pens, pencils and rubbers, and a silent watch.
- At the end of the evening, do something other than work to relax you. If you can manage to take the whole evening off, that's even better.
- Go to bed at a reasonable hour so you have enough sleep.

THE MORNING BEFORE AN EXAMINATION

- Get up in good time to avoid rush and panic.
- Dress carefully, possibly even smartly (to take your mind off the examination).
- Eat breakfast so you won't be hungry during the examination.

IN THE EXAMINATION ROOM

- Be there in good time, but not **too** early.
- Sit as comfortably as possible. Use folded paper to stop your desk rocking.
- Check the number of questions you have to answer and the time available. Divide up your time and write down the 'clock times'.
- Read the questions carefully, and note the settings. In GCSE French the settings can contain vital clues to the answers.
- Do the tasks you are asked to do. This is particularly important in Writing papers, where mark schemes reward 'accomplishment of task'.
- Try to write clearly so that the examiner's task is easier.
- Pace yourself so you have enough time to answer the more difficult questions at the end of the paper in Reading and Writing. If you can't do a question early in the paper, leave it and come back to it later.
- Don't leave blanks – make a sensible guess. This applies especially to multiple-choice questions.
- Use your common sense in Listening and Reading papers. If you don't know what happened, think what the average person might do in identical circumstances.
- When you have finished, check your work **systematically**.
  — In Reading and Listening examinations, have you given enough details?
  — In Writing examinations, check verbs, genders and agreements.
- Ignore the behaviour of other candidates. Many poor candidates demonstratively sit back or go to sleep having 'finished', or even walk out early. Don't be tempted to imitate them.
- After the Speaking Test avoid panicking others by saying how terrible it was, etc. Smile sweetly and wish them good luck.
- When it's all over – celebrate moderately.

So much for general revision skills. As the GCSE Examination in French tests the four language skills separately, let us take preparing for each test in turn. They will in any case take place on several different days over a period of up to three months, so you can certainly prepare for each of the four skills in turn as they are tested. Allow for this when filling in your revision programme on your planner.

6 ▶ PREPARING SPEAKING

> If you are well prepared *Speaking* is a straightforward test

The first test you will do is Speaking. This test often worries candidates, but this really isn't necessary if you are well prepared. For one thing, the Examiner will be your own teacher, who knows what you can do and should be attempting to help you to show off your knowledge. And for another, it is possible to work out from the GCSE syllabus what is likely to come up. A quick look at the relevant chapters of this Revise Guide will give you an idea.

Let us look at some practical things you can do to improve your performance in the **Speaking** test.

1 Make sure you know what the requirements are for the Basic test, and, if you are doing it, for the Higher. If you are not sure what is involved, see the chapters on Basic Speaking and Higher Speaking.

2 Most Speaking tests will be tape-recorded. So some time beforehand, practise speaking into a cassette recorder in order to get used to the whirring noise it makes, the sight of the microphone, and the sound of your own voice on tape. Many good candidates who haven't tried this are overcome by shyness on the day and do badly.

3 Speak up. It will make a better recording and make you feel more confident.

4   For role-play type exercises, you can work out from the list of tasks given in the Vocabulary chapter what situations could be set. There are, for example, only a few things that you might want to do at a petrol station – ask for petrol, say what grade you need, perhaps ask for air, oil and water to be checked, and pay. Once you have worked out the French for that lot, you shouldn't have anything to worry about. You could do this with a friend, making up role-play questions and cards for each other to do. Over time, you could build up quite a range of these to practise. In addition, you should make sure you know the basic phrases which are useful in many situations, for example:

❝❝Know some phrases which are useful in _many_ situations. ❞❞

—Je voudrais . . .
— C'est combien?
— A quelle heure . .
— Où est . . .
— Y a-t-il . . .

5   For general conversation, you can work out again from the list of topics and settings what you are likely to be asked. Remember that you only ever have to be yourself in GCSE French – you never have to pretend to be another person. So having a few well-prepared sentences to say about, for example, your actual hobbies is a wise precaution, and can make for a good flow in a conversation, which is one of the things examiners are looking for. Prepare these topics.

— hobbies
— school
— family
— your daily routine
— your local area
— holidays and visits to French-speaking countries
— your future plans

About a couple of minutes' worth on each should be sufficient.

❝❝Use every opportunity for being tested on Speaking ❞❞

6   If your teacher offers you a practice Speaking exam on your own, be sure to take advantage of it. There is nothing quite like the experience of actually going through the Speaking test, on your own, to show you what it will be like. And, of course, your teacher will be your examiner for Speaking, so it's an especially valuable opportunity.

7   As well as practising with your teacher, you should also practice with a friend from your class. They could, for example, ask you some questions you have prepared and work a cassette recorder for you.

8   Look carefully at all role-play material in your text-book and make sure you can do it from memory.

9   Text-books also contain sets of questions about certain topics such as free time, school, etc. Make sure you can do these too, as preparation for the conversation section.

❝❝ It's hard to say too much; its easy to say too little ❞❞

10 When answering questions, practise avoid incomplete sentences or answers which are just 'oui' and 'non' or, say, the name of a British TV programme ('_Neighbours_'). Look for opportunities to say more than one sentence in reply; for example, add: 'c'est un feuilleton – c'est une émission australienne'. You are most unlikely to say too much, but it is very easy to say too little. Practising what you are going to say and how you are going to say it **beforehand** will pay dividends. Only the very best candidates can think on their feet and achieve reasonable fluency in French, and even they enhance their performance considerably by preparation.

11 Ask your teacher to play you (anonymously) recordings of previous oral examinations, or of sample oral examinations provided by the Examining Group, with both good and bad performances, and to point out the good and bad features to you. It's very instructive.

7 > PREPARING LISTENING

❝ You can hear lots of French *without* going to France ❞

Let us look now at Listening. This is the most difficult skill to revise on your own, because it isn't always easy to come by suitable materials. However, if you take a little trouble it is surprising how much French you can hear without ever setting foot in France. Let us try to list these opportunities.

1 There are quite a lot of French films on TV, on both BBC and Channel 4. Sometimes they are shown quite late, but if you have access to a video recorder you can probably view them at a reasonable hour. Some of the language on them is difficult, but the advantage for you is that there are sub-titles which will help you to absorb the French that you **can** manage that much more easily. Generally, the films that are shown outside France are good films, quite apart from their value to you as a learner of French. Look for:

— late-night programmes on Channel 4
— *Téléjournal* on BBC2
— *Film Club* on BBC2

2 Also on TV, there are beginners' and intermediate courses in French. These are ideal for you. The simpler ones will be well within your grasp, while the more difficult ones may well be at a level comparable with what you are doing in school. You can find out times from *Radio Times* and *TV Times*. Your teacher may know when schools programmes are on. Look for:

— *Dès le début* – easy role-play type situations   BBC

— *France – Français* – conversations with young French people   BBC

— *La Marée et ses secrets* – a 5-part adventure series with straightforward French   BBC

— *A vous la France* – for adult beginners   BBC

— *The French Programme*   ITV

— *Vidéothèque* – extracts based on GCSE topics and settings   ITV
— *Action-télé* (2 and 3) – good comprehension materials and lots of role-plays   ITV

Schools may well have these recorded. You could ask your teacher to make them available to you in the lunch hour if they are not already included in your lessons. It may also be possible to find recordings of older broadcasts in school.

3 Most text-books in use in school for GCSE have cassettes which go with them. You could ask your teacher to make them available to you so you can re-work Listening exercises done in class. You could also ask your school librarian to stock them.

4 There are also courses on sale in booksellers (or – a cheaper option – available in your public library) which are aimed at travellers and tourists, with titles such as *Get by in French* (BBC Publications) and *Survive in French* (Longman). If your local library doesn't have them, you could ask the librarian to get them for you if you can afford to wait a little. Look for the ones with cassettes as a major part of the course. These are likely to be useful in preparing for the Basic level tests as they tend to concentrate on such things as booking hotel rooms, shopping, and dealing with restaurants and filling stations.

5 BBC Schools Radio has the following programmes. The easiest are listed first.
— *Branchez-vous*
— *La Parole aux jeunes*
— *Horizons de France*

And your school may have recorded *Mainstream GCSE* in which Simon Mayo and Susie Grant explain GCSE.
There is also the Radio version of *A vous la France* on Sundays on Radio 4 VHF/Options slot 17.00–17.30.
Find out the times of broadcasts from *Radio Times*, or ask your teacher to make recordings available to you in school.

6 In most parts of Britain, French radio stations can be picked up reasonably well in the vicinity of Radio 4 (either side) on Long Wave. These are music stations, but they also carry news bulletins on the hour. A small daily dose will not be harmful, and may even do you some good!
Wavelengths: Europe 1 – 1647 metres   France Inter – 1829 metres

7   If there are French-speaking visitors in your locality (for example, an exchange with younger pupils), you will probably find that the young French people are pleased to talk to you in French. Ask them about such things as school, their families and their journey as a starting point. The teachers accompanying such parties, too, are worth approaching.

8   If your school is fortunate enough to have a French Assistant(e), be sure to take his/her sessions seriously.

9   Finally, there should be opportunities for you to do Listening practice in your lessons. Make very sure that you take full advantage of those opportunities!

So we have seen that there are quite a number of ways of hearing lots of French spoken. Some of these are more enjoyable than others. The most important thing is to try to hear as much as you can as often as you can, and not to be put off by the apparent speed at which 'they' speak. The more practice you have, the easier it gets. Use your common sense to help you work out what is being said, and remember to listen out for words that you **do** understand to help you to make an intelligent guess about the rest.

8 > PREPARING READING

Reading is a skill which is not too difficult to practise. The more you read, the better. For GCSE, you need to read a variety of texts ranging from train timetables to articles in teenage magazines, so it is unwise to stick to just one sort of reading material. Some suggested sources are listed below.

1   The obvious starting point is your French text-book. It will have a large amount of material in it, specifically chosen to meet the range of topics set for GCSE. You will certainly benefit from spending time working through texts you have previously done in class, or those which your teacher has decided to miss out. Use the vocabulary at the back to help you. Make a note of words (and their meanings) you didn't know without looking them up – that is the first step to learning them.

2   Your school or local library may well have a variety of easy books in French. Some are available with English translations of the same stories. Look out for:

— *Astérix*   — *Barbar the elephant*
— *Tintin*   — *The Mr Men*

These and a very wide range of other material not easily available elsewhere can be obtained from: European Schoolbooks Ltd, Croft Street, Cheltenham, GL53 OHX telephone (0242) 245252.

3   You could ask your teacher if there are any out-of-date text-books in the back of the book cupboard. Old-fashioned first-year books can be quite amusing, and will reinforce your knowledge of things you learned long ago.

4   As well as old text-books, your teacher may have back numbers of magazines designed for learners of French, or you could subscribe to them directly. Popular suitable titles include, in order of difficulty:

— *Bonjour*   — *Chez Nous*
— *Ça Va*

All obtainable from: Mary Glasgow Publications Ltd, Brookhampton Lane, Kineton, CV35 0JB,   Tel: (0926) 640606.

Cartoon-type magazines called *Jeunes* and *Ensemble* are sold by: Language Ideas, 26–27 Market Place, Kingston-upon-Thames, KT1 1JH, Tel: (01) 549 5977.

A more difficult magazine – probably suitable for only the best candidates – is *Authentik*, available from: The Secretary, Authentik, 24 Suffolk Street, Dublin 2, Tel: (001) 771512.

As with listening, a little French reading daily will pay dividends. And the more you do, the easier you will find the exam.

> The more reading you do, the easier you will find the exam

5   French newspapers are available in larger towns and cities. Buy an occasional edition of *France Soir* or the more difficult *Le Figaro*. It's important to be familiar with journalistic style, as some of the texts set in Reading are taken directly from newspapers. Read not only the stories, but also the adverts, large and small. They're very popular with question-setters. French magazines are also available in many public libraries.

9 ▷ PREPARING WRITING

> 66 The key thing is to *get the message across* 99

> 66 You can *predict* many of the phrases you will need 99

For Writing there is no doubt that a high standard of accuracy will improve your marks. However, accuracy can be difficult to improve unless you are systematic. Make sure that you know the fundamentals of **grammar**, for example how verbs are formed in all persons and tenses, when to use the different tenses and how to make adjectives agree. Revise a different grammar topic each week in the run-up to the examination. A skeleton list of the grammar needed for GCSE is given in Chapter 12, together with explanations and examples. The other area to make sure of is **vocabulary**. Learn not only the word, but also its spelling (including accents) and its gender.

As well as accuracy, GCSE examiners will be awarding marks for **'getting the message across'**. So it is **vitally important** to do exactly what the question tells you. You should also be sure to write at least the number of words you have been told to.

You should also make sure of such things as beginnings and ends of letters, and the sorts of phrases which commonly occur in such things as letters booking accommodation, invitations to a pen-friend to stay, and so on. Check in the Writing chapters. Finally, you should look back at any written work you have done over the course. Try doing some of the questions again after noting the mistakes you previously made. Be sure to avoid making them again.

CHAPTER 3

VOCABULARY TOPICS AND SETTINGS

TOPICS

SETTINGS

COMBINATION OF TOPICS AND SETTINGS

ACTIVE AND RECEPTIVE USE

LANGUAGE TASKS

LEARNING VOCABULARY

A STEP FURTHER

GETTING STARTED

For the GCSE in French the Examining Groups have each published in their Defined Content a list of vocabulary and phrases which they require candidates to know. They are not allowed to set questions which depend on knowing words outside the lists, although in Reading and Listening papers they may include up to 5% of words from outside the lists. The vocabulary lists contain about 2000 words; they vary to some extent from one Examining Group to another, and it is not practical to reproduce them all in this book. This chapter includes a combination of some of the vocabulary lists from major Examining Groups so that, if you learn what is given here, you can be pretty sure you have covered what is necessary.

There are hints given at the end of the chapter to help you to learn your vocabulary more effectively. But the main message is to do a little, but often!

ESSENTIAL PRINCIPLES

The Examining Groups do agree on most **topics** which they expect candidates to know about. Check in the table below what your Examining Group requires.

Examining Group	LEAG	MEG	NEA	NISEC	SEG	WJEC
Personal identification, family & friends	yes	yes	yes	yes	yes	yes
House & home, daily routines	yes	yes	yes	yes	yes	yes
Geographical surroundings & local environment	yes	yes	yes	yes	yes	yes
School, education & career	yes	yes	yes	yes	yes	yes
Free time, sports, hobbies & entertainment	yes	yes	yes	yes	yes	yes
Travel	yes	yes	yes	yes	yes	yes
Holidays	yes	yes	yes	yes	yes	no
Meeting people; relationships	no	yes	yes	yes	yes	no
Shopping	yes	yes	yes	yes	yes	yes
Food & drink; café & restaurant	yes	yes	yes	yes	yes	yes
Accommodation	yes	yes	yes	yes	yes	yes
Banks, post office services	yes	yes	yes	yes	yes	yes
Lost property	yes	yes	yes	yes	yes	no
Weather	yes	yes	yes	yes	yes	yes
Sickness, health & hygiene	yes	yes	yes	yes	yes	yes
Accidents and emergencies	yes	yes	yes	yes	yes	yes
Coping with the foreign language	no	no	yes	no	no	yes
The media	no	no	no	no	no	yes
Crime and the law	yes	no	no	no	no	no
Biography	yes	no	no	no	no	no
Yearly routine, festivals	yes	no	no	no	no	no

The Examining Groups vary somewhat in how they classify certain topics. For example, banking is included under shopping by some groups, travel by others, and services by others. The vocabulary given by the Examining Groups is listed here under the following topic headings.

Personal identification	School, education and future career
House and home	Free time and entertainment
Life at home	Travel
Geographical surroundings	Holidays

Accommodation	Food and drink
Social relationships	Services
Health and welfare	Language problems
Shopping	Weather

2 ⟩ SETTINGS

The Examining Groups also give **settings**, that is, the places or scenes in which you will be expected to use the vocabulary. The settings are:

Home	Shops and markets
Town	Café and restaurant
School	Hotels, campsite, etc.
Place of work	Countryside and seaside
Places of entertainment	Dentist, doctor, chemist
Places of interest	Garage and petrol station
Private transport	Bank, exchange office
Public transport	Lost property office, police station
Tourist information office	

3 ⟩ COMBINATION OF TOPICS AND SETTINGS

Each vocabulary topic area may occur in more than one setting. So, for example, you may give your name (personal identification) in virtually any of them. Other topic areas will be more restricted. Shopping, for example, is mainly carried out in shops and markets!

The combinations of settings and topics are perhaps more clearly shown by the following table.

TOPICS \ SETTINGS	Town	Home	School	Place of work	Places of entertainment	Public transport	Private transport	Tourist Information Office	Shops, markets	Café, restaurant	Hotels, campsites etc.	Dentist, doctor, chemist	Garage, petrol station	Bank, exchange office	Lost property, police station
Personal identification			■	■							■	■			■
House and home															
Life at home															
Geographical surroundings															
School, education & future career															
Free time and entertainment															
Travel															
Holidays															
Accommodation															
Social relationships															
Health and welfare															
Shopping															
Food and drink															
Services															
Weather															
Language problems															

You could shade or colour the squares where the topics and settings are most likely to coincide. Personal identification, for instance, is most likely to be required at school, your place of work, at a hotel, at the dentist's, and at the lost property office or police station. So these squares have been shaded in for you. Spend a few moments considering where the other vocabulary topics are most likely to be useful.

4 > ACTIVE AND RECEPTIVE USE

66 Words listed for *receptive use* are words you must *understand*, but not necessarily say or write 99

Vocabulary in the Examining Groups' Defined Content is divided into Active and Receptive use. Words listed for **Active** use are ones you need to be able to say and write. Words listed for **Receptive** use are words you need to be able to understand from speech or by reading, but not necessarily be able to say or write. Of course, if you are able to say or write them, so much the better!

Words for Receptive use are marked (R) in the vocabulary lists after the topic breakdown. Unmarked words are for Active use. However, you are recommended to attempt to learn as many as possible without making a distinction.

5 > LANGUAGE TASKS

66 Ticking off items as you have learned to do them is a useful check on your progress 99

A comprehensive list of the things you need to be able to do is provided below, broken down by topics and into Basic and Higher levels. It may appear a little daunting, but there are many straightforward things in it, such as giving your name and age, which you have been able to do well for a long time.

To help you chart your progress through the tasks, two boxes are provided next to them in which you can tick off items as you have learned them, and again when you have been tested at a later date (by yourself or by a friend).

PERSONAL IDENTIFICATION

You should be able to give information about yourself and others (e.g. members of your family or host family) and seek information from others on the following points.

	Learnt	*Tested*
■ Names (including spelling out your own name)	☐	☐
■ Home address (including spelling out the name of your home town)	☐	☐
■ Telephone numbers	☐	☐
■ Ages and birthdays	☐	☐
■ Nationality	☐	☐
■ General descriptions including sex, marital status, physical appearance, character or disposition of yourself and others.	☐	☐
■ Religion	☐	☐
■ Likes and dislikes (with regard to people and other topics in the syllabus)	☐	☐

HOUSE AND HOME

You should be able to discuss where and under what conditions you and others live, and know the necessary vocabulary to be able to:

	Learnt	*Tested*
■ Say whether you live in a house, flat etc., and ask others the same	☐	☐
■ Describe your house, flat, etc. and its location	☐	☐

	Learnt	*Tested*
■ Find out about and give details of rooms, garage, garden, etc., as appropriate	☐	☐
■ Mention or enquire about availability of the most essential pieces of furniture, amenities, services	☐	☐
■ Say whether you have a room of your own and describe your room or the room where you sleep	☐	☐
■ Say what jobs you do around the home	☐	☐
■ Ask where places and things are in a house	☐	☐
■ Say you need soap, toothpaste, or a towel	☐	☐
■ Invite someone to come in, sit down	☐	☐
■ Thank somebody for hospitality	☐	☐
■ Offer and ask for help to do something about the house	☐	☐
■ Ask permission to use or do things when the guest of a French-speaking family	☐	☐

Learnt Tested

LIFE AT HOME

You should be able to give
and seek information about:

- Members of the family ☐ ☐
- Description of members
  of the family and their
  occupations ☐ ☐
- Description of family pets ☐ ☐
- Daily routine ☐ ☐
- What time you usually get
  up and go to bed, have
  meals, how you spend
  your evenings and
  weekends ☐ ☐
- What you do to help at
  home ☐ ☐
- Whether you have a
  spare-time job. If so, what
  job, what working hours,
  how much you earn ☐ ☐
- How much pocket money
  you get and what you do
  with it ☐ ☐

GEOGRAPHICAL SURROUNDINGS

You should be able to give information about
your home town or village and surrounding
areas, and seek information from others,
with respect to:

- Location ☐ ☐
- Character ☐ ☐
- Amenities, attractions,
  features of interest,
  entertainment ☐ ☐

You should also be able to:

- Express a simple opinion
  about your own town or
  someone else's town ☐ ☐
- Give full descriptions of
  your home town/village or
  that of others, and of the
  surrounding area and
  region ☐ ☐
- Outline possibilities for
  sight-seeing ☐ ☐
- Give your opinion of your
  home town/village: what
  is good about it; what is
  not so good about it; how
  long you have been living
  there; how you would
  improve it ☐ ☐
- Describe and talk about
  the places you have
  visited ☐ ☐

Learnt Tested

SCHOOL

You need to be able to
exchange information and opinions about:

- Your school/college and
  its facilities: state the
  type, size and location of
  your school and describe
  the buildings ☐ ☐
- Daily routines: when
  school begins, ends; how
  many lessons there are
  and how long they last;
  break times and lunch
  times; homework; how
  you travel to and from
  school ☐ ☐
- Your school year and holidays: subjects studied and
  preferences; clubs,
  sports, trips and other
  activities ☐ ☐

EDUCATION AND FUTURE CAREER

In this category you should be able to:

- Discuss what sort of education you have had, propose to continue with, at
  what types of educational
  institution ☐ ☐
- Talk about examinations ☐ ☐
- Talk about special events
  in the school year, e.g.
  plays, sports day, visits ☐ ☐
- Discuss your plans and
  hopes for the future
  including:
    immediate plans for the
    coming months;
    plans for the time after
    the completion of
    compulsory education;
    where you would like to
    work, giving reasons as
    appropriate ☐ ☐

FREE TIME AND ENTERTAINMENT

General

- State your hobbies and
  interests ☐ ☐
- Ask about the hobbies and
  interests of other people ☐ ☐
- Discuss your interest and
  involvement in:
    sport and sporting events
    intellectual and artistic pursuits
    youth clubs, societies ☐ ☐

Learnt Tested

- Give and seek information about leisure facilities ☐ ☐
- Express simple opinions about radio and TV, films, performances ☐ ☐
- Agree or disagree ☐ ☐
- Ask if someone else agrees ☐ ☐
- Describe and comment on the leisure and entertainment facilities of the area you live in ☐ ☐
- Discuss in more detail your interests/activities ☐ ☐
- Discuss films/plays/ concerts, etc. in greater detail ☐ ☐
- Describe how you spent a period of free time, e.g. an evening, weekend ☐ ☐
- Describe what you would like to do if opportunities and finance permitted ☐ ☐

Places of entertainment

- Buy entry tickets for cinema or theatre, concert, swimming pool, football match, sports centre ☐ ☐
- Find out the cost of seats or entry ☐ ☐
- Find out or state the starting/finishing times ☐ ☐
- State or ask what sort of film or play it is ☐ ☐
- Ask if the film or event is/was good ☐ ☐
- Express an opinion (about the film or event) ☐ ☐

TRAVEL

General

- Say how you get to your school/place of work (means of transport, if any; duration of journey) ☐ ☐
- Understand and give information about other journeys ☐ ☐

Finding the way

- Attract the attention of a passer-by ☐ ☐

Learnt Tested

- Ask where a place is ☐ ☐
- Ask the way (to a place) ☐ ☐
- Ask if it is a long way (to a place) ☐ ☐
- Ask if a place is nearby ☐ ☐
- Ask if there is a place or an amenity nearby ☐ ☐
- Understand directions ☐ ☐
- Ask if there is a bus, train, tram or coach ☐ ☐
- Ask someone to repeat what they have said ☐ ☐
- Say you do not understand ☐ ☐
- Thank people ☐ ☐
- Give directions to strangers ☐ ☐
- State and enquire about distances ☐ ☐

Travel by public transport

- Ask if there is a bus, train, tram, tube or coach to a particular place ☐ ☐
- Buy tickets, stating:
  destination
  single or return
  class of travel
  proposed times of departure and arrival ☐ ☐
- Ask about the cost of tickets ☐ ☐
- Ask about times of departure and arrival ☐ ☐
- Ask and check whether it is:
  the right platform
  the right station
  the right line or bus, tram, coach or stop ☐ ☐
- Ask about the location of facilities, e.g. bus stop, waiting room, information office, toilets ☐ ☐
- Ask if and/or where it is necessary to change buses, trains, trams or coaches ☐ ☐
- Ask or state whether a seat is free ☐ ☐
- Understand information given in brochures and tables ☐ ☐
- Write a letter about requirements for travel arrangements ☐ ☐

	Learnt	Tested
Give above information to others	☐	☐
Say what you have lost at the lost property office	☐	☐
Ask how to get to a place by bus, train, tram, tube or coach	☐	☐
Give above information to others	☐	☐
Reserve a seat	☐	☐
Ask for information, time-tables, or a plan	☐	☐
Ask about price reductions and supplements	☐	☐
Make arrangements for taking, leaving or sending luggage	☐	☐
Deal with an element of the unexpected in travel arrangements, e.g. delayed or cancelled departures, mislaid tickets, documents, lost luggage	☐	☐

Private transport

	Learnt	Tested
Buy petrol by grade, volume or price	☐	☐
Ask for the tank to be filled up	☐	☐
Ask the cost	☐	☐
Ask someone to check oil, water and tyres	☐	☐
Ask where facilities are	☐	☐
Ask about the availability of facilities nearby	☐	☐
Check on your route	☐	☐
Obtain and give information about routes, types of roads, traffic rules, parking facilities	☐	☐
Report a breakdown, giving location and other relevant information	☐	☐
Ask for technical help	☐	☐
Pay and ask for a receipt	☐	☐

Travel by air or sea

	Learnt	Tested
Buy a ticket	☐	☐
Ask about the cost of a flight or crossing	☐	☐
Say where you would like to sit	☐	☐
Ask about times of departure and arrival	☐	☐

	Learnt	Tested
Inform someone about your proposed times of arrival and departure	☐	☐
Check which is the right flight, ferry or hovercraft	☐	☐
Ask about the location of facilities	☐	☐
State whether you wish to declare anything at the customs	☐	☐

HOLIDAYS

General

	Learnt	Tested
Say where you normally spend your holidays; how long they last; with whom you go on holiday; what you normally do; and understand others giving the above information	☐	☐
Describe a previous holiday: where you went; how you went; with whom you went, and for how long; where you stayed; what the weather was like; what you saw and did; what your general impressions were; and understand others giving the above information	☐	☐
Describe your holiday plans	☐	☐
Say whether you have been abroad, e.g. to a French-speaking country and give details if applicable	☐	☐
Understand others giving the information	☐	☐
Supply information about travel documents	☐	☐

Tourist information

	Learnt	Tested
Ask for and understand information about a town or region (maps, brochures of hotels and campsites)	☐	☐
Ask for and understand details of excursions, shows, places of interest (location, costs, times)	☐	☐
Give above information about your own area or one you have visited to others, e.g. prospective tourists	☐	☐

Learnt Tested

- React to (i.e. welcome or reject) suggestions about activities and places of interest ☐ ☐
- Write a short letter asking for information and brochures about a town or region and its tourist facilities or attractions ☐ ☐

ACCOMMODATION

General

- Describe accommodation you use or have used ☐ ☐
- Write a short letter asking about the availability and price of accommodation at a hotel, campsite or youth hostel and about amenities available ☐ ☐
- Write a short letter booking such accommodation ☐ ☐
- Read and understand relevant information about accommodation, e.g. brochures ☐ ☐
- Make complaints ☐ ☐

Hotel

- Ask if there are rooms available ☐ ☐
- State when you require a room/rooms and for how long ☐ ☐
- Say what sort of room is required ☐ ☐
- Ask the cost (per night, per person, per room) ☐ ☐
- Say it is too expensive ☐ ☐
- Ask to see the room(s) ☐ ☐
- Accept or reject a room ☐ ☐
- Check in ☐ ☐
- Say that you have (not) reserved accommodation ☐ ☐
- Identify yourself ☐ ☐
- Ask if there is a particular facility (e.g. restaurant) in or near the hotel ☐ ☐
- Ask where facilities are, e.g. telephone, car park, lift, lounge ☐ ☐
- Ask if meals are included ☐ ☐
- Ask what meals are available ☐ ☐
- Ask the times of meals ☐ ☐

Learnt Tested

- Ask for your key ☐ ☐
- Say you would like to pay ☐ ☐

Youth hostel

- Ask if there is any room ☐ ☐
- State when and for how long the rooms are required ☐ ☐
- State how many males and females require accommodation ☐ ☐
- Say you have (not) reserved ☐ ☐
- Identify yourself ☐ ☐
- Ask the cost (per night, per person or facility) ☐ ☐
- Ask if there is a particular facility in or near the hostel ☐ ☐
- Ask where facilities are ☐ ☐
- Say you would like to pay ☐ ☐
- Ask about meal times ☐ ☐
- Ask about opening and closing times ☐ ☐
- Ask about rules and regulations ☐ ☐
- Say you have a sleeping bag ☐ ☐
- Say you wish to hire a sleeping bag ☐ ☐

Campsite

- Ask if there is any room ☐ ☐
- State when and for how long you will be staying ☐ ☐
- Say you have (not) reserved ☐ ☐
- Identify yourself ☐ ☐
- Say how many tents, caravans, people or vehicles it is for ☐
- Say how many children and adults are in the group ☐ ☐
- Ask the cost (per night, per person, per tent, caravan, vehicle or facility) ☐ ☐
- Say it is too expensive ☐ ☐
- Ask if there is a particular facility on or near the site ☐ ☐
- Ask where the facilities are ☐ ☐
- Buy essential supplies ☐ ☐
- Ask about rules and regulations ☐ ☐

Learnt Tested *Learnt Tested*

SOCIAL RELATIONSHIPS

Relations with others (general)

You should be able to:

- Say whether you are a member of any clubs/ groups; if so, which clubs and what activities are involved ☐ ☐
- Give information about your friends ☐ ☐
- Say if you have any friends in foreign countries ☐ ☐

Making acquaintances

- Greet someone and respond to greetings ☐ ☐
- Ask how someone is and reply to similar enquiries ☐ ☐
- Say that you are pleased to meet someone ☐ ☐
- Introduce yourself (see also Personal identification) ☐ ☐
- Introduce an acquaintance to someone else ☐ ☐
- Give, receive and exchange gifts ☐ ☐
- Make a telephone call ☐ ☐

Arranging a meeting or an activity

You should be able to:

- Find out what a friend wants to do ☐ ☐
- Ask what is on TV or at the cinema ☐ ☐
- Express preferences for an activity (e.g. watching TV, going out, visiting a friend) ☐ ☐
- Invite someone to go out (stating when and where) ☐ ☐
- Suggest going to a particular place, event or on a visit ☐ ☐
- Accept or decline invitations ☐ ☐
- State that something is possible, impossible, probable or certain ☐ ☐
- Thank and apologize ☐ ☐
- Express pleasure ☐ ☐
- Ask about, suggest or confirm a time and place to meet ☐ ☐

- Ask about and state the cost (of entry, etc.) ☐ ☐
- Express surprise, regret, doubt, certainty ☐ ☐
- Apologize for late arrival ☐ ☐
- State likes and dislikes ☐ ☐

Current affairs

You should be able to follow the recounting or discussion of current issues and events of general news value, and of interest to 16-year-old students, and to express your reaction to such items.

HEALTH AND WELFARE

General

- State how you feel (well, ill, better, hot, cold, hungry, thirsty, tired), and ask others how they feel ☐ ☐
- Ask about taking a bath or shower ☐ ☐
- Ask for soap, toothpaste, towel ☐ ☐
- Refer to parts of the body where you are in pain or discomfort ☐ ☐
- Call for help ☐ ☐
- Warn about danger ☐ ☐
- Say you would like to rest or go to bed ☐ ☐

Illness and injury

You should be able to:

- Report minor ailments (e.g. temperature, cold, sunburn), and injuries ☐ ☐
- Ask for items in a chemist's and ask if they have anything for particular ailments ☐ ☐
- Say you would like to lie down ☐ ☐
- Respond to an enquiry about how long an ailment or symptom has persisted ☐ ☐
- Say you would like to see a doctor or dentist ☐ ☐
- Deal with contact with the medical services ☐ ☐
- Say whether you take medicine regularly, and if so, what ☐ ☐
- Say whether or not you are insured ☐ ☐
- Tell others about medical facilities, surgery hours ☐ ☐

Learnt Tested

Accident

You should be able to:

- Ask or advise someone to phone the doctor, police, fire brigade, ambulance, consulate, acquaintance, etc. ☐ ☐
- Ask for someone's name and address ☐ ☐
- Suggest filling in a road accident form ☐ ☐
- Describe an accident ☐ ☐
- Report an accident ☐ ☐
- Ask or say whether it is serious ☐ ☐
- Deny responsibility and say whose fault it was ☐ ☐

SHOPPING

General

You should be able to:

- Ask for information about supermarkets, shopping centres, markets, shops ☐ ☐
- Ask where specific shops and departments are ☐ ☐
- Discuss shopping habits ☐ ☐

Shops and markets

You should be able to:

- Ask whether particular goods are available ☐ ☐
- Ask for particular items (mentioning e.g colour, size, whom it is for, etc.) ☐ ☐
- Find out how much things cost ☐ ☐
- Say an item is (not) satisfactory or too expensive, small, big, etc. ☐ ☐
- Say you will (not) take or prefer something ☐ ☐
- Express quantity required (including weights, volumes, containers) ☐ ☐
- Find out opening and closing times ☐ ☐
- Say that is all you require ☐ ☐
- Enquire about costs and prices ☐ ☐
- Pay for items ☐ ☐
- State whether you have enough money ☐ ☐

Learnt Tested

- Understand currencies used in French-speaking countries, including written and printed prices ☐ ☐
- Ask for small change ☐ ☐
- Return unsatisfactory goods and ask for a refund or replacement ☐ ☐

FOOD AND DRINK

General

You should be able to:

- Discuss your likes, dislikes and preferences and those of others ☐ ☐
- Discuss your typical meals, meal times, and eating habits ☐ ☐
- Buy food and drink (see Shops and markets) ☐ ☐
- Explain to a visitor what a dish is, or what it contains ☐ ☐

Café, restaurant and other public places

- Attract the attention of the waiter/waitress ☐ ☐
- Order a drink, snack, or meal ☐ ☐
- Ask for a particular fixed-price menu ☐ ☐
- Say how many there are in your group ☐ ☐
- Ask for a table (for a certain number) ☐ ☐
- Ask about availability of certain dishes and drinks ☐ ☐
- Ask the cost of dishes and drinks ☐ ☐
- Ask for an explanation or description of something on the menu ☐ ☐
- Express opinions about a meal or dish ☐ ☐
- Accept or reject suggestions ☐ ☐
- Ask if the service charge is included ☐ ☐
- Ask about the location of facilities (e.g. toilets, telephone) ☐ ☐

	Learnt	*Tested*

At home

- Express hunger and thirst ☐ ☐
- Ask about time and place of meals ☐ ☐
- Ask for food and table articles (including asking for more, a little, a lot) ☐ ☐
- React to offers of food (accept, decline, apologize, express pleasure) ☐ ☐
- Express likes, dislikes and preferences ☐ ☐
- Express appreciation and pay compliments ☐ ☐
- Respond to a toast, e.g. 'A la vôtre' ☐ ☐

SERVICES

Post office

- Ask where a post office or letter box is ☐ ☐
- Ask how much it costs to send letters, postcards or parcels to a particular country or within the country ☐ ☐
- Say whether you would like to send letters, postcards or parcels ☐ ☐
- Buy stamps of a particular value ☐ ☐
- Find out opening and closing times ☐ ☐
- Say that is all you require ☐ ☐
- Give and seek information about where phone calls can be made ☐ ☐
- Ask for a telephone number and give your own telephone number ☐ ☐
- Answer a phone call, stating who you are ☐ ☐
- Make a phone call and ask to speak to someone ☐ ☐
- Ask someone to telephone you ☐ ☐
- Find out if others can be contacted by phone ☐ ☐
- Tell others you will telephone them ☐ ☐
- Ask for coins ☐ ☐
- Ask for a reversed charge call ☐ ☐
- Send a telegram ☐ ☐

	Learnt	*Tested*

Bank or exchange office

- Say you would like to change travellers' cheques or money (including sterling) ☐ ☐
- Ask for coins or notes of a particular denomination ☐ ☐
- Give proof of identity (e.g. show passport) ☐ ☐
- Cope with any likely eventuality that may arise while using a bank or foreign exchange office to change currency or cheques ☐ ☐

Lost property office

- Report a loss or theft, stating what you have lost, when and where it was lost or left, describing the item (size, shape, colour, make, contents) ☐ ☐
- Express surprise, pleasure, disappointment, anger ☐ ☐

Having things repaired and cleaned

- Report an accident, damage done or breakdown ☐ ☐
- Ask if shoes, clothes, camera, etc. can be repaired ☐ ☐
- Explain what is wrong ☐ ☐
- Ask for, and offer, advice about getting something cleaned or repaired ☐ ☐
- Ask for an item of clothing to be cleaned ☐ ☐
- Arrange for clothing to be washed ☐ ☐
- Find out how long it will take, what it will cost, when an item will be ready ☐ ☐
- Thank, complain, express disappointment, pleasure ☐ ☐
- Suggest the need for repair or cleaning and report or comment on any action taken ☐ ☐

Learnt Tested　　　　　　　　　　　*Learnt Tested*

WEATHER

- Describe or comment on current weather conditions ☐ ☐
- Ask about weather conditions in the country you are visiting ☐ ☐
- Describe the general climate of your own country and ask about the climate in another country ☐ ☐
- Understand simple predictions about weather conditions ☐ ☐
- Understand spoken and written weather forecasts ☐ ☐

LANGUAGE PROBLEMS

- State whether or not you understand ☐ ☐
- Ask someone to repeat what they have said ☐ ☐
- Ask for and understand the spelling out of names, place-names, etc. ☐ ☐

- Ask if someone speaks English or French ☐ ☐
- State how well or how little you speak and understand French ☐ ☐
- Ask what things are called in French or English ☐ ☐
- Ask what words or phrases mean ☐ ☐
- Say you do not know (something) ☐ ☐
- Say that you have forgotten (something) ☐ ☐
- Apologize ☐ ☐
- Ask whether, or state that, something is correct ☐ ☐
- Say for how long you have been learning French and any other languages you know ☐ ☐
- Ask someone to explain something, to correct mistakes ☐ ☐
- Ask how something is pronounced ☐ ☐

6 LEARNING VOCABULARY

> A *regular* daily slot for learning vocabulary will help

> Be methodical in your approach

> Writing out words and phrases is *active* learning

This is one of the chores of learning a foreign language. One thing is certain. If you sit down the night before your first exam and attempt to learn 2000 words, you will know very few indeed the next morning. You would be far better to have a regular time of day (or perhaps two occasions in the day) when you sit down and spend 10–15 minutes learning vocabulary. And the sooner you start, the better – so start today! This really requires somewhere private, or at least somewhere you won't be disturbed. So your room, somewhere quiet in school at break or lunch-time, or even on public transport would be suitable. What is *not* suitable is trying to do it while talking to or listening to someone else, or watching *Neighbours*. Don't kid yourself you are working when you're not.

As well as having a good place to do it, it's as well to be methodical. Work through the vocabulary topics, changing them daily. Don't try to learn too many words at once. And try to relate them to a situation, rather than just working through an alphabetical list. It's more interesting to learn, say, everything to do with changing money than just 40 words which happen to begin with the same letter.

Begin your sessions with a written test on what you did last time. This could be half and half French–English, English–French. Don't cheat, but check your test afterwards with the text-book. If you did well, reward yourself with a treat of some kind. Keep a record of how you have done so you can check your progress.

Rather than simply learning vocabulary in your head from a list, it is better to be **doing** something. The best method is to write out each word or phrase two or three times. (It doesn't matter if you can't read it afterwards. Go for speed!) Make sure of accents. Include the gender for nouns, and the past participle for verbs. If you haven't anywhere to write, you can still test yourself using a piece of card or paper cut or folded as shown (p 27).

First, cover the English column on your list and see if you can say what the French words mean. Then turn the blind over and see if you can say what the French should be (including gender or past participle, as before). You can also use the blind to give yourself a written test. You immediately find out if you were right as you move it down to the next word. No peeping!

Students often like to learn vocabulary with a friend. This is fine as a way of learning what the English version of French words is, and for checking gender and past participles. However, unless someone is writing, then spelling accuracy is not likely to be improved.

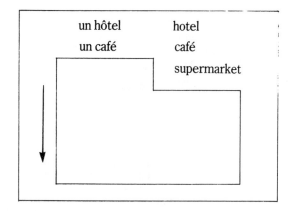

You will know that certain sounds in French can be spelt in several ways (e.g. manger, mangeais, mangé, and the similar mon jet). This means that **precise personal proficiency** is very important. It's no help to you in the exam if your friend can do it. Make sure **you** can do it!

VOCABULARY LISTS

PERSONAL IDENTIFICATION

NAME

Basic

une	identité	*identity*
le	nom	*name*
le	prénom	*first name*
la	signature	*signature*

s'appeler *to be called*
écrire *to write*
épeler *to spell*
signer *to sign*

Madame *Mrs, madam*
Mademoiselle *Miss*
Monsieur *Mr, Sir*
M./Mme/Mlle *Mr, Mrs, Miss*

Basic phrases

Je m'appelle . . . *My name is . . .*

Higher

nom de jeune fille *maiden name*
s'écrire *to be written*
+letters of the alphabet

Higher phrases

Comment ça s'écrit? *How do you spell that?*

HOME ADDRESS

Basic

une	adresse	*address*
un	appartement	*flat*
une	allée	*walk, lane, avenue*
une	avenue	*avenue*
le	boulevard	*boulevard, wide road*
(R) le	code postal	*post code*
(R) le	département	*administrative department (= county)*
(R) le	domicile	*home*
une	enveloppe	*envelope*
la	lettre	*letter*
la	maison	*house*
le	numéro	*number*
le	pays	*country*

la	place	*square*
	premier, etc. (see ordinal numbers in Grammar)	
la	route	*road*
la	rue	*road, street*
la	ville	*town*
le	village	*village*

chez *at the home of*

habiter (à) *to live (at, in)*

Basic phrases

J'habite Bristol } *I live in Bristol*
J'habite à Bristol }
J'habite au premier étage *I live on the first floor*

Higher

le/la concierge *caretaker*
le rez-de-chaussée *ground floor*
en bas *downstairs, below*
en haut *upstairs, above*
hors de *outside*
(R) à proximité de *near to*

demeurer *to live*
habiter (en/au) *to live (in)*
vivre *to live*

Higher phrases

J'habite au rez-de-chaussée *I live on the ground floor*
J'habite en Angleterre *I live in England*
J'habite au Pays de Galles *I live in Wales*

TELEPHONE

Basic

allô? *hello?*
appeler *to call*
avoir le téléphone *to be on the phone*
contacter *to contact*
téléphoner à *to phone*

un   annuaire   *telephone directory*
(R) un avantage   *advantage*
le   faux numéro   *wrong number*
le   téléphone   *telephone*

pratique   *convenient*
quel-   *which, what*

Basic phrases

Jacques Colbert à l'appareil   *Jacques Colbert speaking*
(R) Ne quittez pas   *Do not ring off*
Je me suis trompé(e) de numéro   *I've rung the wrong number*
Quel est ton numéro de téléphone?   *What is your phone number?*

Higher

composer   *to dial*
un inconvénient   *inconvenient*

AGES AND BIRTHDAYS

Basic

un   âge   *age*
un   an
une année   } *year*
un   anniversaire   *birthday*
la   date   *date*
la   date de naissance   *date of birth*
le   lieu de naissance   *place of birth*
le   mois   *month*

avoir __ ans   *to be __ years old*
naître   *to be born*
né(e) le __ à __   *born on the __ at __*

Basic phrases

J'ai seize ans   *I am sixteen*
Je suis né(e) le vingt février dix-neuf cent soixante-treize à Londres   *I was born on 20th February 1973 in London*
Quelle est la date de ton anniversaire?   *What is the date of your birthday?*

Higher

(R) majeur   *18 and over*
(R) mineur   *under 18*
la   naissance   *birth*
la   grande personne   *adult*

NATIONALITY

Basic

la   carte d'identité   *identity card*
un   étranger   *foreigner*
le   passeport   *passport*
la   pièce d'identité   *item of identification*

où   *who*
d'où   *where from*
venir   *to come*

FRENCH-SPEAKING AND COMMON MARKET COUNTRIES

Basic

COUNTRY	ADJECTIVE	INHABITANTS
l' Europe *Europe*	européen *European*	un(e) Européen(nne) *European*
l' Allemagne/FRA *Germany*	allemand *German*	un(e) Allemand(e) *German*
l' Angleterre *England*	anglais *English*	un(e) Anglais(e) *English*
la Grande-Bretagne *GB*	britannique *British*	un(e) Britannique *British*
le Royaume-Uni *UK*		
la Belgique *Belgium*	belge *Belgian*	un(e) Belge *Belgian*
le Canada *Canada*	canadien *Canadian*	un(e) Canadien(ne) *Canadian*
le Danemark *Denmark*	danois *Danish*	un(e) Danois(e) *Danish*
l' Espagne *Spain*	espagnol *Spanish*	un(e) Espagnol(e) *Spanish*
la France *France*	français *French*	un(e) Français(e) *French*
la Grèce *Greece*	grec, grecque *Greek*	un Grec, une Grecque *Greek*
la Hollande *Holland*	hollandais *Dutch*	un(e) Hollandais(e) *Dutchman/woman*
les Pays Bas *Netherlands*	néerlandais *Dutch*	un(e) Néerlandais(e) *Dutch(wo)man*
l' Italie *Italy*	italien *Italian*	un(e) Italien(ne) *Italian*
l' Irlande *Ireland*	irlandais *Irish*	un(e) Irlandais *Irish*
le Luxembourg *Luxemburg*	luxembourgeois	un(e) Luxembourgeois(e) *Luxemburger*
le Portugal *Portugal*	portugais *Portuguese*	un(e) Portugaise(e) *Portuguese*
la Suisse *Switzerland*	suisse *Swiss*	un(e) Suisse *Swiss*

Basic phrases

D'où venez-vous?   *Where do you come from?*
Où êtes-vous né(e)?   *Where were you born?*
Je suis anglais(e)   *I am English (or other)*

Higher

Other parts of the UK and other major countries

Higher

COUNTRY	ADJECTIVE	INHABITANTS
l' Amérique *America*	américain *American*	une(e) Américain(e) *American*
les Etats-Unis *USA*		
la Chine *China*	chinois *Chinese*	une(e) Chinois(e) *Chinese*
l' Ecosse *Scotland*	écossais *Scottish*	une(e) Ecossais(e) *Scotsman*
l' Inde *India*	indien *Indian*	une(e) Indien(e) *Indian*
l' Irlande du Nord *Northern Ireland*	irlandais *Irish*	une(e) Irlandais *Irish*
le Japon *Japan*	japonais *Japonese*	une(e) Japonaise(e) *Japanese*
le Pays de Galles *Wales*	gallois *Welsh*	une(e) Gallois(e) *Welsh*
la Russie *Russia*	russe *Russian*	une(e) Russe *Russian*
l' URSS *USSR*	soviétique *Soviet*	

Higher

> Je suis de nationalité britannique *I am British (or other)*

PEOPLE

Basic

la	dame *lady*	
	(R) Dames *Ladies*	
la	femme *woman, wife*	
la	(jeune) fille *girl*	
le	garçon *boy*	
les	gens *people*	
le	jeune homme *young man*	
l'	homme *man*	
	(R) Hommes *Men*	
le	mari *husband*	
	(R) Messieurs *Gentlemen*	

+ nationalities – see above table

Higher

un(e)	adolescent(e) *adolescent*
un	adulte *adult*
un(e)	célibataire *batchelor*
un(e)	divorcé(e) *a divorcee*
un	étranger/une étrangère *foreigner*
	feminin *feminine*
	fiancé *engaged*
	marié *married*
	séparé (s) *separated*
	masculin *masculine*
le	pays d'origine *country of origin*
une	jeune personne *young person*
le	veuf *widower*
la	veuve *widow*

+ nationalities – see above table

DESCRIBING PEOPLE

(a) CHARACTER AND DISPOSITION

Basic

affreux *awful*
agréable *pleasant*
(R) aimable *friendly*
amusant *amusing*
bête *stupid*
(R) bizarre *odd*
calme *calm*
célèbre *famous*
charmant *charming*
en colère *angry*
content *pleased, happy*
drôle *funny*
énervé *nervous*
fâché *angry*
formidable *great*
fou *mad*
gentil *kind*
heureux *happy*
important *important*
inquiet *anxious*
intelligent *intelligent*
malheureux *unhappy, unfortunate*
méchant *naughty*
paresseux *lazy*
j'ai peur *I'm afraid*
pauvre *poor*
(R) poli *polite*
riche *rich*
sérieux *serious*
sûr *certain*
sympa *nice*
sympathique *nice*
timide *shy*
triste *sad*

à mon avis *in my opinion*
assez *fairly*
en général *usually*
(R) plutôt *rather*
toujours *always*
très *very*
vraiment *really*

aimer *to like*
croire *to believe*
espérer *to hope*
se fâcher *to get angry*
se méfier de *to distrust*
penser *to think*
pleurer *to weep*
réfléchir *to think, reflect*
rire *to laugh*
sourire *to smile*

le caractère *character*
la chance *luck*
une opinion *opinion*
de bonne/mauvaise humeur *in a good/bad mood*
j'en ai marre *I'm fed up*

Basic phrases

Comment est __? *What's __ like?*
Comment trouves-tu __? *How do you find __?*
J'en ai marre du français *I'm fed up with French*
Je suis de bonne humeur aujourd'hui *I'm in a good mood today*

Higher

actif *active*
calme *calm*
capable de *capable of*
déçu *disappointed*
dégoûtant *disgusting*
désagréable *disagreeable*
étrange *strange*
(R) fier *proud*
habile *clever*
(R) honnête *honest*
insupportable *unbearable*
jaloux *jealous*
marrant *funny*
naturel *natural*
normal *normal*
(R) optimiste *optimistic*
(R) pessimiste *pessimistic*
(R) surprenant *surprising*
têtu *obstinate*
tranquille *quiet*

franchement *frankly*
généralement *generally*
naturellement *naturally*
tellement *so*

avoir envie de *to wish to*
avoir le droit de *to have the right to*
avoir honte *to be ashamed*
avoir tort *to be wrong*
conseiller *to advise*
s'entendre *to understand one another, get on well*
effrayer *to frighten*
étonner *to amaze*
se mettre en colère *to get angry*
oser *to dare*
paraître *to appear*
prouver *to prove*
sembler *to seem*
un amour *love*
la confiance *confidence*
un espoir *hope*
un humour *humour*
une imagination *imagination*
le sentiment *feeling*
le souci *care, worry*

Higher phrases

Je m'entends bien avec mon frère *I get on well with my brother*
Le professeur s'est mis en colère *The teacher got angry*
Jean me semble tout à fait sympathique *Jean seems to me to be really nice*
Je lui fais confiance *I have confidence in him/her*
J'ai envie de manger *I want to eat*
J'ai le droit de sortir ce soir *I have the right to go out this evening*
Tu as tort *You are wrong*
J'ai eu honte *I was ashamed*
A mon avis, il faut se méfier de lui *In my opinion, you can't trust him*

(b) PHYSICAL APPEARANCE

Basic

beau *handsome, beautiful*
blanc *white*
bleu *blue*
blond *fair*
bouclé *curly*

bronzé *tanned*
brun *brown*
court *short*
fort *strong*
grand *big, tall*
gris *grey*
gros *big, fat*
jaune *yellow*
jeune *young*
joli *pretty*
(R) laid *ugly*
long *long*
marron *chestnut*
(R) mince *thin*
noir *black*
orange *orange*
pâle *pale*
petit *small*
raide *stiff*
rose *pink*
(R) roux *red (hair)*
sportif *good at sports, keen on sports*
vert *green*
vieux *old*
avoir l'air *to seem*
porter *to wear, carry*
trouver *to find*
(R) reconnaître *to recognize*
(R) ressembler à *to resemble*
la barbe *beard*
les cheveux *hair*
les lunettes *spectacles*
les moustaches *moustache*
les yeux *eyes*

Basic phrases

Il a les cheveux longs *He has long hair*
Il a l'air sportif *He looks athletic*
Elle porte des lunettes *She wears glasses*
Je la trouve jolie *I think she's pretty*

Higher

actif *active*
élégant *elegant, smart*
fragile *weak, fragile, delicate*
robuste *tough*
semblable *alike, similar*
souple *athletic, supple*

absolument *absolutely*
complètement *completely*
tout à fait *totally*

sembler *to seem*
paraître *to appear*

Higher phrases

Elle me semble tout à fait honnête *She seems to me to be totally honest*

THE FAMILY AND RELATIVES

Basic

le/la bébé *baby*
(R) le/la cousin(e) *cousin*
un(e) enfant *child*
la famille *family*
le/la fiancé(e) *fiancé*
la femme *woman, wife*
la fille *girl, daughter*
le fils *son*
le frère *brother*
le garçon *boy*
les gens *people*
la grand-mère *grandmother*
les grands-parents *grandparents*
le grand-père *grandfather*

un	homme	*man*
la	maman	*mummy*
le	mari	*husband*
la	mère	*mother*
le	neveu	*nephew*
la	nièce	*niece*
un	oncle	*uncle*
le	papa	*daddy*
les	parents	*parents, relatives*
le/la	petit(e) ami(e)	*boy/girl friend*
le	petit-fils	*grandson*
la	petite-fille	*grand-daughter*
le	père	*father*
la	soeur	*sister*
la	tante	*aunt*

aîné   *elder*
cadet   *younger*
dernier   *last*
divorcer   *to divorce*
se marier avec   *to marry*

Basic phrases

Je suis enfant unique   *I'm an only child*
Ian, c'est mon frère aîné   *Ian is my elder brother*
Je suis allé avec ma mère voir des parents   *I went with my mother to see relations*
Ma soeur s'est mariée avec un Américain   *My sister has married an American*

Higher

le	beau-père	*father-in-law*
le	beau-fils	*son-in-law*
la	belle-fille	*daughter-in-law*
la	belle-mère	*mother-in-law*
un	époux	*husband*

une	épouse	*wife*
les	petits-enfants	*grand-children*
le	veuf	*widower*
la	veuve	*widow*
	célibataire	*single*
	divorcé	*divorced*
(R)	familial	*of the family*
	séparé	*separated*

Higher phrases

Mon oncle est célibataire   *My uncle is a bachelor*
Ma grand-mère est veuve   *My grandmother is a widow*
Mes parents sont séparés/divorcés   *My parents are separated/divorced*

RELIGION

Higher

catholique   *Catholic*
hindou   *Hindu*
musulman   *Muslim*
protestant   *Protestant*
la religion   *religion*

(+ other religions as appropriate to the student)

LIKES AND DISLIKES

Basic

aimer   *to like*
détester   *to hate*
préférer   *to prefer*
trouver   *to find*

+ material from most other topics in the syllabus

HOUSE

Basic

un	appartement	*flat*
(R)	le bâtiment	*building*
le	bruit	*noise*
la	clé	*key*
(R)	le confort	*comfort*
une	entrée	*entrance*
un	extérieur	*outside*
la	ferme	*farm*
la	grange	*barn*
(R)	une H.L.M.	*council house*
un	immeuble	*building*
un	intérieur	*inside*
(R)	la location	*situation*
la	maison	*house*
le	pavillon	*detached house*
le	rez-de-chaussée	*ground floor*
la	terrasse	*terrace*
la	tour	*tower*
la	vue	*view*

(R) affreux   *awful*
agréable   *pleasant*
(R) ancien   *old, ex- —*
beau   *beautiful, fine*
en bois   *of wood*
en brique   *of brick*
en béton   *of concrete*
(R) calme   *calm, quiet*
cher/pas très cher/pas trop cher   *expensive, not very expensive, not too expensive*
chic   *smart*
confortable   *comfortable*
difficile   *difficult*

élégant   *elegant*
étroit   *narrow*
facile   *easy*
formidable   *great*
grand   *large*
joli   *pretty*
(R) laid   *ugly*
de luxe   *luxurious*
métal   *metal*
moderne   *modern*
nécessaire   *necessary*
neuf   *new*
nouveau   *new*
(R) parfait   *perfect*
petit   *small*
(R) plastique   *plastic*
(R) pratique   *practical*
(R) propre   *clean*
(R) sale   *dirty*
(R) typique   *typical*
utile   *useful*
vieux   *old*

acheter   *to buy*
adorer   *to love*
agrandir   *to increase, to enlarge*
aimer   *to like*
décorer   *to decorate*
déménager   *to move house*
détester   *to hate*
frapper (à la porte)   *to knock (on the door)*
habiter   *to live*
louer   *to rent*
sonner   *to ring*
venir   *to come*

chez   *at the home of*
loin de   *far from*
près de   *near to*
presque   *almost*

Higher
la   différence   *difference*
le   gratte-ciel   *skyscraper*
le   logement   *accommodation*
(R) le loyer   *rent*
(R) le mètre carré   *square metre*
le   meuble   *furniture*
la   peinture   *painting*
(R) le propriétaire   *owner*

bizarre   *odd, strange*
(R) bruyant   *noisy*
essentiel   *essential*
en   bon état   *in good condition*
en   mauvais état   *in poor condition*
en   haut   *upstairs, above*
en   bas   *downstairs, below*
étonnant   *surprising*
tranquille   *peaceful, calm*

critiquer   *to criticize*
vendre   *to sell*
(R) aménager   *to furnish*
loger   *to lodge, accommodate*
nettoyer   *to clean*
(R) tapisser   *to paper*

ROOMS

General

Basic
un   ascenseur   *lift*
le   balcon   *balcony*
le   bouton   *knob, button*
la   cave   *cellar*
la   chambre   *bedroom*
le   chauffage central   *central heating*
le   couloir   *corridor*
la   cuisine   *kitchen*
l'   eau (non) potable (f)   *(non) drinkable water*
l'   électricité (f)   *electricity*
une   entrée   *entrance*
un   escalier   *staircase*
un   étage   *floor, storey*
la   fenêtre   *window*
le   garage   *garage*
le   gaz   *gas*
le   grenier   *loft*
le   jardin   *garden*
la   lampe   *lamp*
(R) la lumière   *light*
(R) le mur   *wall*
le   parking   *parking place*
la   pièce   *room*
le   plan   *plan*
la   porte   *door*
la   salle de bains   *bathroom*
la   salle à manger   *dining room*
la   salle de séjour   *living-room*
(R) le sous-sol   *basement*
le   salon   *lounge, sitting room*
les   toilettes   *toilet*
le   toit   *roof*
le   vestibule   *hall*
(R) le W.C.   *toilet*

allumer   *to light*
appuyer   *to lean, press*
couper   *to cut*

fermer   *to close*
ouvrir   *to open*

voici   *here is . . .*
voilà   *there is . . .*

Basic phrases
Appuyez sur le bouton   *Press the button*
Fermez la porte, svp   *Close the door please*
Coupe le gaz, s'il te plaît   *Turn off the gas please*

Higher
une   ampoule électrique   *electric light bulb*
(R) un aménagement   *furnishings, fittings*
la   cour   *courtyard*
le   débarras   *lumber room*
(R) un entretien   *maintenance*
le   palier   *banister*
le   plafond   *ceiling*
le   plancher   *floor*
la   prise de courant   *power point*
le   radiateur   *radiator*
(R) la serrure   *lock*
le   volet   *shutter*
(R) brancher   *to plug in*
faire du bricolage   *to do odd jobs*
réparer   *to repair*
utiliser   *to use*

(R) aménagé   *fitted, furnished*

Bedroom – la chambre (à coucher)

Basic
une   armoire   *wardrobe*
un   placard   *cupboard*
la   chaîne-stéréo   *stereo*
la   chaise   *chair*
(R) la couverture   *blanket*
un   électrophone   *record player*
la   lampe   *lamp*
le   lit   *bed*
le   magnétophone (à cassettes)   *tape recorder (cassette recorder)*
(R) un oreiller   *pillow*
le   poster   *poster*
le   rideau   *curtain*
le   tapis   *carpet*
le   transistor   *transistor*

plusieurs   *several*
+ adjectives of size and colour, etc.
partager   *to share*

Basic phrases
J'ai une chambre à moi   *I have a room of my own*
Je partage ma chambre avec ma soeur/mon frère   *I share my room with my sister/ brother*

Higher
le   drap   *sheet*
une   étagère   *shelf*
le   matelas   *mattress*
le   micro-ordinateur   *micro computer*
le   miroir   *mirror*
la   moquette   *wall-to-wall carpet*
le   réveil   *alarm clock*

Kitchen – la cuisine

Basic
les   allumettes   *matches*
un   aspirateur   *vacuum cleaner*
une   assiette   *plate*
le   bol   *bowl*
la   casserole   *saucepan*

le   congélateur   *freezer*
le   couteau   *knife*
la   cuillère/cuiller   *spoon*
la   cuisinière à gaz   *gas cooker*
la   cuisinière électrique   *electric cooker*
l'   eau chaude/froide (f)   *hot/cold water*
un   évier   *sink*
la   fourchette   *fork*
le   frigidaire/frigo   *refrigerator*
la   machine à laver   *washing machine*
le   placard   *cupboard*
la   poêle   *frying pan*
la   poubelle   *dustbin*
la   table   *table*
la   tasse   *cup*
la   vaisselle   *crockery*
le   verre   *glass*

Higher
la   bougie   *candle*
le   fer à repasser   *iron*
le   four   *oven*
le   lave-vaisselle   *dishwasher*
le   robinet   *tap*

allumer   *to light*
éteindre   *to extinguish, put out*
faire la lessive   *to do the washing*
faire la vaisselle   *to do the washing up*
jeter   *to throw (out)*

Bathroom – la salle de bains
Basic
la   baignoire   *bath*
la   brosse à dents   *toothbrush*
la   dentifrice   *toothpaste*
la   douche   *shower*
l'   eau (froide/chaude) (f)   *cold/hot water*
la   glace   *mirror*
le   lavabo   *wash-basin*
le   rasoir   *razor*
le   savon   *soap*
la   serviette   *towel*
le   shampooing   *shampoo*

Higher
le   bidet   *bidet*
une   éponge   *sponge*
le   gant de toilette   *flannel*
le   prise-rasoir   *electric razor socket*

Dining room – la salle à manger
Basic
le   buffet   *sideboard*
la   chaise   *chair*
la   cheminée   *fire-place, hearth*
une   horloge   *clock*
le   plat   *dish*
la   table   *table*
le   tableau   *picture*

Higher
le   carafe   *glass jug, carafe*
la   nappe   *table-cloth*
la   serviette   *serviette*
le   vaisselier   *dresser*

**Living room – le salon/
la salle de séjour/le séjour**

Basic
la   bibliothèque   *book-case*
le   cendrier   *ashtray*
la   chaîne-stéréo   *stereo*
le   divan   *sofa*
le   fauteuil   *armchair*
le   magnétophone   *tape recorder*
le   magnétoscope   *video*
(R) le piano   *piano*
la   photo   *photo*
la   plante verte   *plant*
le   tableau   *picture*
la   télévision   *television*
le   vase   *vase*

Higher
le   canapé   *sofa*
le   coussin   *cushion*
une   étagère   *shelf*
la   pendule   *clock*
la   table basse   *coffee table*

Hall – le vestibule
Basic
la   clé   *key*
le   mur   *war*
la   porte (d'entrée) *front door*
le   téléphone   *telephone*

Garden – le jardin
Basic
un   arbre   *tree*
la   fleur   *flower*
le   fruit   *fruit*
le   jardinage   *gardening*
le   légume   *vegetable*
la   plante   *plant*

Higher
un   arbre fruitier   *fruit tree*
(R) le buisson   *bush*
l'herbe (f)   *grass*
les   mauvaises herbes   *weeds*
le   sapin   *fir tree*

arroser   *to water*
cultiver   *to cultivate, to grow*
faire pousser   *to grow*
tondre la pelouse   *to mow the lawn*

Higher phrases
Je fais pousser des légumes   *I grow
   vegetables*
J'ai tondu la pelouse   *I have mown the lawn*

LIFE AT HOME   **PETS AND ANIMALS**

Pets
Basic
un   animal   *animal*
le   chien   *dog*
le   chat   *cat*
le   cochon d'Inde   *guinea-pig*
un   hamster   *hamster*
le   lapin   *rabbit*
un   oiseau   *bird*
la   perruche   *budgerigar*

le   poisson-rouge   *goldfish*
la   souris   *mouse*
la   tortue   *tortoise*

+ adjectives as for physical descriptions of
   people

Basic phrases
As-tu un animal domestique?   *Have you got
   a pet?*

Other livestock

Basic

un	agneau	*lamb*
un	âne	*donkey*
un	boeuf	*bullock*
un	canard	*duck*
un	cheval	*horse*
une	chèvre	*goat*
un	cochon	*pig*
un	coq	*cock*
un	mouton	*sheep*
une	poule	*hen*
une	puce	*flea*
une	vache	*cow*

Higher

une	oie	*goose*
un	taureau	*bull*
un	veau	*calf*

Undomesticated creatures

Basic

une	abeille	*bee*
une	araignée	*spider*
une	grenouille	*frog*
un	insecte	*insect*

Higher

(R)	un escargot	*snail*
(R)	un moineau	*sparrow*
(R)	un renard	*fox*
	un serpent	*snake*
	la truite	*trout*

Parts of animals

la	fourrure	*fur*
la	gueule	*mouth*
la	patte	*paw, foot*
la	plume	*feather*
la	queue	*tail*

DAILY ROUTINE

Basic

(R)	accrocher	*to hang up*
	acheter	*to buy*
	aider	*to help*
	aller à la toilette	*to go to the toilet*
	s'amuser	*to enjoy oneself*
	apporter	*to bring*
	s'asseoir	*to sit down*
	avoir besoin de	*to need*
	boire	*to drink*
	changer	*to change*
	se coucher	*to go to bed*
	coudre	*to sew*
	couper	*to cut*
	débarrasser (la table)	*to clear (the table)*
	déjeuner	*to have lunch, breakfast*
	se déshabiller	*to undress*
	dormir	*to sleep*

écouter de la musique/la radio/des disques *to listen to music/the radio/records*

	écrire	*to write*
	s'endormir	*to go to sleep*
	être prêt à	*to be ready to*
	faire les courses	*to do the shopping*
	faire la cuisine	*to do the cooking*
	faire le lit	*to make the bed*
	faire le ménage	*to do the housework*
	faire la vaisselle	*to wash up*
	faire ses devoirs	*to do one's homework*

garder les enfants *to look after the children/to babysit*

	s'habiller	*to dress*

	jeter	*to throw (away)*
	se laver	*to get washed*

se laver les mains, etc. *to wash one's hands etc.*

	se lever	*to get up, stand up*
	manger	*to eat*
	mettre le couvert	*to lay the table*
	nettoyer	*to clean*
	partager	*to share*
	passer l'aspirateur	*to do the hoovering*
	prendre un café	*to have a cup of coffee*

prendre le (petit) déjeuner *to have lunch (breakfast)*

	préparer un repas	*to prepare a meal*
	prendre un bain	*to have a bath*
	prendre une douche	*to have a shower*
	quitter	*to leave*
	recevoir	*to receive*
	regarder la télévision	*to watch TV*
	repasser	*to iron*
(R)	se reposer	*to rest*
	se réveiller	*to wake up*
	rentrer	*to return home*
	servir	*to serve*
	sortir	*to go out*
	travailler	*to work*
	tricoter	*to knit*

le	week-end	*weekend*
le	petit déjeuner	*breakfast*
le	déjeuner	*lunch, midday meal*
le	goûter	*tea, snack*
le	dîner	*dinner, evening meal*

	généralement	*usually*
	d'habitude	*usually*
	enfin	*at last, in the end*
	ensuite	*afterwards*
	puis	*then*

Basic phrases

J'ai besoin de me laver *I need to wash*

Je me couche normalement à dix heures *I usually go to bed at 10 o'clock*

Est-ce que je peux débarrasser la table? *May I clear the table?*

Je me suis déshabillé(e) avant de me coucher *I undressed before going to bed*

Peux-tu me faire les courses? *Could you do some shopping for me?*

Je me suis lavé les mains *I have washed my hands*

Je voudrais prendre une douche *I would like a shower*

J'aime regarder la télévision *I like watching TV*

Est-ce que tu veux te reposer? *Would you like to rest?*

A quelle heure est-ce que tu te réveilles d'habitude? *What time do you usually wake up?*

Higher

	aller chercher	*to go and get*
	aller voir	*to go and see*
	s'en aller	*to go away*
	arrêter de	*to stop*
	balayer	*to sweep*
	se brosser les cheveux	*to brush one's hair*
	se changer	*to change*
	déranger	*to disturb*
	discuter	*to discuss*
	se disputer	*to argue*

éplucher les légumes *to prepare the vegetables*

essuyer *to wipe*
faire du bricolage *to do odd jobs*
faire cuire *to cook*
faire la lessive *to do the washing*
interdire *to forbid*
s'occuper de *to be busy with*
offrir *to offer*
prêter *to lend*
se promener *to go for a walk*
ranger *to put away*
se raser *to shave*
recommencer *to start again*
réparer *to repair*
utiliser *to use*
vouloir bien *to want to*

Higher phrases

Je m'en vais *I'm going*
Va-t-en! *Go away!*
Va voir qui est là! *Go and see who is there!*
Je me suis changé(e) *I have changed*
Veux-tu bien éplucher les carottes? *Will you please prepare (peel, scrape) the carrots?*
Je vais faire cuire ce lapin dans le four *I'll cook this rabbit in the oven*
Est-ce que je peux t'aider à ranger ta chambre? *Can I help you tidy your room?*
Je vais m'en occuper *I'll do that*
Est-ce que tu peux me prêter 10 francs? *Can you lend me 10 francs?*
Est-ce que je peux vous donner un coup de main? *Can I give you a hand?*
Mon père m'a interdit de sortir ce soir *My father has forbidden me to go out this evening*

POCKET MONEY AND SPARE-TIME JOBS

Basic

(pas) assez *(not) enough*
beaucoup *a lot*
cher *expensive*
gratuit *free of charge*
important *important*
pauvre *poor*

peu de *little*
riche *rich*
acheter *to buy*
coûter *to cost*
commencer *to begin*
faire des économies *to save*
se faire __ F par semaine/par heure *to make __ francs a week/an hour*
finir *to finish*
gagner *to earn*
payer *to pay (for)*
travailler *to work*

argent de poche (m) *pocket money*
(R) la monnaie *(small) change*
le porte-feuille *wallet*
le porte-monnaie *purse*
le prix *price*
un(e) après-midi *afternoon*
la journée *day*
le matin *morning*
le soir *evening*
le weekend *weekend*

Basic phrases

Je fais des économies pour acheter . . . *I'm saving to buy . . .*
Je gagne 20 francs par heure *I earn 20 francs an hour*
Je travaille le week-end *I work at weekends*
Je commence à __ heures et je finis à __ heures *I begin at __ o'clock and finish at __ o'clock*

Higher

appartenir *to belong*
dépenser *to spend (money)*
déposer *to deposit (in the bank)*
emprunter (à) *to borrow (from)*
être à court d'argent *to be short of money*
prêter (à) *to lend (to)*

Higher phrases

Je suis à court d'argent *I am short of money*
Je voudrais emprunter 50 francs *I'd like to borrow 50 francs*
J'ai tout depensé *I have spent everything*
Je gagne beaucoup *I earn a lot*

GEOGRAPHICAL SURROUNDINGS

IN TOWN

Basic

un aéroport *airport*
un arrêt d'autobus *bus stop*
une autoroute *motorway*
le banlieue *suburb*
la banque *bank*
le bâtiment *building*
la bibliothèque *library*
la boîte aux lettres *letter box*
le bruit *noise*
le bureau *office*
(R) la cabine téléphonique *phone box*
le camping *campsite*
la capitale *capital*
la cathédrale *cathedral*
le centre commercial *shopping centre*
le centre-ville *town centre*
le château *castle*
le cinéma *cinema*
(R) la circulation *traffic*
la cité *city/housing estate*
le danger *danger*

une église *church*
un endroit *place*
l' environnement (m) *environment*
(R) l'espace (f) *space*
la fabrique *factory*
la fête *festival*
les feux *traffic lights*
la foire *fair*
la gare *station*
(R) la gendarmerie *police station*
un hôpital *hospital*
une industrie *industry*
un hôtel de ville *town hall*
le magasin *shop*
la mairie *town hall*
le marché *market*
le monument *monument*
le musée *museum*
le parc *park*
le parking *car park*
le passage clouté *pedestrian crossing*
la piscine *swimming pool*
la place *square*
le pont *bridge*

le   port   *port*
la   poste   *post office*
le   stade   *stadium*
le   station-service   *service-station*
le   syndicat d'initiative   *information office*
le   théâtre   *theatre*
la   tour   *tower*
le   trottoir   *pavement*
une   usine   *factory*
la   ville   *town*
le/la voisin(e)   *neighbour*
la   zone piétonne   *pedestrian precinct*

Basic phrases

J'habite à Newcastle depuis trois ans   *I've been living in Newcastle for 3 years*
J'habite à Norwich depuis toujours   *I've always lived in Norwich*

Higher

un   agence de voyages   *travel agency*
les   environs   *surroundings, neighbourhood*
un   événement   *event*
un   habitant   *inhabitant*
le   jardin public   *park*
le   panneau   *board*
le   passage à niveau   *level crossing*
le   passage souterrain   *subway*
le   quartier   *quarter, district*
le   siècle   *century*
le   terrain de camping   *campsite*
la   terrasse de café   *café terrace*

IN THE COUNTRYSIDE

Basic

le   bois   *wood*
la   campagne   *countryside*
la   ferme   *farm*
le   fleuve   *river*
la   forêt   *forest*
une   île   *island*
le   lac   *lake*
le   lieu   *place*
la   mer   *sea*
le   monde   *world*
la   montagne   *mountain*
la   nature   *nature*
le   pays   *country, region*
la   plage   *beach*
la   pollution   *pollution*
la   province   *region, province*
la   région   *region*
la   rivière   *river*
la   vallée   *valley*
le   village   *village*

Higher

les   champs   *fields*
les   environs   *surroundings*
le   paysage   *countryside*
la   qualité   *quality*
(R)   la randonnée   *long walk*

les   specialités locales   *local specialities*
la   terre   *land, earth*

POSITIONS

Basic

autour de   *around*
en bas   *downstairs, below*
chez   *at the home of*
à côté de   *next door to, beside*
dehors   *outside*
à droite   *on the right*
en face de   *opposite*
à gauche   *on the left*
loin de   *far from*
le long de   *along*
au milieu de   *in the middle of*
près de   *near to*
proche de   *near to*
situé à   *situated (at)*
se trouver   *to be situated*

Higher

au sommet de   *at the top of*
en plein air   *in the open air*
encombré de   *congested by*
entouré de   *surrounded by*
hors de   *outside*
n'importe où   *anywhere*
relié à   *linked to*

DESCRIPTIONS

Basic

ancien   *old, ex-* __
agréable   *pleasant*
dangereux   *dangerous*
ennuyeux   *boring*
historique   *historic*
important   *important*
industriel   *industrial*
intéressant   *interesting*
pollué   *polluted*
propre   *clean*
sale   *dirty*
triste   *sad*
varié   *varied*
voisin   *next, neighbouring*

Higher

accueillant   *welcoming*
agricole   *agricultural*
animé   *lively*
charmant   *charming*
laid   *ugly*
naturel   *natural*
(R) paisible   *peaceful*
(R) pittoresque   *picturesque*
profond   *deep*
rare   *rare*
tranquille   *peaceful, quiet*
(R) à peine   *hardly, scarcely*

SCHOOL

BUILDINGS AND TYPES

Basic

la   bibliothèque   *library*
la   cantine   *canteen*
le   CES   *secondary school*
le   collège   *secondary school, college*
une   école primaire   *primary school*
le   gymnase   *gymnasium*
une   infirmerie   *infirmary*

(R)   le laboratoire   *laboratory*
le   lycée   *secondary school (grammar)*
la   salle de classe   *classroom*
la   salle des professeurs   *staffroom*
(R)   une université   *university*
les   vestiaires   *cloak-rooms, changing rooms*
loin   *far*
mixte   *mixed*
public   *public*
privé   *private*

Higher

un	atelier	*workshop, studio*
la	cour	*playground*
le	foyer des élèves	*pupils' common room*
la	pelouse	*lawn*

SCHOOL ROUTINE

Basic

le	bic	*ball-point pen*
le	bulletin	*bulletin*
le	bureau	*office*
le	cahier	*exercise book*
le/la	camarade	*friend*
le	cartable	*school satchel*
le	concert	*concert*
le/la	copain, copine	*friend*
le	cours	*lesson*
le	crayon	*pencil*
le(s)	devoir(s)	*homework*
un	échange	*exchange*
(R)	l'éducation (f)	*education*
un	emploi du temps	*timetable*
(R)	l'enseignement (m)	*teaching*
(R)	un(e) étudiant(e)	*student*
un	exemple	*example*
la	faute	*mistake*
le	livre	*book*
le	livre de classe	*text-book*
la	note	*mark*
un	ordinateur	*calculator, computer*
le	papier	*paper*
la	permission	*permission*
la	phrase	*phrase, sentence*
le	problème	*problem*
le/la	prof	*teacher*
le/la	professeur	*teacher*
la	récréation	*break*
le	repas	*meal*
la	réponse	*answer*
	sixième	*first form (secondary school)*
	terminale	*sixth form*
le	stylo	*ball-point pen*
le	tableau	*picture*
un	uniforme	*uniform*
le	vocabulaire	*vocabulary*

apprendre	*to learn*
assister à	*to be present at*
calculer	*to calculate*
chanter	*to sing*
compter	*to count*
choisir	*to choose*
demander	*to ask (for)*
dessiner	*to draw*
durer	*to last*
écouter	*to listen*
s'entraîner	*to train, practise*
étudier	*to study*
expliquer	*to explain*
faire ses devoirs	*to do one's homework*
faire des progrès	*to make progress*
faire un exercice	*to do an exercise*
faire une expérience	*to do an experiment*
jouer	*to play*
lire	*to read*
manquer	*to be missing*
nager	*to swim*
oublier	*to forget*
poser une question	*to ask a question*
punir	*to punish*
répéter	*to repeat*
réviser	*to revise*

(R)	surveiller	*to supervise*

absent	*absent*
bon	*good*
classique	*classical*
difficile	*difficult*
excellent	*excellent*
facile	*easy*
présent	*present*
sévère	*strict*

en avance	*in advance, early*
en retard	*late*
d'abord	*first of all*
après	*after, later*
ensuite	*afterwards*

Higher

le	congé	*leave, time off*
la	craie	*chalk*
le	demi-pensionnaire	*half-boarder*
la	gomme	*rubber*
le	pensionnaire	*boarder*
la	règle	*ruler, rule*

copier	*to copy*
enseigner	*to teach*
fournir	*to provide*
penser	*to think*
prendre des notes	*to take notes*
quitter	*to leave*
raconter	*to recount, tell*
répondre	*to reply, answer*
(R) se taire	*to be silent*
traduire	*to translate*

Higher phrases

Taisez-vous! *Be quiet!*
Demain, nous avons un jour de
　congé *Tomorrow we have a day off*

SUBJECTS

Basic

la	matière	*subject*
l'	allemand (m)	*German*
l'	anglais (m)	*English*
la	biologie	*biology*
la	chimie	*chemistry*
le	commerce	*commerce*
la	couture	*needlework*
la	cuisine	*cookery*
le	dessin	*drawing*
l'	éducation physique	*physical education*
(R)	l'électronique	*electronics*
l'	espagnol	*Spanish*
les	études menagères	*home economics*
le	français	*French*
la	géographie	*geography*
le	grec	*Greek*
la	gymnastique	*gymnastics*
l'	histoire ancienne (f)	*ancient history*
l'	histoire moderne (f)	*modern history*
l'	informatique (f)	*information technology*
l'	instruction civique (f)	*civics, social studies*
l'	instruction religieuse (f)	*religious education*
l'	italien (m)	*Italian*
les	langues modernes (f)	*modern languages*
le	latin	*Latin*
la	littérature	*literature*
les	maths (f)	*maths*
les	mathématiques (f)	*mathematics*

la	musique	*music*
la	poterie	*pottery*
la	physique	*physics*
la	religion	*religion*
le	russe	*Russian*
la	science	*science*
les	sciences économiques (f)	*economics*
le	sport	*sport*
les	travaux manuels (m)	*crafts*
les	travaux pratiques (m)	*crafts*

+ any other subjects studied by the student

aimer	*to like*	
détester	*to hate*	
préférer	*to prefer*	

bête	*stupid*	
chouette	*great, marvellous*	
compliqué	*complicated*	
difficile	*difficult*	
ennuyeux	*boring*	
facile	*easy*	
intéressant	*interesting*	
marrant	*funny*	

Basic phrases

Je suis fort(e) en anglais   *I'm good at English*

Je suis faible en histoire   *I'm weak in history*

Je suis moyen(ne) en biologie   *I'm average at biology*

MARKS AND EXAMS

Basic

un	examen	*examination*
le	résultat	*result*
	passer un examen	*to take an exam*
	rater un examen	*to fail an exam*
	réussir à	*to pass, succeed*

Basic phrases

Je vais passer mes examens cet été   *I will take my exams this summer*

J'ai réussi à mon examen   *I have passed my exam*

J'ai raté mon examen de physique   *I failed my physics exam.*

Higher

le	brevet	*diploma, certificate*
le	certificat	*certificate*
le	diplôme	*diploma*

	échouer à	*to fail*
	être reçu	*to pass*
	tricher	*to cheat*

Higher phrases

J'ai échoué au bac   *I have failed my 'bac' (A levels)*

J'ai été reçu(e) au bac   *I have passed my 'bac' (A levels)*

FUTURE PLANS AND OCCUPATIONS

Basic

un/une	acteur/actrice	*actor, actress*
le/la	boucher/bouchère	*butcher*
le/la	boulanger/boulangère	*baker*
le/la	charcutier/charcutière	*pork butcher*
le/la	coiffeur/coiffeuse	*hairdresser*
le/la	cuisinier/cuisinière	*cook*

le/la	dentiste	*dentist*
le	directeur	*director, headmaster*
la	directrice	*director, headmistress*
le	docteur	*doctor*
un(e)	électricien/életricienne	*electrician*
un/une	employé(e)	*employee*
un/une	épicier/épicière	*grocer*
un/une	étudiant/étudiante	*student*
le/la	facteur/factrice	*postman, postwoman*
la	femme de chambre	*housemaid*
le/la	fermier/fermière	*farmer*
le	garçon de café	*waiter*
le	gendarme	*policeman*
une	hôtesse de l'air	*air hostess*
un/une	infirmier/infirmière	*nurse*
le	journaliste	*journalist*
le/la	mécanicien/mécanicienne	*mechanic*
le	médecin	*doctor*
le/la	musicien/musicienne	*musician*
le/la	pâtissier/pâtissière	*pastry cook*
le/la	patron/patronne (de restaurant)	*restaurant owner*
le	pilote	*pilot*
le/la	professeur	*teacher*
le/la	secrétaire	*secretary*
le	serveur	*barman, shop assistant*
la	serveuse	*barmaid, shop assistant*
la	vedette	*film star*
le	vétérinaire	*veterinary surgeon*
un	emploi	*job*
le	bureau de change	*exchange office*
une	industrie	*industry*
le	laboratoire	*laboratory*
le	métier	*occupation, profession*
la	poste	*post office*
la	réception	*reception*
une	usine	*factory*

Basic phrases

Je voudrais être . . .   *I would like to be . . .*

Je voudrais travailler dans une usine   *I would like to work in a factory*

Mon père est mécanicien   *My father is a mechanic*

Ma mère est ménagère   *My mother is a housewife*

Higher

un/une	animateur/animatrice	*organizer*
un(e)	avocate(e)	*lawyer*
le	chef	*cook*
(R)	le chirurgien	*surgeon*
le/la	chômeur/chômeuse	*unemployed man/woman*
le/la	commerçant/commerçante	*salesperson, market trader*
le,la	comptable	*accountant*
la	dactylo	*shorthand typist*
le/la	décorateur/décoratrice	*decorator*
le/la	dessinateur/dessinatrice	*designer*
la	femme d'affaires	*businesswoman*
un	homme d'affaires	*businessman*
le/la	jardinier/jardinière	*gardener*
le	maçon	*builder*
le	militaire	*soldier*
un/une	ouvrier/ouvrière	*worker*
le	pompier	*fireman*
le/la	programmeur/programmeuse	*programmer*
le/la	technicien/technicienne	*technician*
la	société	*company*
une	administration	*administration*
un	agence de voyages	*travel agency*
la	profession libérale	*profession*

Higher phrases

Je suis attiré(e) par les professions
  libérales *I am attracted to professional
  work*
J'aimerais être vétérinaire *I would like to
  be a vet*
Je serai en chômage, sinon *Otherwise I
  shall be unemployed*

J'ai l'intention de faire ma licence *I intend
  to take a degree*
Je vais faire mes études à l'université *I am
  going to study at university*
Je ferai mon bac *I will take my 'bac'*
J'aimerais travailler à l'étranger *I would
  like to work abroad*

HOBBIES

Basic

le   club   *club*
la   collection   *collection*
le   disque   *record*
la   distraction   *entertainment*
un   échange   *exchange*
les   échecs(m)   *chess*
une   excursion   *excursion*
une   exposition   *exhibition*
un   instrument   *instrument*
le   jeu   *game*
le   journal   *newspaper*
un   illustré   *illustrated magazine*
les   loisirs(m)   *free time, pastimes*
le   magazine   *magazine*
le   membre   *member*
la   musique   *music*
le   passe-temps   *hobby*
la   pêche   *fishing*
le   programme   *programme*
(R)   la revue   *magazine*
la   société   *society, club*
la   soirée   *evening*
le   sport   *sport*
le   téléjournal   *TV news*
le   temps libre   *free time*
les   vacances (f)   *holidays*
la   visite guidée   *tour (of museum, etc.)*
le   week-end   *weekend*

aimer beaucoup   *to like a lot*
collectionner   *to collect*
danser   *to dance*
écouter   *to listen (to)*
s'ennuyer   *to get bored*
(R) exposer   *to exhibit*
s'intéresser à   *to be interested in*
jouer au football (etc.)   *to play football (etc.)*
jouer de la guitare (etc.)   *to play the guitar
  (etc.)*
préférer   *to prefer*
réaliser   *to realize, put into practice*
regarder   *to watch*
rêver   *to dream*
rire   *to laugh*
sortir   *to go out*
visiter   *to visit*

+ any other activities appropriate to the
  student

(R)   tout le monde   *everyone*
longtemps   *a long time*
quelquefois   *sometimes*
sauf   *except*
souvent   *often*
(R) de temps en temps   *from time to time*
toujours   *always*

chouette   *great, marvellous*
classique   *classical*
mauvais   *bad*
moche   *rotten*

passionnant   *exciting*
pop   *pop*
sensass   *great, sensational*
seul   *alone*
sportif   *athletic, keen on sports*

+ adjectives for describing people – see
  page 29

Basic phrases

Je m'intéresse à la photographie *I'm
  interested in photography*
Je joue quelquefois au tennis *I sometimes
  play tennis*
Je joue de la flûte *I play the flute*
J'aime visiter les châteaux *I like going to
  castles*
Je suis membre d'un club *I am a member
  of a club*
Quelles distractions y a-t-il ici? *What
  entertainments are there here?*
Je vais à la pêche assez souvent *I go
  fishing quite often*
On a fait la visite guidée du musée *We had
  a guided tour of the museum*

Higher

avoir le temps de   *to have the time to*
avoir horreur de   *to hate*
bricoler   *to do odd jobs, to potter*
s'informer   *to learn*
faire de la peinture   *to paint*
pratiquer un sport   *to do a sport*
la   bande dessinée   *cartoon*
la   chorale   *choir*
les   environs   *surroundings*
les   festivités (f)   *festivities*
la   lecture   *reading*
(R)   le tricot   *jumper*
quotidien   *daily*
hebdomadaire   *weekly*
mensuel   *monthly*
populaire   *popular*

Higher phrases

J'ai horreur du tennis *I hate tennis*
Je lis les journaux pour m'informer *I read
  the papers to learn about things*
Je fais partie d'une chorale *I am in a choir*
Ma lecture préférée, c'est les bandes
  dessinées *I like reading cartoons best
  of all*

SPORTING ACTIVITIES

Basic

le   ballon   *ball (e.g. football)*
le   champion   *champion*
le   championnat   *championship*
la   compétition   *competition*
le   courage   *courage, drive*
le   cricket   *cricket*
une   équipe   *team*
le   football   *football*
la   gymnastique   *gymnastics*
(R)   un hobby   *hobby*

le   hockey   *hockey*
le   jouet   *toy*
le   joueur   *player*
le   match   *match*
le   rugby   *rugby*
les   sports d'hiver (m)   *winter sports*
le   stade   *stadium*
(R) le terrain de sport   *sports ground*

se baigner   *to swim, bathe*
courir   *to run*
gagner   *to win*
faire du cyclisme   *to cycle*
faire de la natation   *to swim*
faire une promenade en bateau   *to go boating*
faire une promenade en vélo   *to go for a bike ride*
faire du ski   *to ski*
perdre   *to lose*
se reposer   *to rest*

Basic phrases

On a perdu le match de rugby   *We lost the rugby match*
Je fais souvent du ski   *I often go skiing*
Je me suis baigné(e) dans la rivière   *I bathed in the river*
J'adore faire de la natation   *I love swimming*
Bon courage!   *Good luck! Play well!*

Higher

un   arbitre   *referee*
un   aviron   *oar*
l'   équipement (m)   *equipment*
le   match nul   *draw*
le   titre   *title*

battre   *to beat*
critiquer   *to criticize*
défendre   *to defend*
faire un partie de tennis, etc.   *to play a game of tennis, etc.*
marquer un but   *to score a goal*
marquer un point   *to score a point*
protester   *to protest*
soutenir une équipe   *to support a team*

ENTERTAINMENT

Basic

(R) un/une acteur/actrice   *actor, actress*
une ambiance   *atmosphere*
un   animal sauvage   *wild animal*
une aventure   *adventure*
le   bal   *ball (dancing)*
le   balcon   *balcony*
le   bandit   *bandit*
le   billet   *ticket*
la   boum   *party*
le   chameau   *camel*
la   cassette   *cassette*
la   chanson   *song*
le/la chanteur/chanteuse   *singer*
le   cinéma   *cinema*
le   cirque   *circus*
le   clown   *clown*
le   club   *club*
la   comédie   *comedy*
le   concert   *concert*
la   discothèque   *disco*
le   drapeau   *flag*
un   éléphant   *elephant*
l'   espionnage (m)   *spying, espionage*

le   film d'amour   *love film*
le   film d'épouvante   *horror film*
le   film policier   *crime film*
le   film de science-fiction   *science-fiction film*
la   flûte   *flute*
le   groupe   *group*
la   guerre   *war*
la   guitare   *guitar*
(R) l'information (f)   *information*
la   jeunesse   *youth, young people*
le   lion   *lion*
le   loup   *wolf*
le   magicien   *magician*
la   maison de jeunes   *youth club*
la   matinée   *morning, afternoon performance*
un   opéra   *opera*
un   orchestre   *orchestra*
un   ours   *bear*
le   piano   *piano*
la   pièce de théâtre   *play*
(R) la réunion   *meeting*
le   rhinocéros   *rhinoceros*
(R) le risque   *risk*
la   salle   *room, hall*
(R) la séance   *performance*
le   singe   *monkey*
(R) le spectacle   *entertainment*
la   surprise-partie   *party*
le   théâtre   *theatre*
le   ticket   *ticket*
la   vedette   *(film) star*
la   version anglaise   *English edition (version)*
le   violon   *violin*
le   western   *western*
le   zoo   *zoo*

aller voir   *to go and see*
commencer   *to begin*
dresser un animal   *to train an animal*
enfermer   *to close, lock up*
(R) s'évader   *to escape*
fuir   *to flee*
payer   *to pay (for)*
plaire à   *to please*
réserver   *to reserve*
se sauver   *to run away*

affreux   *awful*
amusant   *amusing*
bien!   *good!*
bon   *good*
comique   *funny*
drôle   *funny*
ennuyeux   *boring*
excellent   *excellent*
extraordinaire   *extraordinary*
formidable   *great, terrific*
intéressant   *interesting*
nouveau   *new*
pas mal   *not bad*
sensationnel   *sensational, marvellous*
super   *terrific, great*
surprenant   *surprising*

+ adjectives for hobbies

(R) agréablement   *pleasantly*
(R) extrêmement   *extremely*
tout à fait   *quite, totally*

être d'accord   *to agree*
avoir raison   *to be right*
penser   *to think*
trouver   *to find*

Basic phrases

Il y avait une bonne ambiance *There was a good atmosphere*

Nous sommes allé(e)s à la boum chez Marie. C'était sensass! *We went to Marie's party. It was great!*

Le film était en version anglaise *The film was in an English version*

Comment as-tu trouvé le concert? *What did you think of the concert?*

Higher

les	actualités	*news*
le/la	comédien/comédienne	*comedian, comedienne*
le	dessin animé	*cartoon*
le	documentaire	*documentary*
un	entr'acte	*interval*
le	feuilleton	*serial*
une	ouvreuse	*usherette*
(R) le	pourboire	*tip*
la	réduction	*reduction*
les	sous-titres (m)	*sub-titles*
le	succès	*success*
le	tube	*hit record*

annuler *to cancel*
apprécier *to appreciate*
conseiller *to advise*
découvrir *to discover*
enregistrer *to record*
(R) être à l'affiche *to be billed, advertised*
protester *to protest*
se réjouir *to be delighted*
tourner un film *to make a film*

favori *favourite*
impressionnant *impressive*
(R) majeur *major*
merveilleux *marvellous*
passionnant *exciting*
pire *worse*
rare *rare*
ridicule *ridiculous*

Higher phrases

Pendant l'entr'acte nous avons vu la vedette qui était à l'affiche *During the interval we saw the star who was on the poster*

J'ai enregistré cette émission sur magnétoscope parce que je voulais regarder le feuilleton sur l'autre chaîne *I recorded this programme on video because I wanted to see the serial on the other channel*

J'ai oublié de donner un pourboire à l'ouvreuse. Elle était furieuse *I forgot to give the usherette a tip. She was furious*

BOX OFFICE SCENES

Theatre

Je voudrais réserver des places pour la pièce du 13 juillet *I would like to reserve seats for the play on 13th July*

Il n'y a plus de places pour ce jour-là, mais il en reste encore pour le lendemain *There are no seats left for that day, but there are some for the following day*

Alors, trois places pour le lendemain *All right, three seats for the following day*

Des places à quel prix? Il reste des places à 25 F et à 30 F *At what price? There are seats left at 25 francs and 30 francs*

Trois places à 30 F, s'il vous plaît *Three seats at 30 francs please*

Sporting event

Je voudrais réserver des places pour le match de samedi, s'il vous plaît *I would like to reserve places for the match on Saturday please*

Oui, combien de places? *Yes. How many places?*

Deux places, s'il vous plaît *Two please*

Concert

Je voudrais réserver des places pour le concert du 11 novembre, s'il vous plaît *I would like to reserve seats for the concert on 11th November please*

Des places à quel prix? Il reste des places à 45 F et à 35 F *What price seats? There are seats left at 45 francs and 35 francs*

Deux places à 35 F, s'il vous plaît *Two seats at 35 francs please*

Cinema

Je voudrais une place pour *Ghandi*, s'il vous plaît *I would like a seat for* Ghandi *please*

Il ne reste plus que des places tout à fait à l'avant ou à l'arrière. Qu'est-ce que vous préférez? *The only seats left are right at the front and at the back. Which would you prefer?*

Une place à l'arrière, s'il vous plaît *A seat at the back please*

Ça vous fait 40F *That'll be 40 francs*

C'est un film en anglais? *Is the film in English?*

Non, il est en version française *No, it's the French version*

TRAVEL ## TRAVEL TO WORK AND SCHOOL

Basic

	en autobus	*by bus*
	en autocar	*by coach*
	à bicyclette	*by bicycle*
la	distance	*distance*
la	gare	*station*
	en métro	*by tube*
	à pied	*on foot*
la	station	*tube station, stop*
	par le train	*by train*
le	transport	*transport*
	en vélo	*by bike*
	en vélomoteur	*by motorized bicycle*
	amener quelqu'un en voiture	*to take someone by car*

s'arrêter *to stop*
arriver à 9 h *to arrive at 9 o'clock*
conduire *to drive*
se dépêcher *to hurry*
déposer quelqu'un en voiture *to drop someone by car*
descendre *to get out*
durer *to last*
entrer *to enter*
être de retour *to be back*
marcher *to walk*
mettre 20 minutes *to take 20 minutes*
(R) se mettre en route *to set out*
monter dans *to get in*
partir *to leave*

préférer   *to prefer*
prendre le train   *to go by train*
quitter   *to leave*
rater   *to miss*
rentrer   *to return*
renverser   *to turn or knock over*
rester   *to remain*
revenir   *to come back*
sortir   *to go out*
traverser   *to cross*
utiliser   *to make use of, to use*
voyager en train   *to go by train*
en avance   *in advance*
d'habitude   *usually*
à l'heure   *on time*
de bonne heure   *early*
rapidement   *quickly*
en retard   *late*
toujours   *always*
lent   *slow*
(R) ponctuel   *punctual*
rapide   *fast*
tard   *late*
tôt   *early*
valable pendant un mois   *valid for a month*

chez moi   *at home, at my house*

See also School, and Future plans and
   occupations

Basic phrases

Ma mère m'amène en voiture   *My mother
   takes me by car*
Elle me dépose devant le collège   *She
   drops me outside school*
Mon père me conduit le soir   *My father
   drives me in the evening*
Je mets 20 minutes pour arriver au
   collège   *It takes me 20 minutes to get to
   school*
Je me mets en route vers huit heures   *I
   start off at about 8 o'clock*
Je préfère arriver de bonne heure   *I prefer
   arriving early*
Je suis de retour vers cinq heures   *I am
   back home at about 5 o'clock*
Je monte dans le train   *I get into the train*

Higher

faire de l'auto-stop   *to hitch-hike*
le   moyen de transport   *means of transport*

FINDING THE WAY

Basic

un   agent de police   *policeman*
le   bureau de change   *exchange office*
le   carrefour   *crossroads*
la   carte   *map*
le   chemin   *way*
(R)   le coin   *corner*
la   direction   *direction*
la   distance   *distance*
une   église   *church*
(R)   les feux   *traffic lights*
le   rond-point   *roundabout*
   (R) toutes directions   *all routes*
le   W.C.   *toilet*

see also Geographical surroundings

aider   *to help*
pour aller à . . .   *to get to . . .*
arriver   *to arrive*
chercher   *to look for*

continuer   *to continue*
faire attention   *to pay attention*
monter dans   *to get in*
passer   *to pass*
passer devant   *to pass in front of*
se perdre   *to get lost*
se renseigner   *to get information, to find
   out*
suivre   *to follow*
se trouver   *to be situated*
traverser   *to cross*
après   *after*
avant   *before*
au bout de   *at the end of*
à côté de   *next to*
derrière   *behind*
devant   *in front of*
en face de   *opposite*
jusqu'à   *as far as*
à __ mètres   *__ metres away*
à __ minutes   *__ minutes away*
près de   *near to*
proche de   *near to*

alors   *then*
à droite   *to the right*
ensuite   *afterwards, then*
à gauche   *to the left*
là   *there*
là-bas   *over there*
à l'est   *to the east*
au nord   *to the north*
à l'ouest   *to the west*
au sud   *to the south*
puis   *then*
tout droit   *straight on*

premier, second, etc.   *first, second etc.*

Basic phrases

Pour aller à Orléans, s'il vous plaît?   *The
   way to Orléans please?*
Prenez la troisième route à droite   *Take
   the third road on the right*

Où est la place Marie Curie, s'il vous
   plaît?   *Where is Marie Curie Square
   please?*
Continuez tout droit   *Go straight on*
C'est au centre de la ville   *It's in the town
   centre*
C'est au bout de l'allée Foch   *It's at the end
   of Allée Foch*
Nous pouvons regarder mon plan de la
   ville   *We can look at my town plan*
C'est à quelle distance d'ici?   *How far is it
   from here?*
C'est à 20 minutes à pied   *It's 20 minutes
   on foot*
C'est à 5 minutes en voiture   *It's 5 minutes
   by car*
C'est à 800 mètres d'ici   *It's 800 metres
   from here*

Il y a combien de kilomètres jusqu'à la
   plage?   *How far is it to the beach?*
A peu près 7 kilomètres   *About 7
   kilometres*

Quel jour est la fête foraine?   *On which day
   is the travelling fair?*
Le syndicat d'initiative vous le dira   *The
   information office will tell you*

Excusez-moi, où est la sortie de
   secours?   *Excuse me, where is the
   emergency exit?*

Vous suivez le couloir jusqu'au panneau 'interdit de fumer' et vous tournez à droite. La sortie est au fond du couloir *You go along the corridor as far as the 'no smoking' notice and you turn to the right. The exit is at the end of the corridor*

Merci beaucoup *Thank you very much*

Il n'y a pas de quoi *It's a pleasure*

De rien *Don't mention it*

Higher

le commissariat de police *police station*

le milieu *middle*

s'égarer *to get lost*

retourner *to return*

s'en aller *to go away*

recommander *to recommend*

le long de *along*

(R) n'importe où *anywhere*

Higher phrases

Où est-ce que je peux me stationner? *Where can I park?*

N'importe où le long de cette rue *Anywhere along this street*

PUBLIC TRANSPORT

Trains

Basic

un aller simple *single ticket*

un aller-retour *return ticket*

(R) une arrivée *arrival*

le billet *ticket*

le buffet *buffet*

la 'Carte Jeune' *young person's rail card*

(R) le chemin de fer *railway*

la deuxième classe *second class*

la première classe *first class*

(R) le compartiment *compartment*

(R) la consigne *left luggage office*

(R) les correspondances (f) *connection*

(R) le départ *departure*

(R) un express *express*

(R) le fumeur *smoker*

(R) le non-fumeur *non-smoker*

la gare *station*

le guichet *ticket office*

un horaire *timetable*

un omnibus *slow train*

le porteur *porter*

le quai *platform*

le rapide *express*

(R) la réduction *reduction*

la réservation *reservation*

le sac *bag*

le sac à dos *rucksack*

la salle d'attente *waiting room*

la S.N.C.F. *French railway*

la sortie *exit*

la station de taxis *taxi rank*

le tarif *price list*

le train *train*

la valise *suitcase*

(R) la voie *track*

bon voyage! *have a good trip!*

(R) le voyageur *traveller, passenger*

(R) annoncer *to announce*

attendre *to wait (for)*

changer *to change*

composter *to date, punch (ticket)*

contrôler *to inspect, check*

descendre *to get out*

durer *to last*

s'installer *to settle*

manquer *to miss*

prendre trois heures *to take three hours*

porter *to wear, carry*

de *from*

en direction de *going to*

(R) en provenance de *coming from*

dernier *last*

occupé *occupied*

prochain *next*

suivant *next, following*

supplémentaire *extra*

Basic phrases

Je voudrais un billet pour Paris, s'il vous plaît *I'd like a ticket for Paris, please*

Un aller simple ou un aller-retour? *Single or return?*

Vous voyagez en première ou en seconde? *Are you going first or second class?*

Vous voulez faire une réservation? *Do you want to reserve a seat?*

Ce sera la voiture 11, compartiment 3, place 5 *That'll be coach 11, compartment 3, seat 5*

C'est un omnibus ou un express? *Is it a slow or fast train?*

A quelle heure part le train? *At what time does the train leave?*

A quelle heure arrive le train? *At what time does the train arrive?*

Vous trouverez les heures de départ et d'arrivée affichées là-bas *You'll find departure and arrival times posted over there*

A quelle heure est le prochain train pour Paris? Et le train suivant? *At what time is the next train for Paris? And the one after?*

Où puis-je laisser mes bagages? *Where can I leave my luggage?*

Vous pouvez les déposer à la consigne ou utiliser la consigne automatique *You can put it in the left luggage office or use the automatic luggage locker*

La salle d'attente est de l'autre côté *The waiting room is on the other side*

D'où part le train pour Calais? *Where does the Calais train leave from?*

Du quai numéro 4 *From platform number 4.*

C'est bien ici, le train pour Calais? *Am I right here for the Calais train?*

Non, ici sont les trains de banlieue. Il faut aller au départ des grandes lignes *No, these are the suburban trains. You have to go to the main-line departures*

Messieurs et Mesdames les passengers sont priés de monter en voiture *Ladies and gentlemen, passengers are requested to board the train.*

Higher

le changement d'horaire *timetable change*

la couchette *couchette, sleeper*

la portière *door (train)*

la destination *destination*

le/la touriste *tourist*

le wagon-restaurant *dining car*

consulter *to consult*

indiquer *to show, indicate*

ralentir *to slow down*
rembourser *to reimburse*
rouler *to travel, move*

Higher phrases

Pouvez-vous m'indiquer le wagon-restaurant? *Can you show me the dining car?*

Buses

un arrêt *stop*
un autobus *bus*
un autocar *coach*
le bus *bus*
le car *coach*
le carnet *booklet*
la gare routière *bus station*
la ligne *line, route*
le numéro *number*
le ticket *ticket*

lent *slow*

+ many of the items for trains

Ships and hovercraft

Basic

le bateau *boat*
la gare maritime *ferry terminal*
la traversée *crossing*

débarquer *to disembark*
(R) embarquer *to embark*

Higher

un aéroglisseur *hovercraft*
le car-ferry *car-ferry*
le ferry *ferry*
un hovercraft *hovercraft*
le port *port*
voler *to fly*

Planes

Higher

un avion *aeroplane*
(R) la ceinture de sécurité *safety belt*
le vol *flight*
atterrir *to land*
décoller *to take off*
voler *to fly*

Going through customs

Basic

(R) la douane *customs*

Higher

le douanier *customs official*
la frontière *frontier, border*
le passeport *passport*

Higher phrases

Avez-vous quelque chose à déclarer? *Have you anything to declare?*
Je n'ai rien à déclarer *I have nothing to declare*
Ouvrez vos valises, s'il vous plaît *Open your cases, please*
J'ai des cigarettes et de l'alcool à déclarer *I have some cigarettes and some alcohol to declare*

At the lost property office

Higher

(R) le bureau des objets perdus *lost property office*
(R) le bureau des objets trouvés *lost property office*

le carnet de chèques *cheque book*
le détail *detail*
la récompense *reward*

accuser *to accuse*
(R) décrire *to describe*
expliquer *to explain*
garder *to keep*
oublier *to forget*
(R) reconnaître *to recognize*
(R) ressembler à *to look like, resemble*

Higher phrases

J'ai perdu mon porte-feuille *I have lost my wallet*
Est-ce que vous pouvez me le décrire? *Can you describe it to me?*

PRIVATE TRANSPORT

General

Basic

(R) attention! *look out*
une aire de repos *picnic area*
une assurance *insurance*
une auto-école *driving school*
le camion *lorry*
la carte verte *green card*
la carte routière *road map*
le casque *helmet*
(R) la chaussée *roadway*
le chauffeur *driver*
le conducteur *driver*
(R) la déviation *diversion*
(R) la fin *end*
le garage *garage*
(R) le mécanicien *mechanic*
la moto *motorbike*
le numéro *number*
le parking *car park*
(R) le péage *toll*
le permis de conduire *driving licence*
le poids lourd *heavy vehicle*
(R) priorité à droite *priority from the right*
(R) le passage protégé *right of way*
la route nationale *major road*
(R) le scooter *scooter*
(R) le stationnement *parking*
(R) les travaux (m) *works*
le vélomoteur *motorized bicycle*
le virage *turn, bend*
la vitesse *speed, gear*

freiner *to brake*
garer *to park*
passer le permis *to take one's test*
rouler *to drive, move*
stationner *to park*
tourner *to turn*

(R) lent *slow*
(R) obligatoire *obligatory*
(R) payant *paying, where one must pay*

Basic phrases

Il faut freiner avant le virage *You have to brake before the bend*
Il est interdit de stationner ici *It is forbidden to park here*

Higher

(R) une amende *fine*
le camion *lorry*
la camionette *van*
le code de la route *highway code*
le disque de stationnement *parking disc*

un   embouteillage   *traffic jam*
une   heure d'affluence   *rush hour*
les   papiers (m)   *papers*
la   police d'assurance   *insurance policy*
le   piéton   *pedestrian*
le   trottoir   *pavement*
le   zone bleue   *blue zone*

(R) circuler   *to move about*
conduire   *to drive*
dépasser   *to overtake*
louer   *to hire*
(R) ralentir   *to slow down*
retourner   *to return*
rouler au pas   *to drive at walking pace*

automatique   *automatic*

Accidents

Basic

un   accident   *accident*
une   ambulance   *ambulance*
la   clinique   *clinic*
le   docteur   *doctor*
le   gendarme   *gendarme, policeman*
la   police   *police*

blessé   *injured*
tuer   *to kill*
se tuer   *to commit suicide*

Higher

la   collision   *collision*
la   marque de voiture   *make of car*

aider   *to help*
cogner   *to bump*
écraser   *to crush*
risquer   *to risk*

s'approcher   *to approach*

dangereux   *dangerous*

The car

Basic

l'arrière   *back*
l'avant   *front*
la   clé de voiture   *car key*
le   coffre   *boot*
(R) un essuie-glace   *windscreen wiper*
le   frein   *brake*
le   moteur   *engine*
la   panne   *breakdown*
la   panne d'essence   *run out of petrol*
(R) le pare-brise   *windscreen*
le   phare   *head light*
le   pneu   *tyre*
(R) le rétroviseur   *driving mirror*
le   siège   *seat*
accélérer   *to accelerate*
allumer   *to put on lights*
s'arrêter   *to stop*
éteindre   *to put out lights*
(R) fonctionner   *to work, function*
marcher   *to work, function*
réparer   *to repair*
tomber en panne   *to break down*

Basic phrases

J'ai allumé les phares   *I have switched on the head lights*
Je suis tombé(e) en panne d'essence   *I have run out of petrol*
Le moteur ne marche pas   *The engine doesn't work*

Higher

la   batterie   *battery*
la   ceinture de sécurité   *safety strap*
la   crevaison   *puncture*
la   portière   *door*
le   volant   *steering wheel*

démarrer   *to start*
dépanner   *to repair*
freiner   *to brake*
passer une vitesse   *to change gear*

Higher phrases

Pouvez-vous me dépanner? J'ai une crevaison   *Can you put my car right. I have a puncture*

At the service station

Basic

l'   air (m)   *air*
l'   eau (f)   *water*
l'   essence (f)   *petrol*
la   fumée   *smoke*
le   gasole   *diesel*
le   gas-oil   *diesel*
l'   huile   *oil*
le   litre   *litre*
le   pompiste   *petrol-pump attendant*
le   super   *4 star*
les   toilettes (f)   *toilet*
le   W. C.   *toilet*
vérifier le niveau d'eau   *to check the water level*
vérifier le niveau d'huile   *to check the oil level*
vérifier les pressions   *to check tyre pressure*

Basic phrases

Faites le plein!   *Fill it up!*
Le plein d'essence, s'il vous plaît   *Fill it up with 2 star please*
Le plein de super, s'il vous plaît   *Fill it up with 4 star please*
C'est un self-service ici   *It's self service here*
Est-ce que vous pouvez laver le pare-brise, s'il vous plaît   *Can you wash the windscreen please?*
Je voudrais aussi acheter une carte routière   *I would also like to buy a road map*
Il me faut de l'huile   *I need oil*
Voulez-vous vérifier le niveau d'eau, s'il vous plaît?   *Would you check the water level please?*

Higher

(R) deux-temps   *two-stroke*
(R) lavage automatique   *carwash*

HOLIDAYS

GENERAL

Basic

un   appareil photo   *camera*
le   bateau à voile   *sailing boat*
la   brochure   *brochure*
(R) le bureau de tourisme   *tourist office*
le   bureau de renseignements   *information office*
le   centre de vacances   *holiday centre*
les   chèques de voyage   *travellers' cheques*
les   chaussures de ski (f)   *ski boots*
le   coquillage   *shellfish*
le   coup de soleil   *sunstroke*

la	crème solaire	*sun cream*
la	crêperie	*pancake shop or stall*
	Douvres	*Dover*
(R)	une école de langues	*language school*
une	excursion	*excursion*
la	falaise	*cliff*
la	forêt	*forest*
le	groupe	*group*
la	liste	*list*
le	monde	*world*
le	monument	*monument*
le	musée	*museum*
	Noël	*Christmas*
	Pâques	*Easter*
le	parapluie	*umbrella*
le	parasol	*parasol*
le	phare	*lighthouse*
la	photo	*photo*
le	pique-nique	*picnic*
la	piscine	*swimming pool*
la	piste	*track*
la	plage	*beach*
le	plan	*plan*
la	planche à voile	*surfboard*
le	port	*port*
(R)	la publicité	*publicity*
(R)	quinze jours	*a fortnight*
la	région	*area*
les	renseignements (m)	*information*
le	sac à dos	*rucksack*
le	séjour	*stay*
les	sports d'hiver (m)	*winter sports*
le/la	touriste	*tourist*
(R)	tout le monde	*everyone*
les	vacances (f)	*holidays*
(R)	la visite	*visit*
la	visite scolaire	*school trip*
le	voyage	*journey*

s'amuser *to enjoy oneself*
avoir du beau temps *to have fine weather*
avoir du mauvais temps *to have bad weather*
descendre dans un hôtel *to stay at a hotel*
(R) se détendre *to relax*
se (faire) bronzer *to get brown*
faire de l'autostop *to hitch hike*
faire de la planche à voile *to go surfboarding*
faire une promenade en bateau *to go out in a boat*
faire une promenade en vélo *to go for a bike ride*
faire du ski *to ski*
faire du ski nautique *to water-ski*
faire du stop *to hitch hike*
faire de la voile *to go sailing*
(R) louer *to hire*
(R) se mettre en route *to set out*
être en vacances *to be on holiday*
partir en vacances *to set out on holiday*
plaire à *to please*
prendre l'avion *to take the plane, to fly*
rester *to stay*
sécher *to dry*
voyager *to travel*

au bord de la mer *by the sea*
à la campagne *in the country*
à l'étranger *abroad*
à la mer *at the sea*
au mois de juin *in June*
à la montagne *in the mountains*
(R) à partir de 20 heures *from 8 p.m. onwards*
en plein air *in the open air*

pendant les vacances *during the holidays*
déjà *already*
(R) tellement *so*

+ adjectives for describing things and people – see Personal identification

+ Geographical items

+ Travel and Accommodation items as appropriate

+ Weather items as appropriate

+ Free time and entertainment as appropriate

Basic phrases

Nous sommes descendu(e)s dans un hôtel à Douvres *We stayed in a hotel in Dover*
J'ai cherché des coquillages au bord de la mer *I looked for shells by the sea*
Nous sommes parti(e)s en vacances au mois d'août *We set off on holiday in August*
Tout le monde était en vacances *Everyone was on holiday*

Higher

un	agence de voyage	*travel agency*
l'	archéologie (f)	*archaeology*
la	ceinture de sauvetage	*life belt*
la	chaise longue	*couch, sun bed*
le	congé	*leave, day off*
le	cours d'été	*summer course*
les	curiosités (f)	*curiosities*
le	dépliant	*leaflet, folder*
les	descriptions (f)	*descriptions*
les	festivités (f)	*festivals*
le	genre	*type, kind*
le	guide	*guide*
l'	hospitalité (f)	*hospitality*
le	jardin zoologique	*zoo*
la	marée basse	*low tide*
la	marée haute	*high tide*
le	pellicule	*film (for camera)*
	Québec	*Quebec*
le	Rhin	*the Rhine*
(R)	le S.I.	*information office*
le	site	*site*
(R)	son et lumière	*sound and light entertainment*
le	spectacle	*entertainment*
la	Tamise	*the Thames*
la	terrasse de café	*café terrace*

accueillir *to welcome*
avoir lieu *to take place*
faire de la plongée sous-marine *to do deep-sea diving*
faire des sports nautiques *to do water sports*
faire les valises *to pack*
s'informer *to find out*
montrer *to show*
organiser *to organize*
se noyer *to drown*
se passer *to take place, happen*
se souvenir *to remember*
ramer *to row*

accueillant *welcoming*
pittoresque *picturesque*

+ proper names of geographical features as appropriate to the student

Higher phrases

Le son et lumière aura lieu à dix heures *The 'son et lumière' performance will take place at 10 o'clock*

Un garçon s'est noyé à la marée haute l'année dernière *A boy drowned at high tide last year*

Est-ce que vous avez un dépliant qui montre ce qui se passe dans la région? *Have you a leaflet showing what is on in the area?*

HOTEL

Description

Basic

un	ascenseur	*lift*
le	bain	*bath*
la	clé	*key*
la	douche	*shower*
une	entrée	*entrance*
un	escalier	*staircase*
un	étage	*floor, storey*
un	hôtel	*hotel*
la	porte d'entrée	*front door*
la	réception	*reception*
le	restaurant	*restaurant*
le	rez-de-chaussée	*ground floor*
la	salle de bains	*bathroom*
la	sortie	*exit*
(R) la	sortie de secours	*emergency exit*
(R) le	sous-sol	*basement*
le	téléphone	*telephone*
la	télévision	*TV*
les	toilettes (f)	*toilets*
la	vue	*view*

confortable *comfortable*
grand *big*
moderne *modern*
pas cher *not expensive*
pas trop cher *not too expensive*
petit *small*
privé *private*
solide *solid*

Higher

bruyant *noisy*
(R) de grand confort *very comfortable*
(R) de grand luxe *luxurious*

Use of the hotel

Basic

le	chèque	*cheque*
la	date	*date*
la	femme de chambre	*maid*
le	garçon	*waiter*
(R) le	patron	*manager*
(R) la	pension	*board*
(R) la	pension complète	*full board*
le	petit déjeuner	*breakfast*
(R) le	supplément	*extra, addition*
la	valise	*suitcase*

arriver *to arrive*
partir *to leave*
pousser/POUSSEZ *to push/PUSH*
prendre un repas *to have a meal*
regretter *to regret*
réserver *to reserve*
réveiller *to wake up*
revenir *to return*
stationner *to park*
téléphoner à *to telephone*
tirer/TIREZ *to pull/PULL*
trouver *to find*
vouloir *to want, wish*
autre *other*
(R) disponible *available*

occupé *occupied*
non-compris *not included*
seul *alone*

avec *with*
pour *for*
sans *without*

Basic phrases

Est-ce qu'il vous reste des chambres de libre? *Have you any free rooms left?*

Non. Je regrette, tout est occupé *No. I'm afraid not, we are full*

Pour combien de personnes et pour combien de temps? *For how many people and for how long?*

Une grande chambre avec deux grands lits, ça vous convient? *A big room with two double beds, is that all right for you?*

Elles coûtent combien? *How much do they cost?*

Vous n'avez rien de moins cher? *Have you anything cheaper?*

Ça ira très bien. Nous les prenons *That'll do fine. We'll take them*

Est-ce que le petit déjeuner est compris? *Is breakfast included?*

Le petit déjeuner est servi à partir de huit heures jusqu'à dix heures *Breakfast is served from 8.00–10.00 a.m.*

Puis-je monter mes bagages maintenant? *May I take my luggage up now?*

Avant, il faut remplir la fiche *Before that you must fill in the form*

Votre passeport, s'il vous plaît *Your passport, please*

Voici votre clé. Chambre numéro vingt-deux *Here is your key. Room number twenty-two*

Il y a un parking à l'arrière *There is a car park at the back*

Higher

apprécier *to appreciate*
appuyer/APPUYEZ *to press/PRESS*
(R) déranger *to disturb*
se plaindre *to complain*
remplacer *to replace*

les	arrhes (f)	*deposit*
le	cintre	*coat-hanger*
la	demi-pension	*half board*
(R) une	incendie	*fire*
(R) le	prix maximum	*maximum price*
(R) le	prix minimum	*minimum price*
le/la	réceptionniste	*receptionist*
(R)	inclus	*inclusive*
	satisfait	*satisfied*

Higher phrases

Je voudrais réserver une chambre pour trois nuits *I would like to reserve a room for three nights*

Je voudrais une chambre qui donne sur la plage *I would like a room looking on to the beach*

Vous avez une chambre avec salle de bains? *Have you a room with a bathroom?*

Malheureusement, ça ne me convient pas. Au revoir, madame *I'm afraid that doesn't suit me. Goodbye, madam*

Tant pis, je prends la chambre *Never mind, I'll take the room*

C'est 150F pour la chambre, service et taxes compris *It's 150 francs for the room, service and VAT included*

Reservation problems

Higher phrases

J'ai fait des réservations par téléphone   *I made reservations by phone*

C'est à quel nom?   *What name?*

C'est bien ça?   *Is that it?*

Vous êtes sûr(e)?   *Are you sure?*

Qu'est-ce que je vais faire?   *What shall I do?*

Je suis très déçu(e)   *I am very disappointed*

Je vous prie de bien vouloir nous excuser   *Please do accept our apologies*

Asking for extras

Higher phrases

Je voudrais des cintres, s'il vous plaît   *I would like some coat-hangers please*

Est-ce que je peux avoir une serviette de bain?   *May I have a bath towel?*

Il manque un oreiller   *A pillow is missing*

On va vous en apporter tout de suite   *We'll bring one straight away*

Complaining

Je voudrais avoir une autre chambre   *I would like another room*

La lampe ne marche pas   *The lamp does not work*

Le lavabo est bouché   *The wash-basin is blocked*

Il n'y a plus de papier hygiénique   *There is no more toilet paper*

Il ne reste plus de savon   *There is no soap left*

Le robinet à eau froide a une fuite   *The cold water tap leaks*

La douche ne marche pas   *The shower does not work*

On va arranger ça tout de suite   *We'll deal with that straight away*

On va s'en occuper immédiatement   *We'll see to that immediately*

YOUTH HOSTEL

Basic

une auberge de jeunesse   *youth hostel*

(R) un avantage   *advantage, facility*

le bureau   *office*

la carte   *card*

la cuisine   *kitchen*

le dortoir   *dormitory*

(R) le drap-sac   *sheet sleeping bag*

l' eau chaude (f)   *hot water*

la nuit   *night*

(R) une paire de draps   *a pair of sheets*

la poubelle   *dustbin*

le sac de couchage   *sleeping bag*

la salle à manger   *dining room*

la salle de jeux   *games room*

le séjour   *stay, living room*

(R) le silence   *silence*

(R) le tarif   *price list*

le visiteur   *visitor*

aider   *to help*

fermer   *to close*

garder   *to keep*

(R) louer   *to hire*

organiser   *to organize*

ouvrir   *to open*

payer   *to pay*

remercier   *to thank*

la bienvenue   *welcome*

complet   *full*

(R) obligatoire   *obligatory*

toute l'année   *all year round*

(R) sauf   *except*

Higher

la carte d'adhérent   *member's card*

la couverture   *blanket*

un inconvénient   *drawback*

le linge   *linen*

les provisions (f)   *food*

le responsable   *the organizer, leader*

balayer   *to sweep*

ranger   *to tidy, put away*

défendu   *forbidden*

CAMPING

Basic

les allumettes   *matches*

(R) le bac à vaisselle   *washing up sink*

(R) le bloc sanitaire   *toilet block*

le bol   *bowl*

la bouteille de gaz   *gas cylinder*

le campeur   *camper*

le camping   *campsite*

la caravane   *caravan*

le carnet de camping   *camping card*

la cuisinière à gaz   *gas cooker*

eau non-potable (f)   *non-drinking water*

(R) un emplacement   *site, pitch*

le feu de camp   *camp-fire*

le journal   *newspaper, diary*

la lampe électrique   *torch*

(R) la laverie   *laundrette*

le lit de camp   *camp bed*

(R) la machine à laver   *washing machine*

(R) le supplément   *extra payment*

la tente   *tent*

(R) le terrain de camping   *campsite*

le véhicule   *vehicle*

camper   *camp*

chercher   *to look for*

coûter   *to cost*

(R) débarrasser   *to clear*

faire du camping   *to go camping*

faire la cuisine   *to cook*

laver   *to wash*

monter la tente   *to put up the tent*

(R) municipal   *of the town*

payer   *to pay*

(R) surveiller   *to supervise*

à emporter   *to take away*

complet   *full*

froid   *cold*

loin   *far*

moderne   *modern*

propre   *clean*

sale   *dirty*

(R) simple   *simple*

quand même   *all the same*

Basic phrases

Est-ce qu'il vous reste de la place pour une caravane?   *Have you room left for a caravan?*

Combien de personnes?   *How many people?*

Nous avons besoin d'un tire-bouchon et de piles   *We need a cork screw and some batteries*

Le camp est éclairé la nuit? *Is the camp lit up at night?*

Il y a un gardien toute la nuit *There is a warden all night*

L'eau est potable *The water is drinkable*

Je vais vous montrer votre emplacement *I will show you your pitch*

Est-ce qu'il est à l'ombre? *Is it in the shade?*

Higher

l'   électricité (f) *electricity*
les installations sanitaires (f) *toilets*
la   lessive *washing (clothes)*
le   matériel du camping *camping equipment*
la   prise de courant *power point*
les provisions (f) *food*
     indiquer *to indicate, show*
     plier *to fold*
     (R) à proximité de *near to*
     serré *congested*

Higher phrases

Est-ce qu'il est permis d'allumer une barbecue? *Is it allowed to light a barbecue?*

Il est défendu de faire du feu dans le camp? *Is it forbidden to light a fire in the camp?*

Est-ce que le camp est fermé la nuit? *Is the camp closed at night?*

HOLIDAY HOME IN FRANCE

Basic

le   gîte *gîte, simple self-catering house*
la   grange *barn*

(R) le terrain *plot, area of land*
    au mois de *in the month of*
    attendre *to wait (for)*
    cueillir des fruits *to pick fruit*
    demander *to ask (for)*
    (R) faire la récolte *to reap the harvest*
    (R) louer *to hire*
    rendre *to give back*
    transformer *to change*
    vouloir voir *to want to see*

    ailleurs *elsewhere*
    indépendant *independent*
    libre *free*
    (R) occupé *busy*

Higher

(R) la chambre d'hôte *guest room*
la   chasse *hunting*
un   ensemble de bâtiments *group of buildings*
(R) la location de vélos *cycle hire*
la   réclamation *complaint, claim*
le   vendange *vine picking*
le   vigneron *vine cultivator*
le   vignoble *vineyard*

    améliorer *to improve*
    (R) aménager *to furnish, equip*
    cultiver *to cultivate, grow*
    égarer *to lead astray*
    se plaindre *to complain*
    se présenter *to introduce oneself*

    en bon état *in good condition*
    en mauvais état *in poor condition*
    hors saison *out of season*
    (R) provisoire *temporary*

SOCIAL RELATIONSHIPS

LETTERS

See the advice on letter-writing in chapters 10 and 11 (Basic and Higher Writing).

General
Basic

un   ami *friend*
(R) le/la camarade *friend*
le   club *club*
le   copain *(boy) friend*
la   copine *(girl) friend*
le   correspondant *(boy) pen-friend*
la   correspondante *(girl) pen-friend*
le   membre *member*
la   musique *music*

     aimer *to like*
     s'amuser *to enjoy oneself*
     connaître *to know*
     danser *to dance*
     écouter *to listen (to)*
     jouer *to play*
     parler *to speak*
     passer *to spend (time)*
     se passer *to happen*

     aussi *also*
     d'habitude *usually*
     souvent *often*
     toujours *always*

Higher

une activité *activity*
une ambiance *atmosphere*

la   conférence *lecture*
(R) la cotisation *subscription*
une équipe *team*
la   jeunesse *young people, youth*
les loisirs *leisure time, pastimes*
la   maison des jeunes *youth club*
la   réunion *meeting*
la   société *society*

     apprécier *to appreciate*
     discuter *to discuss*
     s'entendre avec quelqu'un *to get on well with someone*
     fréquenter *to frequent, go to, attend*
     s'intéresser à *to be interested in*
     s'occuper à *to be busy at*
     participer à *to take part in*

Higher phrases

Je fréquente la maison des jeunes *I go to the youth club*

Il y a une réunion des jeunes ce soir *There is a meeting of young people tonight*

Je ne m'intéresse pas à la politique *I'm not interested in politics*

Greetings, wishes and goodbyes
Basic

     à bientôt *see you soon!*
(R) la bienvenue *welcome*
     à ce soir *see you this evening*
     à demain *till tomorrow*
     à samedi (etc.) *till Saturday (etc.)*
     à tout à l'heure *see you later*
     au revoir *goodbye*

bon anniversaire   *happy birthday*
bon voyage   *have a good trip*
bon week-end   *have a good weekend*
bonne année   *have a good year/Happy New Year*
bonne chance   *good luck*
bonne fête   *happy birthday*
bonne nuit   *goodnight*
bonjour   *good morning, hello*
bonsoir   *good evening*
comment allez-vous?   *how are you?*
Félicitations!   *Congratulations!*
Joyeux Noël!   *Happy Christmas!*
Salut!   *Hi! Hello!*
à votre santé!   *to your health, cheers*

MAKING ACQUAINTANCES

Basic

accompagner   *to accompany*
aller chercher   *to go and get*
assurer   *to assure, insure*
présenter   *to present, introduce*
se présenter   *to introduce oneself*
remercier   *to thank*
rencontrer   *to meet*
revenir   *to return*
souhaiter   *to wish*
se voir   *to see one another*
le/la camarade   *friend*
un   échange   *exchange*
les   gens (m)   *people*
(R) le jumelage   *twinning*
le   plaisir   *pleasure*
la   surprise   *surprise*

aimable   *pleasant, friendly, kind*
enchanté   *delighted*
insupportable   *unbearable, dreadful*
ravi   *delighted*
de retour   *back*

Basic phrases

Je te présente Marie   *May I introduce Marie to you?*
Enchanté(e)   *Pleased to meet you*
Je suis ravi(e) de vous voir   *I am delighted to see you*
On va se voir demain, n'est-ce pas?   *We'll meet tomorrow, won't we?*

Higher

(R) le/la collègue   *colleague*
le   discours   *talk, speech*
une intention   *intention*
la   proposition   *suggestion*
les   relations   *relationships*

contacter   *to make contact with*
étonner   *to amaze*
faire la connaissance de quelqu'un   *to make the aquaintance of someone*
féliciter   *to congratulate*
remarquer   *to notice*

Higher phrases

Je vous souhaite la bienvenue   *I welcome you*
Je trouve ces gens insupportables   *I find these people unbearable*
Je suis ravi(e) de faire votre connaissance   *I am delighted to meet you*

ARRANGING A MEETING OR ACTIVITY

Basic

une invitation   *invitation*
le   parc   *park*
la   promenade   *walk*
le   rendez-vous   *meeting*
un   idiot   *fool*
le   dommage   *damage, pity*
accepter   *to accept*
accompagner   *to accompany*
aimer   *to like*
s'amuser   *to enjoy oneself*
arriver   *to arrive*
attendre   *to wait (for)*
(R) avoir lieu   *to take place*
coûter   *to cost*
danser   *to dance*
décider   *to decide*
demander   *to ask (for)*
s'excuser   *to apologize*
inviter   *to invite*
oublier   *to forget*
penser   *to think*
préférer   *to prefer*
prendre rendez-vous   *to arrange to meet*
(R) proposer   *to suggest*
recevoir des amis   *to have friends round*
(R) refuser   *to refuse*
regretter   *to regret*
remercier   *to thank*
rencontrer   *to meet*
rendre visite à quelqu'un   *to visit someone*
rester   *to stay*
venir   *to come*
se voir   *to see one another*
d'accord   *agreed*
bof!   *oh well!*
certainement   *of course*
chouette!   *great!*
désolé(e)   *very sorry*
devoir   *to owe, ought to*
formidable   *great, terrific*
impossible   *impossible*
libre   *free*
avec plaisir   *with pleasure*
possible   *possible*
sur   *on*
urgent   *urgent*
zut!   *damn!*

+ places of entertainment – see Free time and entertainment
+ times
+ locations – see Geographical surroundings

Basic phrases

Tu veux m'accompagner au cinéma?   *Would you like to come to the cinema with me?*
D'accord. Où est-ce qu'on va se rencontrer?   *Of course. Where shall we meet?*
Devant le cinéma à huit heures   *Outside the cinema at 8 o'clock*
Entendu   *Agreed*
A quelle date?   *What date?*
C'est dommage. J'ai trop de devoirs   *It's a shame. I have too much homework*
Ça dépend   *It depends*
Ça ne fait rien   *It doesn't matter*
Ça suffit   *That's enough*

Higher

aller voir   *to go and see*
annuler   *to cancel*
avoir envie de   *to want to*
avoir le droit de   *to have the right to*
avoir le temps de   *to have the time to*
bavarder   *to chat*
empêcher   *to prevent*
exagérer   *to exaggerate*
promettre   *to promise*
offrir   *to offer*
refuser   *to refuse*
rejoindre   *to join*
retourner   *to return*
se trouver   *to be situated*
suggérer   *to suggest*
supposer   *to suppose*

sans doute   *without doubt*
de bonne heure   *early*
ensemble   *together*
tant mieux   *all the better*
tant pis   *never mind*
tiens!   *oh!*
(R) volontiers   *gladly*

Higher phrases

Où est-ce qu'on va se rencontrer?   *Where shall we meet?*
Ça m'est égal, franchement   *To be honest, I don't mind*
Je vous en prie   *Please*
Ce n'est pas la peine   *It's not worth it*
Tiens! Le grand bal aura lieu demain   *Oh! The big dance is tomorrow*

CURRENT AFFAIRS

Higher

une actualité   *piece of news*
un article   *article*
le cas   *case*
le catastrophe   *disaster*
(R) le chômage   *unemployment*
la crise   *crisis*
une élection   *election*
(R) un employeur   *employer*

l' energie (f)   *energy*
une enquête   *enquiry*
une époque   *period of time*
un événement   *event*
le gouvernement   *government*
(R) la grève   *strike*
la guerre   *war*
un immigré   *immigrant*
(R) l'impôt (m)   *tax*
les informations (f)   *news*
le maire   *mayor*
(R) la manifestation   *demonstration*
le niveau de vie   *standard of living*
une opération   *operation*
la politique   *politics, policy*
le premier ministre   *prime minister*
le président   *president*
le problème   *problem*
la question   *question*
la sécurité sociale   *social security*
la solution   *solution*
le syndicat   *trade union*
le titre   *title*
la violence   *violence*
admirer   *to admire*
(R) améliorer   *to improve*
augmenter   *to increase, augment*
avoir lieu   *to take place*
déclarer   *to declare*
défendre   *to defend, to forbid*
diminuer   *to diminish*
se passer   *to take place, to happen*
persuader   *to persuade*
(R) se produire   *to be produced*
promettre   *to promise*
protester   *to protest*
remarquer   *to notice*

de droite   *on the right*
étonnant   *surprising*
de gauche   *on the left*
grave   *serious*
important   *important*
probable   *probable*
récent   *recent*
social   *social*

HEALTH AND WELFARE

PARTS OF THE BODY

Basic

la bouche   *mouth*
le bras   *arm*
le coeur   *heart*
la dent   *tooth*
le doigt   *finger*
le dos   *back*
une épaule   *shoulder*
(R) un estomac   *stomach*
la gorge   *throat*
la jambe   *leg*
la main   *hand*
le nez   *nose*
un oeil (plural: les yeux)   *eye(s)*
une oreille   *ear*
le pied   *foot*
le sang   *blood*
la tête   *head*
le ventre   *stomach*

Higher

la cheville   *ankle*
le genou   *knee*
la langue   *tongue*

la peau   *skin*
la poitrine   *chest*
un os   *bone*

HYGIENE

Basic

le bain   *bath*
la brosse à dents   *toothbrush*
le dentifrice   *toothpaste*
(R) un essuie-mains   *hand towel*
le maquillage   *make-up*
la pâte dentifrice   *toothpaste*
le rasoir   *razor*
le savon   *soap*
la serviette   *towel*
le shampooing   *shampoo*

se laver   *to wash*
prendre un bain   *to have a bath*
prendre une douche   *to have a shower*
se maquiller   *to put on make-up*
se raser   *to shave*

propre   *clean*
sale   *dirty*

Higher

se brosser les dents   *to brush one's teeth*

MEDICAL PROBLEMS

Basic

aller bien   *to be well*
aller mal   *to be ill*
aller mieux   *to be better*
avoir chaud   *to be warm*
avoir faim   *to be hungry*
avoir froid   *to be cold*
avoir soif   *to be thirsty*
dormir   *to sleep*
se faire mal   *to hurt oneself*
piquer   *to sting, bite*
(R) se reposer   *to rest*
(R) soulager   *to relieve*

(R) en forme   *in form*
fatigué   *tired*

la   fièvre   *fever, high temperature*
l'   indigestion (f)   *indigestion*
le   mal de mer   *sea sickness*
(R) le rhume   *cold*
la   santé   *health*
la   température   *temperature*

Basic phrases

Je ne vais pas bien   *I am not well*
Je vais mieux maintenant   *I'm feeling better now*
J'ai chaud   *I'm warm*
Il a faim   *He is hungry*
Elle s'est fait mal à la jambe   *She has hurt her leg*
Une moustique l'a piqué   *A mosquito has bitten him*
J'ai de la fièvre   *I have a high temperature*

Higher

s'allonger   *to lie down*
avaler   *to swallow*
avoir mal à l'estomac   *to have stomach ache*
avoir mal à la gorge   *to have a sore throat*
avoir mal à la jambe   *to have a bad leg*
avoir mal à la tête   *to have a headache*
avoir mal au bras   *to have a bad arm*
avoir mal au coeur   *to feel sick*
avoir mal au dos   *to have a bad back*
avoir mal au ventre   *to have stomach ache*
avoir mal aux dents   *to have toothache*
avoir mal aux yeux   *to have sore eyes*
avoir un rhume   *to have a cold*
se blesser   *to get injured*
se brûler la main   *to burn one's hand*
se casser le bras   *to break one's arm*
se cogner   *to get a knock*
conseiller   *to advise*
consulter   *to consult*
se coucher   *to go to bed, to lie down*
se couper le doigt   *to cut one's finger*
crier   *to shout*
(R) être admis à l'hôpital   *to be admitted to hospital*
se fouler la cheville   *to twist, sprain one's ankle*
(R) guérir   *to heal, cure*
s'inquiéter   *to worry*
mordre   *to bite*
mourir   *to die*
se noyer   *to drown*
pleurer   *to weep, to cry*
saigner   *to bleed*

se sentir bien   *to feel well*
se sentir mal   *to feel ill*
souffrir   *to suffer*
surveiller sa température   *to take one's temperature*
(R) se taire   *to be silent*
tomber   *to fall*
tousser   *to cough*
(R) vomir   *to vomit*
vouloir   *to want, wish (to)*

une   ambulance   *ambulance*
une   aspirine   *aspirin*
une   assurance   *insurance*
le   cabinet   *cabinet*
le   cachet   *tablet*
(R) la clinique   *clinic*
(R) le comprimé   *tablet*
(R) le coton hydrophile   *absorbent cotton wool*
le   coup de soleil   *sun burn*
la   crème   *cream*
la   crise   *crisis*
la   cuillerée   *spoonful*
le   dentiste   *dentist*
la   diarrhée   *diarrhoea*
le   docteur   *doctor*
la   douleur   *pain*
la   fièvre   *fever, high temperature*
la   fois   *time, occasion*
les   frais   *expenses*
le   gonflement   *swelling*
la   grippe   *flu*
une   heure   *hour*
un   hôpital   *hospital*
(R) une insolation   *sun stroke*
le   jour   *day*
les   lunettes   *spectacles*
la   maladie   *illness*
le   médecin   *doctor*
(R) la médecine   *medicine (as a subject)*
le   médicament   *medicine, treatment*
la   naissance   *birth*
(R) une opération   *operation*
un   opticien   *optician*
une   ordonnance   *prescription*
le   pansement   *dressing, plaster*
la   pastille   *throat pastille*
(R) le patient   *patient*
la   pharmacie   *chemist's shop*
le   pharmacien   *chemist*
(R) la pilule   *pill*
(R) la piqûre   *sting, bite*
le   plâtre   *plaster*
le   problème   *problem*
(R) le remède   *remedy*
le   rendez-vous   *appointment*
la   salle de consultation   *surgery*
la   santé   *health*
le   sirop   *medicine*
le   sparadrap   *plaster, elastoplast*
la   sympathie   *sympathy*
le   tube   *tube*
la   voix   *voice*

antiseptique   *antiseptic*
assuré   *insured*
blessé   *injured*
capable   *capable*
constipé   *constipated*
enrhumé   *with a cold*
faible   *weak*
fragile   *delicate*
grave   *serious*
inquiet   *anxious*
mort   *dead*
sensible   *sensitive*

souffrant   *ill, suffering*
vivant   *alive*

gravement   *seriously*
mieux   *better*

Higher phrases

J'ai mal au coeur   *I feel sick*
Je me suis brûlé la main   *I have burnt my hand*
Elle s'est cassé le bras   *She has broken her arm*
Anne s'est foulé la cheville   *Anne has twisted her ankle*
Elle souffre   *She's not well*
C'est un beau coup de soleil   *That's quite a sunburn*
Une insolation, c'est très dangereux   *Sunstroke is very dangerous*

ACCIDENTS

un   accident   *accident*
une   adresse   *address*
un   agent de police   *policeman*
attention!   *look out!*
le   car   *coach*
la   collision   *collision*
le   commissariat   *police station*
le   constat   *statement*
le   consulat   *consulate*
le   cycliste   *cyclist*
le   danger   *danger*
mon dieu!   *my goodness!*
le   dommage   *damage*
une   excuse   *excuse*
la   faute   *fault*
la   gendarmerie   *police station*
monsieur l'agent   *'officer'*
le   motocycliste   *motorcyclist*
oh là là!   *oh dear!*
pardon   *sorry*
le   passant   *passer-by*
la   permission   *permission*
le   piéton   *pedestrian*
la   police   *police*
le   police-secours   *police rescue service*
le   sapeur-pompier   *fireman*
le   poste de police   *police station*
le   problème   *problem*
la   priorité   *priority*
le   responsable   *the leader*
le   risque   *risk*
le   sens   *direction*
(R) le témoin   *witness*
le   véhicule   *vehicle*
accuser   *to accuse*
aider   *to help*
appeler   *to call*
s'arrêter   *to stop*

attendre   *to wait (for)*
avoir le droit   *to have the right*
avoir peur   *to be afraid*
brûler   *to burn*
courir   *to run*
crier   *to shout*
déclarer   *to declare*
dépasser   *to overtake*
se dépêcher   *to hurry*
s'excuser   *to apologize*
faire attention   *to pay attention*
heurter   *to knock, bump into*
informer   *to inform*
se mettre en colère   *to get angry*
pardonner   *to forgive*
payer   *to pay (for)*
pleurer   *to weep, to cry*
poser   *to put down*
protester   *to protest*
(R)   ralentir   *to slow down*
regarder   *to watch, to look at*
(R)   remplir   *to fill*
renverser   *to knock or turn over*
réparer   *to repair*
(R) respecter   *to respect*
rouler   *to drive, move*
tomber   *to fall*
tourner   *to turn*
traverser   *to cross*
(R) tuer   *to kill*
blessé   *injured*
certain   *certain*
désolé   *very sorry*
faux   *false, wrong*
grave   *serious*
mort   *dead*
mouillé   *wet*
sûr   *certain*
(R) surprenant   *surprising*
urgent   *urgent*
vrai   *true*

d'accord   *agreed*
doucement   *gently*
gravement   *seriously*
hélas!   *alas!*
là   *there*
plus tard   *later*
(R) pourtant   *however*
presque   *almost*
tant mieux   *so much the better*
tant pis   *never mind*
tiens!   *oh!*
tout à coup   *suddenly*
tout de suite   *straight away*
vite   *quickly*

au feu!   *fire!*
au secours!   *help!*

+ vocabulary from Travel

SHOPPING   GENERAL

Basic

l'   alimentation (f)   *food*
une   allumette   *match*
un   ascenseur   *lift*
la   boîte   *box, tin, can*
la   boucherie   *butcher's shop*
la   boulangerie   *baker's shop*
la   bouteille   *bottle*
la   boutique   *small shop*

le   bureau de tabac   *tobacconist's shop*
le   cadeau   *present*
le   café   *café, coffee*
la   caisse   *cash desk, till*
la   carte   *card, map*
la   carte postale   *postcard*
(R) le centre commercial   *shopping centre*
la   charcuterie   *pork butcher's shop, cold meats*
la   chose   *thing*
le   coiffeur   *hairdressing salon*
le   crayon   *pencil*

la crémerie *dairy*
le disque *record*
(R) la douzaine *a dozen, about twelve*
une enveloppe *envelope*
une épicerie *grocer's shop*
un étage *floor, storey*
le gramme *gramme*
l' hypermarché *hypermarket*
le journal *newspaper*
le kilo *kilogramme*
le libre-service *self-service*
la liste *list*
le litre *litre*
la livre *pound*
le magasin *shop*
le magazine *magazine*
le marché *market*
le mètre *metre*
la monnaie *change*
le morceau *bit, piece*
le paquet *parcel*
le parfum *perfume*
la parfumerie *perfume shop*
la pâtisserie *cake shop*
la pharmacie *chemist's shop*
(R) les plats cuisinés(m) *cooked dishes*
la poissonerie *fish shop*
le pot *jar, pot*
la quincaillerie *hardware shop*
le rayon *shelf, department*
la réduction *reduction*
le rez-de-chaussée *ground floor*
le sac *bag*
(R) le solde *sale*
la sorte *sort, kind*
le sous-sol *basement*
le souvenir *souvenir*
le stylo *ball-point pen*
le supermarché *supermarket*
la tranche *slice*

acheter *to buy*
aimer *to like*
aller chercher *to go and get*
avoir *to have*
coûter *to cost*
désirer *to want*
faire les courses *to do the shopping*
fermer *to close*
montrer *to show*
ouvrir *to open*
préférer *to prefer*
prendre *to take*
remercier *to thank*
se trouver *to be situated*
vendre *to sell*
vouloir *to want (to)*
voler *to steal*

autre *other*
cher *dear, expensive*
court *short*
différent *different*
grand *large*
(R) juste *exact*
long *long*
petit *small*
premier *first*
quel *which, what*
rouge *red*

beaucoup *a lot, many*
ça va *that's all right*
demi *half*
merci *thank you*
moins *less*

á partir de . . . *from . . .*
pas de . . . *no . . .*
plus (un peu plus) *more (a little more)*
plusieurs *several*
quelque *some*
(R) quoi *what*
de rien *don't mention it*
(R) sauf *except*
tout *all*
trop *too, too much*
je voudrais *I would like*

Higher

le commerçant *shopkeeper, market trader*
le déodorant *deodorant*
le guide *guide*
le jouet *toy*
le loisir *leisure*
le maquillage *make-up*
le marchand *salesman*
la moitié *half*
le papier à lettres *writing paper*
le patron *manager, boss*
le pellicule *film*
(R) la quantité *quantity*
(R) la réclamation *complaint*
le sport *sport*
le tabac *tobacco*
le, la vendeur/vendeuse *sales assistant*
la vitrine *shop window*

échanger *to change, exchange*
essayer *to try (on)*
offrir *to offer*
payer *to pay (for)*
se plaindre *to complain*
rembourser *to reimburse*

bon marché *cheap*
(R) lequel *which*
à part *apart from*
sauf *except*

IN THE SHOP

Basic

un anorak *anorak*
une aspirine *aspirin*
l' argent (m) *money*
la baguette *french stick of bread*
la banane *banana*
la banque *bank*
le beurre *butter*
le billet de cent francs *100-franc note*
le biscuit *biscuit*
la boisson *drink*
le bonbon *sweet*
(R) le cachet *cachet*
le carnet de chèques *cheque book*
la carotte *carrot*
le centime *centime*
le centimètre *centimetre*
la cerise *cherry*
le chapeau *hat*
la chaussette *sock*
la chaussure *shoe*
la chemise *shirt*
le chèque *cheque*
le choix *choice, selection*
le chou *cabbage*
le client *customer*
le collant *tights*
la confiture *jam*
(R) le coton *cotton*

la couleur *colour*
la cravate *tie*
une eau minérale *mineral water*
une erreur *mistake*
le filet *net bag*
la fraise *strawberry*
le franc *franc*
le fromage *cheese*
le fruit *fruit*
le gâteau *cake*
le haricot *bean*
un imperméable *raincoat*
le jambon *ham*
le jean *jeans*
le jus de fruit *fruit juice*
(R) le jour férié *holiday*
la jupe *skirt*
la laine *wool*
le lait *milk*
la laitue *lettuce*
les légumes *vegetables*
la liste *list*
la livre *pound, 500 grammes*
la livre sterling *pound sterling*
le maillot de bain *bathing costume*
le manteau *coat*
le marchand *salesman*
le médicament *medicament, medicine*
la mode *fashion*
le mouchoir *handkerchief*
(R) ni repris/ni échange *no return or exchange*
le nylon *nylon*
un oeuf *egg*
un oignon *onion*
une orange *orange*
le pain *bread*
le paquet *packet, parcel*
le pantalon *pair of trousers*
le parapluie *umbrella*
le pâté *pâté*
les pâtisseries (f) *cakes, pastries*
la pêche *peach*
les petits pois *peas*
la pièce *each one*
(R) le plastique *plastic*
(R) la pointure *size (shoes)*
la pomme *apple*
la pomme de terre *potato*
le pot *jar, pot*
le prix *price*
le produit surgelé *frozen food*
le pull (over) *pullover*
le pyjama *pyjamas*
la qualité *quality*
le raisin *grape*
la robe *dress*
la salade *lettuce, salad*
la sandale *sandal*
le saucisson *sausage*
le sel *salt*
(R) le slip *underpants*
le sucre *sugar*
la taille *height, size*
le thé *tea*
la tomate *tomato*
la viande *meat*
le veste *jacket*
les vêtements *clothes*
le vin rouge/blanc *red/white wine*
le yaourt *yoghurt*

aider *to help*
accepter *to accept*
avoir besoin (de) *to need*

demander *to ask (for)*
essayer *to try (on)*
peser *to weigh*
porter *to carry, wear*
voler *to steal*
blanc *white*
bleu *blue*
bon marché *cheap*
compris *included*
étroit *narrow*
gratuit *free (no charge)*
jaune *yellow*
(R) large *broad*
(R) léger *light*
long *long*
(R) lourd *heavy*
même *same*
(R) normal *normal*
neuf *new*

assez *enough, fairly*
beaucoup *a lot, many*
combien *how much, how many*
en *in (e.g. en cuir – in leather)*
ça fait *that makes*
mais *but*
mille *thousand*
par jour *by day*
par nuit *by night*
par personne *per person*
peu *little*
plus *more*
trop *too, too much*
zéro *nil*

Higher

le blouson *jacket*
la botte *boot*
le centimètre *centimetre*
le chariot *trolley*
le chemisier *blouse*
(R) le comptoir *counter*
la confiserie *sweet shop*
le coton *cotton*
le cuir *leather*
(R) un escalier roulant *escalator*
un étagère *shelf, set of shelves*
la faute *mistake*
faire des achats *to go shopping*
faire du lèche-vitrines *to window shop*
le gérant *manager*
la librairie *bookshop*
la mesure *measure*
(R) le métal *metal*
la paire (de) *pair (of)*
le panier *basket*
le poids *weight*
(R) la promotion *offer*
les provisions (f) *food*
quelque chose de . . . *something . . .*
le short *pair of shorts*
le tricot *jumper*
la vitrine *shop window*
le voleur *thief*

aimer mieux *to prefer*
compter *to count*
conseiller *to advise*
devoir *to owe*
distribuer *to distribute*
manquer *to lack*
ne pas marcher *not to work*
plaire *to please*
rapporter *to bring back*
rendre *to give back*
se vendre bien/mal *to sell well/badly*

clair   *light (in colour)*
déchiré   *torn*
entier   *complete*
frais   *fresh*
foncé   *dark (in colour)*
large   *broad*
mûr   *ripe*
rayé   *striped*

exactement   *exactly*
mieux   *better*
(R) par-dessous   *underneath*
(R) par-dessus   *above*
vaut   *is worth*

Basic phrases

Active use

Oui/non   *Yes/no*
C'est à moi   *It's my turn, it's mine*
C'est mon tour   *It's my turn*
Je voudrais des . . . et des . . .   *I would like some . . . and some . . .*
J'ai aussi besoin de . . .   *I also need . . .*
Combien coûte ce/cette . . .?   *What does this . . . cost?*
Combien font ces . . .?   *How much are these . . .?*
C'est combien, les . . .?   *How much are the . . .?*
J'en voudrais une demi-livre, svp   *I would like half a pound please*
Avec ceci, je vais prendre . . .   *Also, I'd like . . .*
Les plus/moins gros/grosses   *The biggest/smallest*
Oui, s'il vous plaît   *Yes please*
Je voudrais aussi de la . . .   *I'd also like some . . .*
Oui, comme ça   *Yes, like that*
Est-ce que vous avez des . . .?   *Have you any . . .?*
Est-ce qu'il y a des . . .?   *Are there any . . .?*
Oui, ce sera tout   *Yes that'll be all*
Je vous dois combien?   *How much do I owe you?*
Je n'ai qu'un billet de (100) francs   *I only have a 100-franc note*

Receptive use

On vous sert?   *Are you being served?*

C'est à qui, maintenant?	*Whose turn is it now*
A qui le tour?	
Qu'est-ce qu'il y a pour votre service?	*What would you like?*
Qu'est-ce qui vous faut?	
Vous désirez?	
Que voulez-vous?	

Voici. Et ensuite?   *There. Anything else?*
Je n'en ai pas/plus   *I haven't any/left*
C'est 8 francs le kilo   *It's 8 francs a kilo*
Et avec ceci   *Anything else?*
De quelle sorte?   *what kind?*
Celles-ci?   *These?*
Comme ça?   *Like this?*
Oui, j'en ai encore   *Yes I have some more*
Et avec ça, ce sera tout?   *Is that all?*
Alors, ça fera . . . francs   *That makes . . . francs*
Vous avez la monnaie?   *Have you any change?*
Ce n'est pas grave   *It doesn't matter*
Voici votre monnaie   *Here's your change*

Higher phrases

Active use

Qu'est-ce que vous avez comme . . .?   *What have you got in the way of . . .?*
Je peux choisir les . . .?   *May I choose the . . .?*
Je voudrais un morceau de . . .   *I'd like a piece of . . .*
Un peu plus grand, svp   *A little bigger, please*
Que me conseillez-vous comme . . .?   *Which . . . would you recommend?*
Vous pouvez me l'envelopper?   *Could you wrap it for me?*
Il me faut aussi des . . .   *I also need . . .*
Quels sont les meilleurs?   *Which are the best?*
Je les prends   *I'll take them*
Je vais réfléchir   *I'll think about it*
Vous n'avez rien de moins cher?   *Have you nothing cheaper?*
D'où vient ce . . .?   *Where does this . . . come from?*
Est-ce que vous vendez du . . .?   *Do you sell . . .?*
Où pourrais-je en trouver?   *Where could I find some?*

Receptive use

J'ai ces . . . et ces . . .   *I have these . . and these . . .*
Oui, certainement   *Yes, of course*
Non, les clients ne se servent pas   *No, customers do not serve themselves*
Comme ceci?   *Like this?*
Mais oui, bien sûr   *Yes, of course*
Il vient de . . .   *It comes from . . .*
D'habitude, j'en ai mais il ne m'en reste plus   *Usually I have some, but I have none left*
Ça se vend au poids   *It's sold by weight*

FOOD AND DRINK

MEAT, FISH, VEGETABLES, FRUIT

Basic

l'   agneau (m)   *lamb*
le   bifteck   *beef steak*
le   boeuf   *beef*
le   canard   *duck*
la   côte   *rib*
le   filet   *fillet steak*
le   jambon   *ham*
le   lapin   *rabbit*
le   mouton   *mutton*
le   porc   *pork*
le   poulet   *chicken*

le   rôti   *roast meat*
le   steak   *steak*

le   crabe   *crab*
la   crevette   *shrimp*
les   fruits de mer (m)   *sea food*
une   huître   *oyster*
le   maquereau   *mackerel*
la   morue   *cod*
les   moules   *mussels*
la   sardine   *sardine*
le   sole   *sole*
la   truite   *trout*

un   artichaut   *artichoke*
la   carotte   *carrot*
le   champignon   *mushroom*
le   chou   *cabbage*
le   chou-fleur   *cauliflower*
le   concombre   *cucumber*
les   épinards (m)   *spinach*
un   haricot   *bean*
la   laitue   *lettuce*
un   oignon   *onion*
les   petits pois   *peas*
(R)   le poireau   *leek*
la   pomme de terre   *potato*
le   riz   *rice*
la   salade   *salad, lettuce*
la   tomate   *tomato*

un   abricot   *apricot*
un   ananas   *pineapple*
la   banane   *banana*
la   cerise   *cherry*
la   fraise   *strawberry*
la   framboise   *raspberry*
la   groseille   *goosberry*
le   melon   *melon*
la   noix   *nut*
la   pêche   *peach*
la   poire   *pear*
la   pomme   *apple*
la   prune   *plum*
le   raisin   *grape*

Higher
le   veau   *veal*
le   citron   *lemon*

OTHER FOOD

Basic
une   assiette anglaise   *cold meat and salad*
la   baguette   *stick of bread*
le   beurre   *butter*
le   biscuit   *biscuit*
le   bonbon   *sweet*
le   chocolat   *chocolate*
la   confiture   *jam*
la   crêpe   *pancake*
le   croissant   *crescent roll*
le   croque-monsieur   *toasted cheese and ham
        sandwich*
(R)   les crudités (f)   *raw vegetables*
le   déjeuner   *lunch*
le   petit déjeuner   *breakfast*
le   dessert   *dessert*
le   dîner   *dinner*
une   épaule de mouton   *shoulder of mutton*
les   frîtes   *chips*
le   fromage   *cheese*
le   gâteau   *cake*
la   glace   *ice cream*
un   hors d'oeuvre   *starter*
le   légume   *vegetable*
un   oeuf   *egg*
une   omelette   *omelette*
le   pain   *bread*
le   pâté   *pâté*
le   plat du jour   *dish of the day*
la   pâtisserie   *cake*
le   pique-nique   *picnic*
le   poisson   *fish*
le   potage   *soup*
les   provisions (f)   *food*
la   purée   *mashed potato*
la   quiche lorraine   *egg and cheese flan*

le   repas   *meal*
la   salade   *salad, lettuce*
le   sandwich   *sandwich*
le   saucisson   *sausage*
le   sel   *salt*
la   soupe   *soup*
le   sucre   *sugar*
la   tarte   *flan*
(R)   la terrine   *potted meat*
(R)   la vanille   *vanilla*
le   vinaigre   *vinegar*
le   yaourt   *yoghurt*

Higher
les   chips   *crisps*
la   mayonnaise   *mayonnaise*
la   moutarde   *mustard*
le   poivre   *pepper*

DRINKS

Basic
(R)   un apéritif   *aperitif*
la   bière   *beer*
la   boisson   *drink*
le   café   *black coffee*
le   café crème   *white coffee*
le   chocolat   *chocolate, hot chocolate*
le   cidre   *cider*
le   citron pressé   *fresh lemon juice*
le   Coca   *Coca-cola*
une   eau minérale   *mineral water*
le   jus de fruit   *fruit juice*
une   orange pressé   *fresh orange juice*
le   lait   *milk*
la   limonade   *lemonade*
le   thé   *tea*
le   vin blanc/rouge   *white/red wine*

Higher
(R)   un pression   *draught beer*

OTHER WORDS

Basic
une   addition   *bill*
une   assiette   *plate*
le   bar   *bar*
le   bol   *bowl*
la   bouteille   *bottle*
la   cafetière   *coffee pot*
la   carte   *card, menu*
le   couteau   *knife*
la   cuiller/cuillère   *spoon*
le   dîner   *dinner*
une   entrée   *main dish, entrance*
la   fourchette   *fork*
le   garçon   *waiter*
le   goût   *taste*
le   menu   *menu*
        merci   *thankyou*
(R)   une odeur   *smell*
le   parfum   *flavour*
le   patron   *manager*
la   personne   *person*
le   plateau   *tray*
le   quart   *quarter*
le   restaurant   *restaurant*
le   service   *service*
la   soucoupe   *saucer*
(R)   la spécialité   *speciality*
la   table   *table*
la   tasse   *cup*
le   téléphone   *telephone*

la   toilette *toilet*
le   verre *glass*

adorer *to love*
aimer *to like*
avoir faim/soif *to be hungry/thirsty*
boire *to drink*
choisir *to choose*
coûter *to cost*
désirer *to want, wish*
détester *to hate*
dîner *to have dinner*
manger *to eat*
passer *to pass*
préférer *to prefer*
prendre *to take*
préparer *to prepare*
recommander *to recommend*
(R) servir *to serve*
trouver *to find*
je (ne) voudrais (pas) *I would (not) like*

bien *good, well*
bien cuit *well cooked*
bon *good*
chaud *hot*
compris *included*
délicieux *delicious*
demi *half*
excellent *excellent*
fraud *cold*
malade *ill*
mauvais *bad*
à point *done to a turn*
rôti *roast*
seul *alone*

assez *enough, fairly*
beaucoup *a lot, many*
combien *how much, how many*
comme *as, how*
comment *how*
(R) en sus *in addition*
encore *more*
exactement *exactly*
de la maison *home-made*
peu *little*
sans *without*
très *very*
voilà! *there you are!*

à votre (ta) santé *to your health, cheers*
bon appétit *enjoy your meal*

Higher
le   carafe *jug*
le   chef *cook*
le   couvert *table place, cover charge*
une erreur *mistake*
les félicitations *congratulations*
le   gaz *gas*
(R) le pichet *pitcher, jug*
le   pourboire *tip*
la   recette *recipe*
le   serveur *server, waiter*
la   serveuse *waitress*
la   théière *teapot*
apporter *to bring*
apprécier *to appreciate*
approuver *to approve*
avoir envie de *to wish to*
commander *to order*
désapprouver *to disapprove*
devoir *to owe*
féliciter *to congratulate*
insulter *to insult*
se mettre en colère *to get angry*

offrir *to offer*
se plaindre *to complain*
plaire *to please*
protester *to protest*
vouloir *to want, wish (to)*
souhaiter *to wish*

appétissant *appetizing*
doux *mild, sweet*
piquant *tart, biting*
saignant *underdone*
(R) salé *salty*
satisfait *satisfied*
(R) sucré *sweet*
(R) varié *varied*
à la votre/tienne *to your health, cheers*
aussi *also*
bravo! *well done!*
complètement *completely*
égal *equal*
entièrement *entirely*
inadmissible *unforgiveable*
lequel *which*
service (non) compris *service (not) included*
ça suffit *that's enough*

ATTRACTING THE WAITER'S ATTENTION

Basic phrases
Active use
1 Attracting attention

Garçon, s'il vous plaît!
Madame! *Waiter, please*
Mademoiselle! *Waitress, please*
Monsieur!

2 Initiating and concluding exchange

Bonjour *Good morning/afternoon*
Merci madame, etc. *Thank you madam, etc*
Au revoir *Goodbye*

Higher phrases
Active use
1 Asking for a table

table libre *free table*
Avez-vous une table pour . . .
  personnes? *Have you a table for . . . people?*
réserver une table *to reserve a table*
faire une réservation *to make a reservation*

Receptive use

Oui, bonjour messieurs'dames *Yes, ladies and gentlemen*

Merci bien *Thank you very much*
Au revoir *Goodbye*
Bonne journée, soirée, etc. *Have a good day, evening, etc.*
Oui, par ici s'il vous plaît *Yes, over here please*
Non, je regrette *No, I'm sorry*

ORDERING A MEAL

Basic phrases
Active use

choisir *to choose*
On peut commander? *May we order?*
Je voudrais le menu, svp *I'd like the menu, please*
Je vais prendre . . . *I'll have . . .*

Receptive use

Vous avez choisi? *Have you chosen?*

Bien sûr, certainement *Of course*

Que désirez-vous? *What would you like?*

Qu'est-ce que vous prendrez? *What will you have?*

Higher phrases
Active use

à la place *in place*

au lieu de *instead of*

menu à 55 F *menu at 55 francs*

Pour commencer . . . *To begin with . . .*
Pour suivre . . . *To follow . . .*
Ce sera tout, merci *That will be all, thankyou*

Qu'est-ce que tu prendras/vous prendrez? *What are you having?*

Qu'est-ce que tu veux/vous voulez? *What do you want?*
Pour lui/elle/eux *For him/her/them*

Je voudrais un steak, svp *I would like a steak please*
    à point *medium*
    (bien) cuit *well done*
    saignant *rare*

Je voudrais . . . *I would like . . .*
Quel dommage! *What a pity!*
Alors, je prendrais . . . *Right, I'll have . . .*

Receptive use

Prenez-vous un apéritif? *Are you having an aperitif?*

Quelle boisson prendrez-vous? *What drink would you like?*

Votre commande, svp? *Your order please*

Vous avez choisi? *Have you chosen?*
Oui, et ensuite? *Yes, and after that?*
Et pour terminer? *And to finish with?*

Et pour vous, mademoiselle? *And for you, mlle?*

Pour monsieur, ce sera . . . *And you sir, you'll have . . .?*

Vous le voulez comment, votre steak? *How would you like your steak?*

Ce sera en supplément *That will be extra*

Désolé(e), il n'en reste plus *I'm very sorry, we have non left*

café compris *coffee included*
boissons en sus *drinks extra*
service 15% (non) compris *service 15% (not) included*

REQUESTING EXTRAS AND CLARIFICATION

Basic phrases
Active use

1 Additions
Svp, on peut avoir . . .? *Could we have . . .?*
    de l'eau/du vin *water/wine*
    de l'huile *oil*
    du sel *salt*
    du sucre *sugar*

Vous pouvez changer . . .? *Would you change . . .?*
    le verre/l'assiette *the glass/plate*

Il manque . . . *We are short of . . .*
    un couteau *a knife*
    une cuillère *a spoon*
    une fourchette *a fork*
    une tasse *a cup*
    un verre *a glass*

Vous pouvez nettoyer la table, svp *Could you clean the table please?*

Receptive use

Tout est bien? *Is everything all right?*

Mais oui, certainement *Yes, of course*

Je vais vous en chercher un/une *I'll go and get you one*

Tout de suite *Straight away*

Higher phrases
Active use

1 Additions
On peut avoir (encore) . . .? *Could we have some more . . .?*
    du vinaigre *vinegar*
    de la moutarde *mustard*
    du poivre *pepper*

2 Clarifications
Qu'est-ce que c'est . . .? *What is . . .?*

Pouvez-vous expliquer ce que c'est? *Could you explain what it is?*

Qu'est-ce qu'il y a comme . . .? *What have you got in the way of . . .?*

Est-ce que vous avez encore . . .? *Have you any more . . .?*
Reste-t-il des . . .? *Are there any . . . left?*

Ça prendra combien de temps? *How long will it take?*

Ça ne sera pas trop long, j'espère *I hope it won't be too long*

Ça sera bientôt prêt? *Will it soon be ready?*

Le service est-il compris? *Is service included?*
Le vin est-il compris? *Is the wine included?*

Receptive use

C'est une sauce *It's a sauce*

C'est un plat servi avec . . . *It's a dish served with . . .*

C'est un vin de la région *It's a local wine*

Oui, bien sûr *Yes, of course*

Il y a des . . . et des . . . *These are . . . and . . .*

Oui, nous en avons encore *Yes, we have some more*

Non, je suis désolé(e), il ne nous en reste plus *No, I'm sorry, we have none left*

Ça prendra . . . minutes *It'll take . . . minutes*

Oui, le service est compris *Yes, service is included*

Non, le service n'est pas compris *No, service is not included*

Oui, les boissons sont comprises *Yes, drinks are included*

Non, le vin n'est pas compris *No, the wine is not included*

REQUESTING THE BILL AND DEALING WITH PAYMENT

Basic phrases

Active use

L'addition, svp   *The bill, please*
On peut avoir l'addition, svp?   *Could we have the bill, please?*

Je n'ai pas assez d'argent!   *I haven't enough money!*

Higher phrases

régler l'addition   *to settle the bill*

Vous acceptez les cartes de crédit?   *Do you accept credit cards?*

Vous faites erreur   *You are mistaken*
La note, svp   *The account, please*
among friends:
Je vous invite   *I'll treat you*
C'est moi qui paie   *I'll pay/This is on me*

Receptive use

Tout de suite   *Straight away*
Certainement   *Certainly*
Ça vous fait . . . francs   *That makes . . . francs*
Voici votre monnaie   *Here is your change*
Nous n'acceptons pas les chèques   *We don't accept cheques*

SERVICES

POST OFFICE

Basic

une adresse   *address*
   par avion   *by air mail*
la boîte aux lettres   *letter box*
le bureau de poste   *post office*
la carte postale   *postcard*
(R) le colis   *parcel*
   combien   *how much*
un étranger   *foreigner*
(R) le facteur   *postman*
(R) fragile   *fragile*
(R) le guichet   *counter position*
la lettre   *letter*
(R) P. et T. ⎫
(R) P.T.T. ⎬ *Post Office*
le paquet   *package*
la poste   *post*
   poster   *to post*
le tabac   *tobacconist*
(R) le tarif   *price list*
le timbre   *stamp*
le timbre à un franc   *one-franc stamp*

Higher

(R) un annuaire   *telephone directory*
(R) à l'appareil   *on the phone, 'speaking'*
la cabine téléphonique   *telephone box*
le coup de téléphone   *phone call*
(R) le courrier   *post, mail*
(R) la fente   *slot*
le formulaire   *form*
(R) le jeton   *token*
la lettre recommandée   *recorded letter*
la levée du courrier   *postal collection*
le mandat postal   *postal order*
le moment   *moment*
le numéro   *number*
une opération de guichet   *counter service*
une opératrice   *(female) operator*
   en panne   *out of order*
   de la part de   *on behalf of*
la pièce   *coin*
   en PCV   *reversed charges*
   poste restante   *post to be collected*
la seconde   *second*
le télégramme   *telegram*
le téléphone   *telephone*
(R) la tonalité   *tonality, sound (of telephone)*
   s'adresser   *to apply to*
   appeler   *to call*
   composer le numéro   *to dial the number*
   compter   *to count*
(R) décrocher le combiné   *to take off the receiver*
   distribuer le courrier   *to deliver the post*

écouter   *to listen (to)*
entendre   *to hear*
faire erreur   *to make a mistake*
mettre à la poste   *to post*
se munir de   *to provide oneself with*
parler   *to speak*
payer au mot   *to pay by the word*
(R) ne quittez pas   *do not ring off*
(R) raccrocher   *to put the receiver down*
rappeler   *to re-call*
remplir   *to fill*
sonner   *to ring*
téléphoner   *to telephone*
toucher un chèque/un mandat   *to cash a cheque, an order*
libre   *free*
occupé   *occupied*
urgent   *urgent*
allô   *hello*
bien   *good, well*
c'est combien?   *how much is it?*
ici   *here*
mal   *bad(ly)*
quand   *when*
qui   *who*

Active use

Je voudrais envoyer cette lettre   *I would like to send this letter*

Je voudrais aussi envoyer ce paquet à l'étranger   *I would also like to send this package abroad*
C'est combien, une lettre pour la Suisse?   *How much is a letter to Switzerland?*

Je voudrais envoyer de l'argent. Qu'est-ce que je dois faire?   *I would like to send some money. What should I do?*

100 francs   *100 francs*

Voilà, il est rempli. Voici l'argent   *There, it's filled in. Here's the money*

Je voudrais envoyer un télégramme   *I would like to send a telegram*

Laquelle?   *Which one?*

Voilà, est rempli. Il y a 17 mots   *There, it's complete. There are 17 words*

Je voudrais aussi appeler quelqu'-un au téléphone. Où pourrais-je trouver les annuaires?   *I would also like to ring someone. Where can I find the directories?*

Je peux téléphoner aux renseignements d'abord?   *Can I ring for information first?*

Voilà, j'ai fini   *There. I have finished*

Pouvez-vous m'expliquer comment on téléphone en Angleterre? *Can you explain how to phone to England?*

Qu'est-ce que c'est la tonalité? *What's the tone?*

Je peux utiliser la cabine là dehors? *Can I use the box outside?*

Receptive use

Par avion? *By air?*

Je vais la peser. Violà. Ça vous fait . . . francs *I'll weigh it. There. It costs . . francs*

Combien voulez-vous envoyer? *How much do you want to send?*

Vous pouvez envoyer un mandat. Il faut remplir ce coupon *You could send a postal order. You have to fill in this coupon*

Remplissez cette formule *Complete that form*

Celle-là, sur le comptoir *That one, on the counter*

Bien. Ça vous fait . . . francs en tout *Good. That will cost . . . francs altogether*

Vous pouvez les consulter ici à la poste. Ils sont à côté des cabines téléphoniques *You can look at them here in the post office. They are next to the phone boxes*

Oui, bien sûr. C'est gratuit *Yes, of course. It's free*

La communication a duré 5 minutes. Ça coûte . . . francs *The call lasted 5 minutes. That costs . . . francs*

Eh bien, il faut composer le 19 et attendre la tonalité. *Well, dial 19 and wait for the tone*

La sonnerie, quoi! *The ringing!*

Après, vous faites le code pour la Grande-Bretagne, le 44, et puis le numéro de votre correspondant sans oublier le code de la région *Then, you dial the code for Great Britain, 44, then the number you wish, not forgetting the local code*

BANK OR EXCHANGE OFFICE

Higher

l'	argent (m)	*money*
la	banque	*bank*
le	billet de cent francs	*100-franc note*
le	bureau de change	*exchange office*
la	caisse	*cash desk, till*
(R) la carte bancaire		*banker's card*
la	carte de crédit	*credit card*
le	centime	*centime*
le	chèque	*cheque*
le	chèque de voyage	*travellers' cheque*
la	commission	*commission*
(R) le cours de change		*rate of exchange*
le	franc	*franc*
le	guichet	*counter window*
la	livre sterling	*pound sterling*
la	moitié	*half*
la	monnaie	*change*
le	numéro de compte	*account number*
le	passeport	*passport*
la	pièce	*coin*
la	pièce d'identité	*proof of identity*
	accepter	*to accept*
	changer	*to change*
	passer à la caisse	*to go on to the cash desk*
	prendre une commission	*to take a commission*

signer *to sign*
valoir *to be worth*
pour cent *per cent*
vaut *is valid, is worth*
Combien vaut la livre? *What is the pound worth?*

Active use

Je voudrais changer des livres, svp *I would like to change some pounds, please*

Des chèques de voyage *Travellers' cheques*

Un passeport, ça va? *Is a passport all right?*

Voilà *There*

Combien vaut la livre? *What is the pound worth?*

Receptive use

Oui, bien sûr. Des billets de banque ou des chèques de voyage? *Of course. Bank notes or travellers' cheques?*

Il y a une commission de 3% sur les chèques de voyage *There is a commission of 3% on travellers' cheques*

Donnez-moi vos chèques de voyage et une pièce d'identité *Give me your travellers' cheques and some proof of identity*

Oui, naturellement *Of course*

Tenez, signez là *Sign here please*

Merci *Thankyou*

Le cours du change est à . . . francs. Voilà votre ticket. Vous pouvez passer à la caisse maintenant. *The rate of exchange is . . . francs. Here's your ticket. You can go to the cash desk now.*

Voici votre argent. Bon séjour! *Here's your money. Have a good stay!*

LOST PROPERTY

Higher

un	appareil-photo	*camera*
un(e) après-midi		*afternoon*
la	bicyclette	*bicycle*
le	bureau des objets perdus	*lost property office*
le	cambrioleur	*burglar*
la	caméra	*cine camera*
le	carnet de chèques	*cheque book*
la	ceinture	*belt*
le	centimètre	*centimetre*
la	clé	*key*
le	consulat	*consulate*
la	couleur	*colour*
la	date	*date*
la	description	*description*
le	dommage	*damage, pity*
la	fiche	*form*
le	flash	*flash gun (photography)*
(R) la forme		*form, shape*
(R) la marque		*make, brand name*
le	matin	*morning*
le	métal	*metal*
la	montre	*watch*
le	mouchoir	*handkerchief*
(R) le moyen		*means*
le	nom	*name*
le	parapluie	*umbrella*
le	passeport	*passport*
la	pièce d'identité	*proof of identity*

la　poche　*pocket*
le　porte-monnaie　*purse*
le　portefeuille　*wallet*
la　récompense　*reward*
le　règlement　*regulation, settlement*
le　sac à dos　*rucksack*
le　sac à main　*handbag*
　　une sorte de　*a kind of*
la　taille　*size, height*
la　valise　*suitcase*
le　vélomoteur　*motor-assisted bicycle*
le　vol　*theft*
le　voleur　*thief*

accuser　*to accuse*
il s'agit de　*it's a question of, it's about*
appartenir　*to belong*
s'arranger　*to manage*
(R) cambrioler　*to break in*
chercher　*to look for*
découvrir　*to discover*
décrire　*to describe*
devoir　*to owe*
disparaître　*to disappear*
douter　*to doubt*
égarer　*to mislead, mislay*
étonner　*to astonish*
emprunter　*to borrow*
il faut　*it is necessary*
laisser　*to let, leave*
marquer　*to mark*
oublier　*to forget*
pardonner　*to forgive*
perdre　*to lose*
prouver　*to prove*
(R) reconnaître　*to recognize*
(R) remplir　*to fill, fill in*
rendre　*to give back*
retrouver　*to find*
se rendre compte　*to realize*
savoir　*to know*
signer　*to sign*
ça ne sert à rien　*that's no use*
se souvenir　*to remember*
trouver　*to find*
voler　*to steal*
acun(e)　*no, none*
carré　*square*
certain　*certain*
clair　*light (colour)*
content　*pleased*
court　*short*
déçu　*disappointed*
différent　*different*
étroit　*narrow*
fâché　*angry*
foncé　*dark (colour)*
formidable　*great*
furieux　*furious*
grand　*big*
heureux　*happy, lucky*
impossible　*impossible*
jaune　*yellow*
large　*broad*
long　*long*
mince　*thin*
neuf　*new*
petit　*small*
plein　*full*
possible　*possible*
rectangulaire　*rectangular*
rond　*round*
solide　*solid*
sûr　*sure*
tout neuf　*brand new*

vide　*empty*
vieux　*old*

après　*after*
aucun　*no, none*
aujourd'hui　*today*
avant　*before*
avant-hier　*the day before yesterday*
(R)ceci　*this one*
cela　*that one*
comme　*as, like*
(R) dedans　*inside*
dessous　*underneath*
dessus　*above*
(R) dont　*whose, of which*
hier　*yesterday*
(R) lequel　*which*
mon dieu!　*good heavens!*

partout　*everywhere*
puisque　*since, as*
sur　*on*
tiens!　*goodness!*
zut!　*blow!*

avec succès　*with success*
en train de　*in the process of*
(R) nulle part　*nowhere*
pas de chance　*no luck*
quoi de neuf?　*What's new?*

HAVING THINGS REPAIRED OR CLEANED

Higher
la　batterie　*battery*
le　bouton　*button, knob*
le　bruit　*noise*
la　cordonnerie　*shoe repairer's shop*
la　critique　*criticism, complaint*
　　dans ce cas　*in this case*
(R)　un électricien　*electrician*
(R)　un embrayage　*engaging (of clutch)*
un　état　*state, condition*
le　flash　*flash gun (photography)*
le　frein　*break*
la　fuite　*leak*
le　garage　*garage*
le　garagiste　*garage owner*
une　inondation　*flood*
la　laverie automatique　*car wash*
la　lampe de poche　*torch*
la　machine à laver　*washing machine*
(R)　la marque　*make, brand*
le　mécanicien　*mechanic*
le　moteur　*engine*
le　nettoyage à sec　*dry cleaning*
la　panne　*breakdown*
　　en panne　*out of order, broken down*
la　pièce de rechange　*spare part*
la　pile　*battery*
le　plombier　*plumber*
le　radiateur　*radiator*
la　réclamation　*complaint*
le　réparateur　*the repair man*
la　réparation　*the repair*
(R)　la roue de secours　*spare wheel*
la　sécurité　*security*
le　trou　*hole*
(R)　les vitesses (f)　*gears*

accepter　*to accept*
casser　*to break*
critiquer　*to criticize*
devoir　*to owe*
déchirer　*to tear*

échanger *to change*
emprunter *to borrow*
faire nettoyer *to have cleaned*
faire réparer *to have repaired*
il faut *it is necessary*
(R) fier *to trust*
(R) fixer *to fix*
(R) garantir *to guarantee*
laisser tomber *to drop*
laver *to wash*
marcher *to work, function*
nettoyer à sec *to dry clean*
se plaindre *to complain*
promettre *to promise*
proposer *to propose*
prouver *to prove*
raccommoder *to mend*
refuser *to refuse*
rembourser *to reimburse*
remercier *to thank*
remplacer *to replace*
(R) rendre *to give back*
renverser *to turn over, reverse*
réparer *to repair*
reprendre *to take back*
revenir *to come back*
(R) suggérer *to suggest*
vérifier *to check*

bizarre *odd, strange*
bon *good*
capable *capable*
crevé *punctured*
déçu *disappointed*
désolé *very sorry*
gentil *kind*
impossible *impossible*
mauvais *bad*
possible *possible*
prêt *ready*
propre *clean*
reçu *received*
sale *dirty*
satisfait *satisfied*
solide *solid*

combien de temps *how long*
demain *tomorrow*
après-demain *the day after tomorrow*
hélas! *alas!*

malgré *in spite of*
naturellement *of course*
pas de quoi *don't mention it*
ce n'est pas la peine *it's not worth it*
je vous en prie *please, not at all*

AT THE CHEMIST

Higher phrases
une angine *tonsilitis*
antiseptique *antiseptic*
se couper *to cut oneself*
saigner du nez *to have a nose bleed*
le traitement *treatment*

Active use

J'ai une angine *I have tonsilitis*

J'ai la grippe *I have flu*

Un insecte m'a piqué *I have been bitten (stung) by an insect*

Je saigne du nez *I have a nose bleed*

Je viens de tomber *I have just had a fall*
Je n'arrête pas de tousser *I can't stop coughing*

Receptive use

Voilà des comprimés efficaces pour la gorge. *Here are some tablets which are good for the throat*

Il vaut mieux rester au lit et attendre que le docteur vous donne une ordonnance pour des médicaments *You had better stay in bed and wait for the doctor to give you a prescription for some medicine*

Voici une crème/un traitement très efficace contre les piqûres d'insecte *Here is a very good cream/treatment for insect bites*
Il vaut mieux vous allonger tout de suite *You had better lie down straight away*
Je vais vous soigner. Voici un flacon d'antiseptique et des pansements/du sparadrap pour protéger votre main *I will deal with that. Here is a bottle of antiseptic and some bandages/plasters to protect your hand*
Voici un bon sirop/remède *Here is a good syrup/remedy*

WEATHER

Basic
un an *year*
une année *year*
un(e) après-midi *afternoon*
un automne *autumn*
une averse *shower, downpour*
le brouillard *fog*
la chaleur *heat*
le ciel *sky*
le climat *climate*
(R) le degré *degree*
un éclair *lightning*
un été *summer*
la glace *ice*
un hiver *winter*
le matin *morning*
la mer *sea*
la météo *weather forecast*
le mois *month*
la neige *snow*
le nuage *cloud*
la nuit *night*

une ombre *shadow*
un orage *storm*
la pluie *rain*
la prévision *forecast*
le printemps *spring*
la saison *season*
le soir *evening*
le soleil *sun*
la température *temperature*
la tempête *storm*
le temps *weather*
le tonnerre *thunder*
le vent *wind*

faire beau, chaud, froid *to be fine, warm, cold*
faire jour *to be light*
geler *to freeze*
neiger *to snow*
pleuvoir *to rain*

agréable *pleasant*
beau *fine*
bleu *blue*
chaud *warm, hot*
couvert *cloudy*
doux *mild*
ensoleillé *sunny*
fort *strong*
froid *cold*
humide *damp*
léger *light*
lourd *heavy, sultry*
mauvais *bad*
meilleur *better*
prochain *next*
(R) rare *rare*
sec *dry*

à peine *hardly, scarcely*
aujourd'hui *today*
demain *tomorrow*
il y a *there is*
il y aura *there will be*
maintenant *now*
(R) normalement *normally*
quel *what, which*
quelquefois *sometimes*
(R) rapidement *quickly*
(R) rarement *rarely*
souvent *often*

Basic phrases
Quel temps fait-il? *What's the weather like?*
Il pleut, neige, gèle, etc. *It's raining, snowing, freezing, etc.*

Higher
une amélioration *improvement*
la brume *mist*
le coucher de soleil *sunset*
une éclaircie *bright period*
la grêle *hail*
le lever du soleil *sunrise*
la marée *tide*
un orage *storm*
le passage *passage, passing*
la précipitation *precipitation (usually of rain)*
(R) la prévision *forecast*
(R) la visibilité *visibility*

s'adoucir *to become mild*
en avoir marre *to be fed up with*
plaire *to please*
pleuvoir à verse *to pour with rain*
(R) prévoir *to forecast*
se refroidir *to become cold*
souffler *to blow*
tonner *to thunder*
brumeux *misty*
couvert *cloudy*
frais *chilly*
maximum *maximum*
minimum *minimum*
neigeux *snowy*
nuageux *cloudy*
orageux *stormy*
pluvieux *rainy*
triste *sad*
(R) variable *variable*

après-demain *the day after tomorrow*
cependant *however*
dans ce cas *in this case*
dehors *outside*
en plein soleil *in full sunshine*
en général *usually*
généralement *usually*
grace à *thanks to*
il fait lourd *it's close, sultry*
malgré *in spite of*
de temps en temps *from time to time*
tout à l'heure *shortly, soon, a few moments ago*

THE WEATHER FORECAST

Higher
le bulletin météo(rologique) *weather bulletin*
éclater *to burst*
fondre *to thaw, melt*
la météo marine *shipping report*
la photo satellite *satellite photo*
la pression *pressure*

Basic
(R) un accent *accent*
l' anglais (m) *English*
la chose *thing*
un exemple *example*
(R) la faute *fault*
la fois *time, occasion*
le français *French*
la langue *language, tongue*
(R) le machin *thing*
le mot *word*
la phrase *phrase, sentence*
la question *question*
une sorte de *a kind of*
le truc *thing*

apprendre *to learn*
avoir raison *to be right*
c'est-a-dire *that's to say*
comprendre *to understand*

demander *to ask*
se dire *to be said*
écouter *to listen (to)*
écrire *to write*
s'écrire *to be written*
excusez-moi *excuse me*
je m'excuse *I'm sorry*
lire *to read*
oublier *to forget*
parler *to speak*
penser *to think*
poser *to put (a question)*
pouvoir *to be able*
regretter *to regret*
répéter *to repeat*
répondre *to reply*
savoir *to know*
vouloir dire *to mean*

correct *correct*
désolé *very sorry*
différent *different*
exact *exact*
excellent *excellent*
faux *wrong, false*
vite *quickly*
vrai *true*

assez *enough, fairly*
bien *good, well*
bof! *oh well!*
comment *how*
au contraire *on the contrary*
depuis *since*
en général *usually*
lentement *slowly*
(R) longtemps *a long time*
mal *badly*
peu *little*
très *very*
trop *too (much)*

aider *to help*
avoir tort *to be wrong*
conseiller *to advise*
corriger *to correct*
critiquer *to criticize*
douter *to doubt*
entendre *to hear*
épeler *to spell*
expliquer *to explain*
faire attention *to pay attention*
prononcer *to pronounce*
traduire *to translate*
se tromper *to make a mistake*

absolument *absolutely*
(R) autrement dit *in other words*
bravo! *well done!*
couramment *fluently*
égal *equal, the same*
quoi *what*

Higher

le doute *doubt*
le progrès *progress*
la voix *voice*

'FALSE FRIENDS'

Check the following words carefully. They resemble English words but have *different* meanings. The similar English words and their correct translation are given opposite. These words can be misleading too!

assister à	to be present at	aider	to assist
les cabinets	lavatories	les placards, les meubles á tiroirs (m)	cabinets
le car	coach	l'auto (f), la voiture	car
causer	to chat	faire	to cause
la cave	cellar	la caverne	cave
la crêpe	pancake	le crêpe	crepe
se dresser	to rise up	s'habiller	to dress
la figure	face	la taille (body) le chiffre (number)	figure
la journée	day	le voyage	journey
la lecture	reading	la conférence	lecture
la librairie	bookshop	la bibliothèque	library
la location	hiring, renting	la situation	location
le médecin	doctor	le médicament	medicine
la ménagère	housewife	le directeur, le gérant	manager
la monnaie	loose change	l'argent (m)	money
passer	spend (time)	réussir (exam etc.)	pass
le pensionnaire	boarder	le (la) retraité(e)	pensioner
le pétrole	crude oil	l'essence (f)	petrol
le photographe	photographer	la photographie	photograph
la place	square	l'endroit (m)	place
le plat	dish	une assiette	plate
le record	record (sports)	le disque	record (music)
rester	to stay	se reposer	rest
sensible	sensitive	raisonnable	sensible
travailler	to work	voyager	travel
le water (closet)	toilet	l'eau (f)	water

A STEP FURTHER

Some people find it useful to learn ten words about a particular subject. For example, you could write down ten words about transport.

la voiture	l'avion
le vélo	la moto
l'autobus	le ferry
le taxi	le bateau
le train	l'aéroglisseur

Now make up a sentence for each one: Je vais à Calais en voiture, etc.

Other topics which lend themselves to this treatment include:

clothes	fruit
weather	vegetables
school subjects	food in general
furniture	sports
shops	hobbies
professions	buildings

There are many other possibilities.

Another suggestion for the vocabulary fiend is to get a box similar to an 'After Eight' box, eat the mints and discard the wrappers, and then cut up bits of card from cereal packets to fit in. You then write the French on one side at the top and the English on the other, gradually replacing words you know with new ones. You can then test yourself, and make the tests as easy or as difficult as suits you.

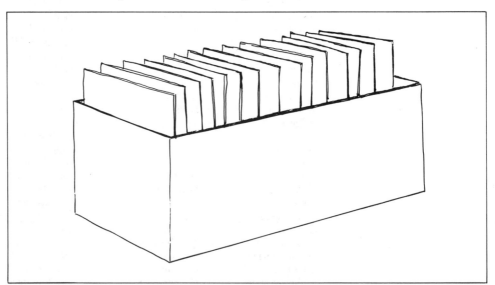

As well as formal learning of vocabulary, the more French you read and listen to, the better your understanding will become. So **do** follow the hints given in Chapter 2.

If you have the chance to pay a visit to a French-speaking country, remember to make the most of it by trying out what you have learned. Even if you are only making a day trip, it is surprising how much reading matter you can pick up free or very cheaply from the tourist office and handouts in shops, etc. Much of that will be very helpful for the topics tested in GCSE French.

In any case, learn a little but often, with variety, testing yourself as you go, and writing things down to improve your writing. The more French you read and listen to, the better.

BASIC SPEAKING

FORMAT OF THE EXAMINATION

EXAM GROUP REQUIREMENTS

ROLE-PLAYS

USEFUL PHRASES FOR ROLE-PLAYS

TOPICS AND SETTINGS FOR ROLE-PLAYS

PRACTICE ROLE-PLAYS

CONVERSATION

TOPICS AND SETTINGS FOR CONVERSATION

CONVERSATION QUESTIONS AND ANSWERS

PRACTICE EXERCISES

A STEP FURTHER

GETTING STARTED

Everybody has to take the Basic Speaking test. So it's important to make a good job of it. If you are not aiming for a high grade (D or above) and are therefore not entered for anything more than Basic Reading, Listening and Speaking, the Basic Speaking test makes up a third of your marks. If you **are** entered for a lot of Higher papers as well, you may find the Basic Speaking fairly simple. However, as it counts for as many marks as each of the Higher tests, you would do well to make a good job of Basic Speaking.

Candidates who gain good marks in Basic Speaking will be able to manage in straightforward situations likely to be met by a visitor to a French-speaking country. They will also be able to answer simple questions about themselves and their own lives and routines. They will pronounce French well enough to be understood by a French speaker who is making an effort to understand them.

ESSENTIAL PRINCIPLES

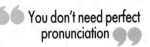

1 ▷ FORMATION OF THE EXAMINATION

The Examining Groups, although they have minor differences, agree broadly about the shape of the Speaking test. (Arrangements are different for the IGCSE.)

— It will be done between March and June at a time to be decided by your teacher.

— It will be conducted by your own teacher.

— It will almost certainly be recorded on cassette, so that the Examining Group can check that it has been properly conducted. This is for your protection.

— Your teacher may well mark what you have done, or the recording may be sent away to be marked.

— It will typically take about ten minutes.

— You will have ten minutes to prepare the role-play beforehand, usually while the previous candidate is taking his or her test.

2 ▷ EXAM GROUP REQUIREMENTS

There will normally be two or three role-play situations to do, followed by between ten and twenty simple questions on a limited range of straightforward topics, which your teacher may well weave into a natural conversation. The questions won't be officially laid down by the Examining Group, but it will not be difficult to work out beforehand the sorts of things that could be asked. So practice of them will certainly be possible.

❝ You can work out the things you are likely to be asked ❞

The role-plays will require you to take the initiative (for example asking for something in a shop) and may also require you to answer questions from strangers and friends. Some role-plays will have five things for you to say, while others have three. But the technique of dealing with them is the same.

In its 'General Level' Speaking Test, SEG includes a picture or a written document (e.g. a school timetable) on which it sets five specific questions to be answered. These can be rephrased by the teacher if you don't understand, although if this is done it can reduce the mark you earn.

❝ You don't need perfect pronunciation ❞

Your pronunciation must be good enough for a sympathetic native speaker who is making an effort to understand. It does not, therefore, have to be perfect in every detail. Indeed, as long as you don't mumble too much and do attempt a French accent, you need not concern yourself further with pronunciation at this level.

The table shows the requirements of the different Examining Groups.

Examining Group	LEAG	MEG	NEA	NISEC	SEG*	WJEC
Time in minutes	10	10	5–10	10	10	10
Tape-recorded	yes	yes	yes	yes	yes	yes
With own teacher	yes	yes	yes	yes	yes	yes
Own teacher marks it	yes	school option	no	yes	yes	school option
Examining Group marks it	no	school option	yes	no	no	school option
Number of role-plays	2	2	3	2	2	2
Conversation	yes	yes	yes	yes	yes	yes
Five questions on picture or text	no	no	no	no	yes	no

* 'General Level'

3 > ROLE-PLAYS   Let us look at the sort of question that might well be set as role-play.

> You are in a café in Calais with a friend. Your teacher will play the part of the waitress and will start the conversation.
>
> a) Order two coffees
> b) Ask if she has any croissants
> c) Order two croissants

 Change the English into what you would *actually* say

The first thing to be realized is that you have to change the English here into what you would actually say. So (although you aren't allowed to write this down while preparing) you have to change the wording into speech, i.e.:

a) 'Two coffees, please'
b) 'Have you any croissants?'
c) 'Two croissants, please'

So what you would actually say will be something like:

a) Je voudrais deux tasses de café, s'il vous plaît
b) Vous avez des croissants?
c) Deux croissants, s'il vous plaît

Try to get the message across

It's important to remember that the **exact** form of what you say doesn't matter as long as you 'get the message across'. The marking schemes mainly reward the skill of getting what you want. So for a) in the example above, it would have been perfectly acceptable to say 'Deux cafés'. You would still have been served your coffees, so it's worth full marks.

Here is another example of a role-play, this time with five things to say.

> You call on a friend to talk about what to do for the evening. The role of your friend will be played by your teacher.
>
> a) Ask whether he/she is free this evening
> b) Ask whether he/she would like to go to town
> c) Say there is a good film on at the cinema
> d) Tell your friend it starts at 8.30
> e) Arrange to meet at the cinema

Work out how to do this one, using the same intermediate (middle) stage as before, putting the instructions into English speech marks. You should come up with something like:
a) 'Are you free this evening?'
b) 'Would you like to go to town?'
c) 'There is a good film at the cinema'
d) 'It begins at 8.30'
e) 'Till 8.15, at the cinema'

Now try to work out what you might say in French before checking with the sample dialogue below. No peeping!

a)   Tu es libre ce soir?
      or Est-ce que tu es libre ce soir?
      or Est-ce que tu fais quelque chose ce soir?
b)   Tu veux aller en ville?
      or Est-ce que tu veux aller en ville?
c)   Il y a un bon film au cinéma
      or Un film qui est excellent passe au cinéma
      or Au cinéma on passe un bon film
d)   Il commence à huit heures et demie
      or Le film commence à huit heures et demie
e)   On se voit à huit heures et quart, devant le cinéma, alors
      or Jusqu'à huit heures et quart, devant le guichet

Whatever you came up with, as long as the message of a role-play is transmitted you will be awarded reasonable marks. Obviously, completely correct French will communicate well. But some marks for 'getting the message across' will be awarded for such versions as shown on the next page.

EXAMINER'S COMMENTS
ON STUDENT ANSWERS

66 Communicates well 99

66 Some ambiguity – is it past or present? 99

66 Conveys the message, albeit with glaring defects in the French 99

66 Gets the message across pretty well. In the context, most people would understand that this was the start time 99

66 Good 99

a) Libre, ce soir, toi?

b) Tu aller en ville?

c) Film bon cinéma

d) Huit heures et demie - le film

e) A bientôt, devant le cinéma

66 Role-play is a good test of practical communication 99

like the first (p69) or the second version given here (above). If you are closer to the second version, take heart – you will in GCSE French be able to score something reasonable for a performance like that. You are, after all, communicating, and one of the major aims of the GCSE is to use the language for the purposes of practical communication.
use the language for the purposes of practical communication.

If your attempts are more sophisticated, you should remember that there is no one right answer to the role-plays, and that you can certainly improvise if you happen to have forgotten an item of vocabulary. I had a candidate in 1988 who had been told to buy cherries. He couldn't remember the word for cherries, but managed to describe 'des petits fruits noirs qui se trouvent souvent dans les gâteaux de la forêt noir'. He got his mark for communicating.

4 > USEFUL PHRASES FOR ROLE-PLAYS

There are phrases for role-play which can be applied to many situations. Make sure you know the ones on this list, and *add to it* as you discover others. If you are very pressed for time, the first three on the list will help in most situations.

Je voudrais . . .	I would like . . .
C'est combien?	How much is it?
A quelle heure?	At what time?
Attendez!	Wait!
Avec plaisir	It's a pleasure/Certainly
D'accord	OK
Entendu	Agreed/Understood
Excusez-moi	Excuse me
Il me faut . . .	I need . . .
J'ai besoin de . . .	I need . . .
Je dois . . .	I have to . . .
Je peux . . . ?	Can I . . . ?
Je ne peux pas . . .	I can't . . .
Je veux . . .	I want (to) . . .
Je ne veux pas . . .	I don't want (to) . . .
Je suis desolé(e)	I'm sorry
Où est . . . ?	Where is . . . ?
Où se trouve . . . ?	Where is . . . ?
Pour aller à . . . ?	How do I get to . . . ?
Pouvez-vous m'aider?	Can you help me?
Pouvez-vous me dire . . . ?	Can you tell me . . . ?
Y a-t-il un — par ici?	Is there a — near here?

5 > TOPICS AND SETTINGS FOR ROLE-PLAYS

In order to help you to revise the sorts of conversation which will come up in role-play, the most common topics are listed below.

- finding your way
- shopping
- cafés and restaurants
- hotels, youth hostels and campsites
- trains, trams, buses and taxis
- bank, post office, customs, tourist office
- garages and petrol stations
- places of entertainment
- staying with a family abroad
- school
- dealing with minor illness and dental problems

Make sure you have worked out likely role-plays for these. You can do this with a friend, and check the results with the various chapters in your text-book. Remember not to make them too difficult.

6 > PRACTICE ROLE-PLAYS

The following role-play exercises give you an idea of the sort of thing which might be set at Basic level for each of the situations listed. After the role-plays there are suggested answers. There are also comments about the role-plays which should help you to tackle other, similar ones with confidence.

Finding the way

You are in the main street of your home town when you happen to come across some French tourists who have stopped their car to make enquiries of a policeman. As there are obvious difficulties you offer to help.

Say that

— you speak a little French and you would like to help.
— there is a car park nearby.
— they should take the next turning left.*
— parking is free.
— the car park closes at eight o'clock in the evening.

(WJEC)

* Directions are very common.

Shopping

In a greengrocer's shop

You are shopping for fruit and vegetables in France, the examiner will play the part of the shopkeeper.

a) Ask for 1 kg of apples.
b) Ask for 5 small oranges.
c) Ask if the potatoes are good.
d) Ask for 3 kgs of potatoes.
e) Ask how much the bill* comes to.

(NISEC)

* Useful in many circumstances.

Café/restaurants

CANDIDATE INSTRUCTIONS
1   Order a large white coffee* for yourself.
2   Order a lemonade for your friend.
3   Ask where the toilets are.

(LEAG)

* Make sure you know all about the different sorts of coffee.

Hotels .

CANDIDATE INSTRUCTIONS

1   Say that your father/mother has reserved two rooms.
2   Give your surname and nationality.
3   Ask what floor the rooms are on.
4   Check that breakfast is included* in the price.
5   Ask where the car can be parked.

(LEAG)

* Compris is a very useful concept.

Youth hostels

You are on a hiking holiday in France with a friend and you have just arrived at a youth hostel where you hope to spend the night.

Find out
— whether the hostel has a room for two people for two nights.
— the cost per night.
— whether you can have an evening meal.
— at what time* breakfast is served.
— whether they have any maps of the region.

(WJEC)

* A quelle heure? crops up in many role-plays.

Camp sites

You arrive at a camp site. Your teacher will play the part of the warden.

1   Ask if they have room* for a caravan and three people.
2   Ask how much it costs.
3   Say you are sorry, but it's too expensive.

* Asking for room is very common.

Trains

At the railway station

You are at the information office of a French railway station to find out about trains to Calais. The examiner will play the part of the clerk.

a) Ask if there are trains to Calais.
b) Ask what time the train arrives in Calais.
c) Ask if it is necessary to change* trains.
d) Ask from which platform the train leaves.
e) Ask if there is a restaurant on the train?

(NISEC)

* Many train role-plays involve changing!

Trams/buses

You are in the information office of a French coach station. Your teacher will play the part of the counter assistant, and will start the conversation.

a) Say you want two seats for Paris.
b) Tell him it's for tomorrow.
c) Ask what time* the coach leaves.

(NEA 16+ 1987)

* Times of departure are very useful in transport role-plays.

Taxis

You get into a taxi at Bayeux.

1   Say you would like* to go to the village of Arromanches.
2   You would like* to get out at the museum.
3   Ask how far it is to Arromanches.

* Note how often Je voudrais is useful.

Banks

You go into a bank. Your teacher will play the part of the clerk.

1   Tell him/her you want to change a travellers' cheque for £25.*
2   Say you have forgotten to bring your passport.
3   Ask what time the bank closes.

* Make sure you know the words for £ sterling.

Post office

You are in a post office in France. Your examiner will play the part of the counter-clerk.

Your tasks are:

to greet the clerk	to enquire where the letter-box is
to post a parcel	to say thank you and goodbye*
to buy stamps	

(SEG)

* Be thankful for easy tasks like thanking and greeting!

Customs

You are at the border between France and Belgium. Your teacher will play the part of the customs officer.

1   Tell him/her that you have four bottles of wine with you.
2   Explain that a friend gave* them to you as a present.
3   Ask how much you have to pay.

* Note that some straightforward perfect tenses may occur in Basic role-play.

Tourist office

CANDIDATE INSTRUCTIONS
1   Ask for a map of the city.
2   Thank the person for the map and say that you would also like some leaflets on Paris.
3   Ask if the Eiffel Tower is open* today.
4   Ask how much it costs to go up the Eiffel Tower.
5   Ask if you can buy metro tickets at the Office.

(LEAG)

* Enquiring about opening times is a common task.

Garages

Study the following situations and be prepared to perform the roles indicated. Your conversation must be in French and you should include greetings and goodbyes as appropriate.

You are travelling through France by car with your family. You call at a petrol station and, as you speak French, your parents ask you to talk to the attendant. The role of the attendant will be played by the Examiner.

1   You require a full tank of petrol.*
2   You require two litres of oil.
3   Enquire about cost.
4   You will have to respond to any other questions or comments about your journey.

(MEG)

* Asking for a full tank is one of the obvious things for service station role-plays.

Places of entertainment

At the cinema

You are at the ticket office of a cinema in France. The examiner will play the part of the person in the ticket office.

a) Ask how much a seat is.
b) Ask for two* seats at 30F.
c) Ask if it is a long film.
d) Ask if it ends at 22 hours.
e) Ask for a programme for August.

(NISEC)

* It's worth knowing how to ask for two seats.

Staying with a family

This is your first day in a French family. Ask your host or hostess:
the time of breakfast
where to put your money and passport,
if you can phone your parents,
what the plans are for tomorrow,
to speak more slowly please.*

(SEG)

* You can see how useful this might be!

School

At your pen-friend's house

You are talking about school to your French pen-friend. The examiner will play the part of your friend.

a) Ask at what time lessons begin in the morning.*
b) Ask how many lessons there are per day.*
c) Say how many lessons you have per day.
d) Ask what your friend's favourite subject is.*
e) Say what your favourite subject is.

(NISEC)

* These are really the likeliest tasks for a school role-play.

Minor illnesses

You are staying with a French family and come down to breakfast after being ill the previous day. Your teacher will play the part of your friend's father, and will start the conversation.
a) Tell him you are much better and thank him.
b) Tell him you have slept* well.
c) Tell him you would like some coffee with milk.

(NEA 16+ 1987)

* Another straightforward perfect tense here.

POSSIBLE ANSWERS TO PRACTICE ROLE-PLAYS

The answers given below are possible solutions to the questions. They are not the only answers which would earn good marks. Getting the message across is the most important point!

Finding the way

Je parle un peu de français. Est-ce que je peux vous aider?
Il y a un parking près d'ici?
Prenez la première rue à gauche.
C'est un parking gratuit.
Le parking ferme à huit heures du soir.

Shopping

a) Un kilo de pommes, s'il vous plaît.
b) Cinq petites oranges, s'il vous plaît.
c) Est-ce que les pommes de terre sont bonnes?
d) Je voudrais trois kilos de pommes de terre, s'il vous plaît.
e) C'est combien?

Café/restaurants

1   Un grand café crême pour moi, s'il vous plaît.
2   Une limonade pour mon ami(e).
3   Où sont les toilettes, s'il vous plaît?

Hotels

1 Mon père (ma mère) a résérvé deux chambres.
2 Je m'appelle Jarvis. Nous sommes anglais.
3 C'est à quel étage, s'il vous plaît?
4 Est-ce que le petit déjeuner est compris?
5 Où est-ce qu'on peut garer notre voiture?

Youth hostels

Est-ce que vous avez de la place pour deux personnes pour deux nuits?
C'est combien par personne par nuit?
Est-ce qu'on peut dîner ici?
A quelle heure est-ce que le petit déjeuner est servi?
Est-ce que vous avez des cartes de la région?

Camp sites

1 Est-ce que vous avez de la place pour une caravane et trois personnes?
2 C'est combien par personne et par journée?
3 Je regrette, monsieur/madame, mais c'est trop cher pour nous.

Trains

a) Est-ce qu'il y a des trains pour Calais?
b) A quelle heure arrive le train à Calais?
c) Est-ce qu'il faut changer?
d) Le train part de quel quai?
e) Y a-t-il un wagon-restaurant?

Trams/buses

a) Je voudrais deux places pour Paris, s'il vous plaît.
b) C'est pour demain.
c) A quelle heure part le car?

Taxis

1 Je voudrais aller à Arromanches, s'il vous plaît.
2 Je voudrais descendre au musée.
3 Arromanches est à quelle distance d'ici?

Banks

1 Je voudrais changer un chèque de voyage sur vingt-cinq livres sterling.
2 J'ai oublié mon passeport.
3 A quelle heure ferme la banque aujourd'hui?

Post office

Bonjour monsieur/madame.
Je voudrais envoyer ce paquet.
Je voudrais cinq timbres pour l'Angleterre.
Où est la boîte aux lettres, s'il vous plaît?
Merci monsieur/madame. Au revoir.

Customs

1 J'ai quatre bouteilles de vin avec moi.
2 Un ami m'a donné le vin comme cadeau.
3 Combien est-ce que je dois payer?

Tourist office

1 Je voudrais un plan de la ville, s'il vous plaît.
2 Je voudrais aussi des brochures sur Paris.
3 Est-ce que la Tour Eiffel est ouverte aujourd'hui?
4 C'est combien pour monter à la Tour Eiffel?
5 Est-ce que je peux acheter des tickets de métro ici?

Garages

1 Faites le plein, s'il vous plaît.
2 Je voudrais deux litres d'huile.
3 Ça fait combien?
4 The examiner asks: Vous êtes en vacances en France?
   Oui. Nous sommes en vacances.
   The examiner asks: Vous allez où aujourd'hui?
   Nous allons à Paris.

Places of entertainment

a) Ça coûte combien, une place?
b) Je voudrais deux places à trente francs.
c) Est-ce que c'est un long film?
d) Est-ce que le film est fini à vingt-deux heures?
e) Donnez-moi un programme pour le mois d'août, s'il vous plaît.

Staying with a family

A quelle heure est-ce qu'on mange le petit déjeuner?
Où est-ce que je peux mettre mon argent et mon passeport?
Est-ce que je peux téléphoner à mes parents?
Qu'est-ce qu'on fait demain?
Parlez moins vite, s'il vous plaît.

School

a) A quelle heure commencent les classes le matin?
b) Combien de leçons y a-t-il par jour?
c) Nous avons huit leçons par jour, chez nous.
d) Quel est ton sujet préféré?
e) Mon sujet préféré, c'est les maths.

Minor illnesses

a) Ça va mieux, merci.
b) J'ai bien dormi.
c) Je voudrais du café au lait.

7 ▷ CONVERSATION

❝Avoid one-word answers❞

Normally you will have 10–20 simple questions (depending on the Examining Group). Your teacher will attempt to weave them into a conversation, but he or she also has to cover a certain number of topic areas, and may well jump around a bit. Don't be put off if this happens. What **you** have to do is to answer the questions adequately.

Try to avoid one-word answers such as 'Oui' or 'Non', or the name of a British TV programme ('*Neighbours*'). Look for opportunities to say at least one sentence in reply to each question.

Your teacher should be asking you questions which do not have a yes/no answer. However, if you are aware that the ideal situation is for you to 'show off' a little of what you can do, you can avoid the pitfall of the one-word answer. So, for example, if you are asked, 'Avez-vous un frère?', it is much more sensible to reply, 'Non, mais j'ai une soeur' than just plain 'Non'.

❝If necessary, fib a little. It's better than drying up!❞

Another important thing to remember is that your teacher is more interested in your French than in the strict truth. He or she is hardly likely to send a private detective round to check whether or not you own a dog, if he or she asks you about pets. So if you are asked about something and you don't have the specialist vocabulary ready (if, for example, you keep a budgie at home but you can only remember 'chien'), then fib a little. Too many candidates stumble over such details and clam up – doing considerable harm to their mark. That said, of course, it is even better if you **do** know the French for budgie (une perruche)!

8 ▷ TOPICS AND SETTINGS FOR CONVERSATION

The topics you are likely to be asked about will include:

- yourself, home and family
- your school
- holidays, a visit abroad

- free time, sports and hobbies
- morning and evening routines
- your home town, village or area
- your friends

Make sure you have something prepared to say about each of these, even if it is only a few sentences.

9 >	**CONVERSATION QUESTIONS AND ANSWERS**

Learn the lists your teacher gives you

Below are some questions which might well be asked. They are given in the 'vous' form, but your teacher may well use the 'tu' form. Check beforehand. Of course, if your teacher gives you a list to learn from, make sure you work through it, because, after all, he or she will actually be doing the Speaking test with you!

A possible answer is given after each question, and italics indicate things which you will need to tailor to your own circumstances.

YOURSELF, HOME AND FAMILY

1 Comment vous appelez-vous?
Je m'appelle *Ian Wilkinson*
(My name is . . .)

2 Quel âge avez-vous? Quelle est la date de votre anniversaire?
J'ai *seize* ans
(I'm 16)
Mon anniversaire, c'est *le trois septembre*
(My birthday is on the . . .)

3 Est-ce que vous avez des frères ou des soeurs?
Oui, j'ai *deux frères et une soeur*
(Yes, I have two brothers and a sister)
Non, je suis enfant unique
(No, I am an only child)

4 Que fait votre père (votre mère) dans la vie?
Mon père est *mécanicien*. Ma mère est *ménagère*
(My father is a mechanic. My mother is a housewife)

5 Est-ce que vous avez un animal à la maison?
J'ai *un cochon d'Inde et deux chats*
(I've got a guinea pig and two cats)
Non. Je n'en ai pas. *Mon pere n'aime pas les animaux.*
(No, I haven't got any. Dad doesn't like animals)

6 Est-ce que vous avez une chambre individuelle à la maison?
Oui, j'ai une chambre à moi
(Yes, I've got my own room)
Non, je partage ma chambre avec *mon frère*
(No, I share a room with my brother)

YOUR SCHOOL

1 Qu'est-ce que vous étudiez au collège?
J'apprends le français, *l'anglais, les maths, la géographie, l'histoire, la biologie, la chimie et les sports*
(I do French, English, maths, geography, history, biology, chemistry and games)

2 Quelle est votre matière préférée?
Je préfère le français, naturellement!
(My favourite subject is French, of course!)

3 Depuis combien de temps apprenez-vous le français?
J'apprends le français depuis *cinq* ans
(I have been learning French for five years)

4 A quelle heure commencent les cours à votre collège le matin?
Au collège, les cours commencent à *neuf heures*
(At school, lessons start at 9.00)

HOLIDAYS, A VISIT ABROAD

1   Où est-ce que vous avez passé vos vacances l'année dernière?
    J'ai passé mes vacances *aux Cornouailles, à Truro*
    (I spent my holidays in Cornwall, at Truro)

2   Quel temps faisait-il?
    La plupart du temps il faisait chaud, mais il a plu pendant deux jours
    (Most of the time it was hot, but it rained for two days)

3   Qu'est-ce que vous avez fait en vacances?
    J'ai *nagé dans la mer, je me suis bronzé(e), j'ai fréquenté des discothèques*
    (I swam in the sea, sunbathed and went to discos)

4   Quels projets de vacances avez-vous pour cette année?
    J'ai l'intention de *visiter la Belgique*
    (I intend going to Belgium)

5   Avez-vous déjà visité la France? Quand? Où étiez-vous?
    Oui, j'ai déjà visité la France. J'ai passé *deux jours à Bayeux il y a deux ans*
    (Yes, I have been to France. I spent two days at Bayeux two years ago)
    Non, pas encore. Peut-être l'année prochaine
    (No, not yet. Perhaps next year)

FREE TIME, SPORT AND HOBBIES

1   Quels sont vos passe-temps?
    Je lis beaucoup, j'écoute des disques, je joue au tennis et je joue de la guitare
    (I read a lot, I listen to records, I play tennis and I play the guitar)

2   Qu'est-ce que vous faites, le week-end?
    Le samedi, *je travaille dans un magasin.* Le soir, *je sors avec des amis.* Le dimanche, *je fais mes devoirs*
    (On Saturdays I work in a shop. In the evening I go out with friends. On Sundays I do my homework)

3   Qu'est-ce que vous avez vu à la télévision hier soir?
    J'ai vu *Neighbours. C'est un feuilleton*
    (I saw *Neighbours*. It's a soap opera)

4   Faites-vous du sport? Où? Quand? Est-ce que vous y jouez bien?
    Oui, je joue au tennis et je fais du cyclisme
    (Yes I play tennis and go cycling)
    Je joue normalement au club de tennis, ou dans le centre sportif. J'y joue *assez bien.*)
    (I normally play in the tennis club or at the sports centre. I play quite well)
    Non, je ne suis pas sportif (sportive)
    (No, I'm not sporty)

MORNING AND EVENING ROUTINES

1   A quelle heure est-ce que vous vous levez normalement?
    Je me lève normalement à *sept heures et demie*
    (I normally get up at 7.30)

2   Qu'est-ce que vous mangez comme petit déjeuner?
    Je mange *du toast, des cornflakes et une pomme*
    (I eat toast, cornflakes and an apple)

3   Venez-vous au collège à pied?
    Oui, je viens à pied
    (Yes, I walk here)
    Non, je viens *en autobus, et quelquefois à bicyclette*
    (No, I come by bus, and sometimes by bike)
    Non, *mon père m'amène en voiture*
    (No, my Dad brings me by car)

4   A quelle heure quittez-vous la maison le matin?
    Je quitte la maison à *huit heures et quart*
    (I leave the house at a quarter past eight)

5   A quelle heure est-ce que vous mangez le soir?
    Chez nous, on mange à *cinq heures et demie*
    (At our house, we eat at 5.30)

6   A quelle heure est-ce que vous vous couchez, d'habitude?
    D'habitude je me couche à *dix heures*
    (I generally go to bed at 10)

YOUR HOME TOWN, VILLAGE OR AREA

1   Où habitez-vous?
    J'habite *Preston*
    (I live in Preston)

2   C'est où exactement, Preston?
    C'est *dans le nord-ouest de l'Angleterre*
    (It's in the north-west of England)

3   Est-ce que c'est une grande ville?
    Oui, c'est une ville assez grande. Il y a *cent mille* habitants
    (Yes, it's quite a big town. There are 100,000 inhabitants)
    Non, Sudbury est assez petit. Il y a *vingt-cinq mille* habitants
    (No, Sudbury's quite small. There are 25,000 inhabitants)

4   Qu'est-ce qu'il y a à voir dans votre région?
    Il y a *les montagnes, un musée industriel, un beau château et des villages pittoresques*
    (There are the hills, an industrial museum, a nice stately home and picturesque villages)

YOUR FRIENDS

1   Comment s'appelle votre meilleur ami (meilleure amie)?
    Il/Elle s'appelle *Chris*
    (He/She is called Chris)

2   Qu'est-ce que vous faites ensemble?
    Nous allons *au cinema et à la piscine* ensemble, *nous faisons du sport*, et nous allons *en ville* ensemble
    (We go to the cinema and the swimming pool together, we play sport, and we go to town together)

PRACTICE EXERCISES

In its 'General Level' Speaking test, SEG includes a picture or a written document (e.g. a school timetable) on which it sets five specific questions to be answered. These can be rephrased by the teacher if you don't understand, although if this is done it can reduce the mark you earn. Below are two samples of the sort of thing they might use, and possible answers to the questions are given for you to study.

NOM: MARIE CARTIER   **CLASSE:** SECONDE

HEURES	LUNDI	MARDI	MERCREDI	JEUDI	VENDREDI	SAMEDI
8 – 9		Latin		Géographie		
9 – 10	Français	Français	Math	Physique	Français	
10 – 11	Français	Allemand		Anglais	Français	Education Physique
11 – 12	Anglais	Anglais	Sc. E.S	Sc. E.S	Allemand	Education Physique
2 – 3	Physique	Géographie		Latin	Mathématiques	
3 – 4	Allemand	Mathématiques		Histoire	Histoire	
4 – 5		Physique		Physique	Latin	
5 – 6						

(SEG)

1 Dans quelle classe est Marie Cartier?
2 Combien de leçons a-t-elle le mardi?
3 A quelle heure est-ce que les cours commencent le vendredi?
4 Quels jours est-ce que les cours commencent à huit heures?
5 Que fait-elle entre midi et deux heures?

Answers to questions:
1 Elle est en seconde
2 Elle en a sept
3 Les cours commencent à neuf heures
4 Les cours commencent à huit heures le mardi et le jeudi
5 Elle mange le déjeuner

1 Le monsieur à droite, qu'est-ce qu'il donne à la femme?
2 Pourquoi?
3 Que fait la dame à côté de lui?
4 Que fait la dame à gauche?
5 Le monsieur au centre, qu'est-ce qu'il veut faire?

(SEG)

Answers to questions:
1 Il donne de l'argent à la femme
2 Parce qu'il achète le pain
3 Elle attend
4 Elle choisit de la viande
5 Il veut entrer avec son chien

A STEP FURTHER

There are many ways of improving your fluency. Most of them boil down to actually doing some speaking.

— Practise reading out loud. This can improve your ability to get your tongue round the sounds of French.
— Talk in French to the cat or your teddy or the goldfish. They may not respond much, but at least you get the feeling of talking to someone. (NB: This is not as good as practice with a human!)
— Prepare the conversation topics thoroughly, so that you know the French for your parents' professions, your specialized hobbies, etc. Ask your teacher or the French assistant(e) for specific words. They are employed to tell you such things!
— Make sure you have worked through role-plays for all settings. Use ones in this book, but don't neglect your text-book. And your teacher may have CSE text-books and past papers which contain lots of them.
— Take advantage of any mock Speaking test which is offered to you at school. The chances are you will have only one opportunity to practise individually with your teacher. Don't be so foolish as not to prepare thoroughly for it. After all, it is your teacher who will be doing the Speaking test with you!

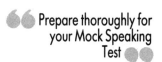 Prepare thoroughly for your Mock Speaking Test

HIGHER SPEAKING

FORMAT OF THE EXAMINATION

EXAM GROUP REQUIREMENTS

HIGHER LEVEL ROLE- PLAYS

TOPICS AND SETTINGS FOR ROLE-PLAYS

PRACTICE ROLE-PLAYS

HIGHER LEVEL CONVERSATION

CONVERSATION QUESTIONS AND ANSWERS

PRACTICE EXERCISES

GETTING STARTED

All candidates for Higher Speaking have to begin by doing Basic Speaking. So you should familiarize yourself with the exercises for that test.

Candidates who do well in Higher Speaking will be able to function quite well in French situations, and will be able to give a good amount of detail about themselves and things which have happened. They will pronounce French reasonably well, although it will be possible to gain full marks without perfect reproduction of a native speaker's accent.

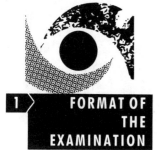

ESSENTIAL PRINCIPLES

1 ▷ FORMAT OF THE EXAMINATION

The arrangements for conducting and marking the Higher Speaking are much the same as for the Basic. In summary, therefore:

— It will be done between March and June.
— It will be conducted by your own teacher.
— It will almost certainly be recorded on cassette.
— It may either be marked by your teacher, or the recording sent away to be marked.
— It will typically take about 15 minutes.
— You will have 15 minutes to prepare the role-plays and other exercises beforehand, usually while the previous candidate is taking his or her test.
— Usually the Higher will immediately follow the Basic, and often the conversation for Basic and Higher is rolled into one, starting off with easy questions (as per Basic) and then moving on to the more lengthy discussion of various topics.

2 ▷ EXAM GROUP REQUIREMENTS

Those who are correctly entered for Higher Speaking should be able to:

■ perform role-plays over the whole range of vocabulary areas in the syllabus
■ ask and reply to questions on activities and events which are within the experience of a 16-year-old
■ conduct a lengthy unrehearsed free conversation ranging over a number of topics
■ pronounce French well enough to be understood by a native speaker without difficulty, with reasonably good intonation and stress

Higher candidates will normally have to do:
■ all the exercises for Basic level
■ an extra role-play with an element of unpredictability
■ an extended conversation

For candidates taking SEG GCSE French, there is a similar but different set of exercises for the Written or Visual Stimulus question. For MEG candidates entered for the Higher Part 2 paper, there is a 'narrator' exercise, where you have to recount a story, journey or incident with the aid of notes and diagrams. Examples of these exercises are given later in this chapter.

Look at the table to see what your Examining Group asks its candidates to do for Higher Speaking, **in addition to** Basic Speaking. Please note that the timings given for the Higher Speaking in the table include the time taken to do the Basic exercises, which those entered for Higher Speaking will probably do much quicker than candidates taking only Basic Speaking.

Examining Group	LEAG	MEG	NEA	NISEC	SEG*	WJEC
time in minutes#	20	Part 1: 12 Part 2: 15	10–15	15	17	15
role-plays	1	1	2	2	2	2
picture and/or text stimulus	no	Part 2 only	no	no	yes	no
general conversation	yes	yes	yes	yes	yes	yes
* 'Extended Level'		# Total time including Basic				

3 > HIGHER LEVEL ROLE-PLAYS

The extra features for Higher are the additional role-plays. These differ from those in Basic Speaking in two ways:

— they cover the whole range of the syllabus
— they have an element of unpredictability in them which you will not really be able to prepare for. So they test your ability to 'think on your feet' a little more.

The 'unpredictable element' will be shown on the card like this:

Respond to the examiner's question.
Say which bus you want to take [after just having found out bus times].
Reply to the examiner's remark.

Your teacher will normally have a script and will not be able to ask you an unreasonable question. But you do have to be able to understand what your teacher has said to you so that you can react correctly!

The role-plays will normally have a setting with them. Some of the Examining Groups rely very much on the contents of the setting for making the situation work, and you would be well advised to read it carefully so that you understand, for example, at what time of day you need to arrive at a particular place according to the setting. Good candidates can easily be trapped by such questions because they haven't familiarized themselves thoroughly enough with the situation.

Otherwise, the technique of turning the instructions into what you would actually say before attempting to work out the French for conveying the message, as outlined in the Basic Speaking chapter, applies here, too.

> **Getting the message across is still the vital point**

Once again, the main focus of the mark schemes for Higher role-play is whether you get the message across. So if you are stuck, describe and paraphrase in the same way as you would have done at Basic level.

Let us now look at a typical **role-play** at Higher level.

While you are on holiday in France with your family, your car breaks down. You telephone a garage. Your teacher will play the part of the mechanic.

a) Tell him/her the car has broken down
b) Say when it happened
c) Explain where it is
d) Answer the mechanic's question
e) Make an appropriate response

You will have to deal with working out the French in the same way as for Basic role-plays, that is, deciding what you would actually say before putting it into French. So for a) you need to say, 'My car has broken down' before you work out what that would be in French, which might be 'Ma voiture est en panne'; 'J'ai une panne de voiture'; 'Je suis tombé(e) en panne', or even 'Ma voiture ne marche pas'. Once again, there will be credit for getting the message across. But there is also credit for the quality of your French.

Tasks d) and e) in the example are more of a problem. You obviously cannot prepare what you are going to say beforehand. Your teacher has a script which will tell him or her what question to ask you. After you have done task c) explaining where the vehicle is, you will be asked, 'De quelle couleur est votre voiture?' and, when you have replied (i.e. done task d)), you will be told, 'Bon. Alors je serai là dans 10 minutes', to which the 'appropriate response' might be, 'Ah merci bien, monsieur'. So although there **is** an element of the unexpected, as you can see, it is not usually fiendishly difficult.

The next example is included with the teacher's sheet so that you can see what information he or she has. A student answer and examiner comments are provided.

Candidate's Card

> You are staying in a small village outside Blois and you are going to England tomorrow by train. You have to get to Blois by midday. You need to make some local enquiries. The examiner plays the role of a helpful passer-by. You may need to make notes, so the examiner will give you some rough paper.
>
> Ask: 1 The times of the buses to Blois
>   2 Whether there is a direct service
> Then when you have found out those two pieces of information:
>   3 Say which bus you want to take
>   4 Ask how much a single ticket costs
>   5 Thank the passer-by for the information

Examiner's notes

1	Times of buses	There are two possible buses:
		Dep. Arr. Blois
		8.00 9.49
		9.05 11.04
		In both cases you need to change at Bracieux.
		Mais il faut changer à Bracieux.
2	Direct service	Oui, il y a un service direct. Mais il part à 11h et arrive à 12.30.
3	Which bus?	If candidate chooses the direct service, remind him that he said he wanted to arrive at midday. Vous voulez être à Blois à quelle heure?
4	Cost	22 francs aller simple.
		If candidate just asks for the price of a ticket without saying a single ticket, ask:
		Aller-retour ou aller simple?
5	Thank passer-by	Il n'y a pas de quoi.

(MEG)

The conversation might sound something like this:

Candidate: Pardon, monsieur. (1) A quelle heure y a-t-il un car pour Blois?

Examiner: Un moment. Oui. Il y a deux possibilités. Le car de huit heures arrive à Blois à neuf heures quarante-neuf, et le car de neuf heures cinq arrive à onze heures quatre. Mais il faut changer à Bracieux.

Candidate: (Writes down times) C'est direct? (2)

Examiner: Oui, il y a un service direct. Mais il part à 11h et arrive à 12 h 30.

Candidate: Je vais prendre le service a 11h. (3)

Examiner: Vous voulez être à Blois à quelle heure?

Candidate: Ah, oui, à midi. (4) Je vais prendre le car à 9 h 05 et changer à Bracieux. (5) C'est combien? (6)

Examiner: Aller-retour ou aller simple?

Candidate: Aller simple.

Examiner: 22 francs aller simple.

Candidate: Merci bien, monsieur. (7)

Examiner: Il n'y a pas de quoi.

1 A nice start – entering into the spirit of the role-play.
2 Simple – but communicates perfectly.
3 Candidate has not read the setting carefully!
4 Redeems her error.
5 Good use of something heard from the examiner, and again, in the spirit of the situation.
6 Simple – but communicates perfectly.
7 Further proof that not all items are fiendishly difficult.

4 ▷ TOPICS AND SETTINGS FOR ROLE-PLAYS

Higher level role-plays cover the range covered by Basic level role-plays. They also cover some of the more difficult settings. These include:

- lost property
- repairs and complaints
- more serious medical problems
- accidents and emergencies
- telephoning and more complex use of a post office
- banking and currency exchange
- travel by air

Make sure you have worked out likely role-plays for these, using the list of language tasks in the Vocabulary chapter to jog your memory. Remember to include an element of unpredictability in your role-plays. It's probably wise to write a teacher's sheet for each pupil role. Then practise with a friend.

The following role-play exercises give you an idea of the sort of thing which might be set at Higher level for each of the situations listed. After the role-plays there are suggested answers. There are also comments about the role-plays which should help you to tackle other, similar ones with confidence.

Lost property

At the lost property office
While on holidays in France you lose your purse/wallet. You go to a lost property office to enquire if it has been left there.

The examiner will play the part of the employee.
a) Say that you lost* your purse/wallet in the market this morning.
b) Describe the purse/wallet* and say what it contains.
c) Give your name and address in France.

(NISEC)

*Note that perfect tense required, as well as vocabulary for describing a purse or wallet.

Repairs

You have been staying with a French friend and you are going home tomorrow. You have to collect your camera from the shop where you left it to be repaired and find that it is not ready. Your teacher will play the part of the shopkeeper* and will start the conversation.

(NEA)

*You have to prepare for what might well be asked by a shopkeeper.

The teacher's sheet reads:

Bonjour monsieur/mademoiselle. Je peux vous aider?
Quand est-ce que vous m'avez apporté l'appareil pour la réparation?
Vous avez votre ticket?
Je suis désolé, mais il n'est pas prêt. Pouvez-vous revenir samedi prochain?
Vous partez demain monsieur/mademoiselle? Alors je vous rendrai l'appareil tel qu'il est.

Complaints

You have just finished a meal in a Paris restaurant which you have visited with two members of your family. All three of you have complaints. Your steaks were not cooked enough and the service was slow. You have to explain the complaints to the head waiter. Your teacher will play the part of the head waiter, and will start the conversation.*

(NEA)

*You need to really put yourself in the customer's shoes here! Make sure you read all the details of a role-play like this!

The teacher's sheet reads:

Bonsoir monsieur/madame. Vous avez bien mangé?
Est-ce que vous avez dit ça au garçon qui vous a servis?
Est-ce que vous vous êtes plaint?
Pourquoi (pas)?
Qu'est-ce que vous avez mangé, monsieur?
Combien de minutes avez-vous attendu avant d'être servi?
Malheureusement nous avons des problèmes aujourd'hui.
Je vous ferai une réduction de cinquante francs. Ça vous va, monsieur?

More serious medical problems

At the doctor's

You are on holiday in France. You have caught a cold and have a high temperature. You go to the doctor's. The examiner will play the part of the doctor.

a) Say what is wrong with you.*
b) Say you have been ill for one day.
c) Ask when you should take the medicine.*

(NISEC)

*You have to know certain specified vocabulary for this role-play.

Emergencies

At the garage

You are travelling by car with your family in France. The car breaks down and you have to give the necessary information at the garage.

The examiner will play the part of the garage mechanic.

a) Say that you are on holiday in France and that your car has broken down.
b) Say that the brakes are not working.
c) Describe exactly where the car is.*

(NISEC)

*Some scope for imagination.

Telephoning

You had arranged to meet your French friend at 8 o'clock at the town hall but unfortunately you arrived late and your friend had gone. You are now telephoning your friend to apologize. Your teacher will play the part of your friend, and will start the conversation.

a) You greet him, apologize, and say you missed the bus.
b) You tell him that you arrived at the town hall but you were half an hour late.
c) You try to arrange another meeting.*

(NEA)

*This requires you to think up an appropriate activity and a time and place.

Currency exchange

At the bank

You are in a bank in France; you want to change your traveller's cheques. The examiner will play the part of the bank clerk.

a) Say that you would like to change traveller's cheques for £50.
b) Say that you do not have your passport and give the reason.
c) Say that you have your student card and ask if that will do.*

(NISEC)

*This requires special vocabulary.

POSSIBLE ANSWERS TO PRACTICE ROLE-PLAYS

The answers given below are possible solutions to the questions. They are not the only answers which would earn good marks. Getting the message across is the most important point!

Lost property

a) J'ai perdu mon porte-monnaie (porte-feuille) ce matin au marché.
b) C'était un porte-monnaie en cuir noir. Il y avait 100F dedans.
c) Je m'appelle Mark Lawson. Je suis chez les Legrand, 29 chemin de Neubourg.

Repairs

The conversation might go something like this:

Shopkeeper: Bonjour monsieur/mademoiselle. Je peux vous aider?
You: Je suis venu(e) chercher mon appareil photo. Vous me le réparez.
Shopkeeper: Quand est-ce que vous m'avez apporté l'appareil pour la réparation?
You: Lundi dernier.
Shopkeeper: Vous avez votre ticket?
You: Voilà, monsieur/madame.
Shopkeeper: Je suis désolé, mais il n'est pas prêt. Pouvez-vous revenir samedi prochain?
You: Ce n'est pas possible. Je pars en Angleterre demain matin.
Shopkeeper: Vous partez demain monsieur/mademoiselle? Alors je vous rendrai l'appareil tel qu'il est.

Complaints

The conversation might go something like this:

Head waiter: Bonsoir monsieur/madame. Vous avez bien mangé?
You: Non. Les steaks n'étaient pas assez cuits.
Head waiter: Est-ce que vous avez dit ça au garçon qui vous a servis?
You: On ne l'a pas remarqué tout de suite.
Head waiter: Est-ce que vous vous êtes plaint?
You: Non, monsieur.
Head waiter: Pourquoi pas?
You: Je n'aime pas me plaindre, monsieur.
Head waiter: Qu'est-ce que vous avez mangé, monsieur?
You: Nous avons mangé trois steaks avec de la salade et des frites. Et on a attendu longtemps.
Head waiter: Combien de minutes avez-vous attendu avant d'être servi?
You: Quarante-cinq.
Head waiter: Malheureusement nous avons des problèmes aujourd'hui.
You: Quand même, nous avons mal mangé ici.
Head waiter: Je vous ferai une réduction de cinquante francs. Ça vous va, monsieur?
You: Oui, monsieur. Merci bien.

More serious medical problems

a) Je suis enrhumé(e) et j'ai de la fièvre.
b) Je suis malade depuis vingt-quatre heures.
c) Quand est-ce que je dois prendre le médicament?

Emergencies

a) Je suis en vacances en France et ma voiture est en panne.
b) Les freins ne marchent pas.
c) La voiture est sur la N7, à 500 mètres d'ici.

Telephoning:

The conversation might go something like this:

Your friend: Allô, ici Pierre Dupont.
You: Voici Anne. Je m'excuse. Je suis arrivée en retard à l'hôtel de ville.
Your friend: Alors, qu'est-ce qui s'est passé?
You: Je suis arrivée à huit heures et demie, mais tu n'étais plus là.
Your friend: Pourquoi es-tu arrivée tellement en retard?
You: Parce que j'ai raté le bus.
Your friend: Eh bien, est-ce qu'on peut fixer un autre rendez-vous?
You: Oui. Quand est-ce qu'on va se voir?
Your friend: Cette fois, c'est à toi de proposer ce qu'on fera.
You: Si on allait au cinéma dimanche prochain?
Your friend: D'accord. A huit heures, alors, devant l'hôtel de ville. Qu'est-ce que tu en penses?

Currency exchange

a) Je voudrais changer des travellers pour cinquante livres sterling, s'il vous plaît.
b) Je n'ai pas mon passeport. Je l'ai laissé chez mon ami.
c) J'ai ma carte d'étudiant(e). Est-ce que cela suffira?

6 ⟩ HIGHER LEVEL CONVERSATION

The *general conversation* at Higher level will cover much of the same ground as the Basic, but in *much* more detail. In particular, your teacher will be trying to find out:

■ if you have a good command of past tenses
■ if you correctly distinguish between the imperfect and the perfect
■ if you can use the future tenses
■ whether you really can carry on a spontaneous, unrehearsed conversation at some length

❝❝ Look out for *open-ended* questions **❞❞**

So look out for open-ended questions like 'Décrivez votre collège'. This should be the signal for you to launch into a full description of your school, your subjects, times, likes and dislikes, your opinions about such matters as uniform, etc. This is relatively straightforward for those candidates who have prepared it and have looked up the vocabulary that they need to deal with their specialist interests. You are very unlikely to say too much. If you do, your teacher will interrupt and move on to the next topic he or she wishes to discuss, duly impressed by your fluency.

❝❝ Look out for questions testing your knowledge of *tenses* **❞❞**

Learn to spot when your teacher is trying to find out if you can demonstrate your knowledge of particular tenses. If you are asked a question in the perfect, for example 'Qu'est-ce que tu as fait hier?', then answer it using the perfect tense. The same applies for future, present and conditional. As far as tenses are concerned, you should **mirror the tense of the question you have been asked**.

It sometimes happens that a teacher does not ask enough open-ended questions after completing the straightforward Basic questions to allow a candidate to shine. Take the initiative if this happens. To a simple question like 'Avez-vous des frères ou des soeurs?' you could answer, 'Oui. On est cinq dans la famille. J'ai un frère Wayne, qui a dix ans et qui s'intéresse beaucoup a l'informatique, et une soeur Mandy, qui a treize ans. Elle est collégienne. Mon père . . .' Show what you can do.

<table>
<tr><td>**7 ⟩ CONVERSATION QUESTIONS AND ANSWERS**</td><td>Below are some questions which you would do well to prepare answers for, although once again, if your teacher gives you his or her list, use that! I have indicated the sort of thing you might like to prepare under each one. However, at Higher level, the onus is very much on you to have your own material prepared.</td></tr>
</table>

HOME AND FAMILY, MORNING AND EVENING ROUTINES

1   Décrivez-moi votre famille.
    On est cinq dans la famille. J'ai un frère Wayne, qui a dix ans et qui s'intéresse beaucoup à l'informatique, et une soeur Mandy, qui a treize ans. Elle est collégienne. Mon père est mécanicien et ma mère est ménagère. Je m'entends bien avec ma soeur, mais mon frère m'ennuie tout le temps avec son ordinateur. Nous sommes tous blonds, à part mon père qui a perdu la plupart de ses cheveux! Mon père est normalement gentil, mais il se fâche quand je rentre tard le soir. Maman nous aide beaucoup, et elle fait des études . . . etc.

2   Parlez-moi de votre routine matinale.
    Bon, alors, je me lève à sept heures, je mets la radio, et puis je vais prendre une douche dans la salle de bain. Après m'être séché(e) je m'habille. Normalement je mets mon uniforme scolaire – que je n'aime pas du tout – mais le week-end je m'habille en jeans avec un pull. Je viens de m'acheter un pull tout à fait chouette. Je me prépare du toast et une tasse de thé comme petit déjeuner, et en semaine je quitte la maison vers huit heures et quart. Normalement j'oublie quelque chose, et je reviens le chercher. Je vais au collège en vélo.

3   Où se trouve votre maison? Est-ce que vous aimez habiter là? Pourquoi?
    Ma maison se trouve dans la banlieue de Leeds. C'est un quartier très agréable. J'aime la maison parce que j'y habite depuis toujours, et parce que j'aime ma chambre. On l'a décorée l'année dernière, et j'ai choisi les couleurs, et la moquette.

4   décorée l'année dernière, et j'ai choisi les couleurs, et la moquette.
    On mange de la soupe, des légumes, de la viande, et peut-être un yaourt. Mon plat préféré, c'est le macaroni au fromage, mais j'aime aussi le rôti de boeuf que nous mangeons de temps en temps – le dimanche soir, d'habitude.

SCHOOL

1   Parlez-moi de votre collège. Quels en sont les avantages et les inconvénients?
    Mon collège est assez grand, avec mille élèves. C'est un collège mixte. Les bâtiments sont assez vieux, mais on les a repeints il y a deux années. Normalement on est obligé de porter un uniforme – des chaussures noires, des chausettes blanches, un pantalon gris ou une jupe grise, un pullover bleu et une chemise blanche. Il y a une cravate rouge et bleu pour les garçons. Les professeurs sont assez gentils.

2 Quelle est votre matière préférée? Pourquoi?

J'aime bien les leçons d'anglais et de physique, parce que je trouve ces sujets-là intéressants. Le français – je ne l'aime pas tellement. Le professeur est trop stricte.

3 Est-ce que vous pensez continuer vos études l'année scolaire prochaine? Qu'est-ce que vous allez faire, et pourquoi?

Je vais continuer mes études l'année prochaine. Je vais faire de la géographie, des maths, et de l'allemand. Ces matières m'intéressent beaucoup. Je passerai mon bac dans deux années. Après cela, j'espère faire ma licence, mais je ne sais pas où. Je voudrais peut-être devenir journaliste, mais ce n'est pas certain en ce moment.

FREE TIME, SPORT AND HOBBIES

1 Dites-moi ce que vous avez fait pendant le week-end dernier.

Le samedi je me suis levé(e) tard, car j'étais fatigué(e). J'ai pris le petit déjeuner, et puis je suis allé(e) en ville, où j'avais rendez-vous avec mon camarade Chris. Nous avons acheté des disques ensemble, et puis nous sommes rentré(e)s. Vers quatre heures j'ai regardé une émission favorite à la télé. Le soir, je suis sorti(e). Je suis allé(e) à une boum chez Mary. C'était extra. Je suis rentré(e) très tard à la maison. Le dimanche, je n'ai rien fait. Mais j'ai préparé mon examen de français!

2 Que comptez-vous faire samedi prochain?

J'irai en ville, et j'ai l'intention d'acheter un nouveau pantalon. Après cela, je vais rencontrer des amis, et nous allons voir le nouveau film qui passe au cinéma. C'est un film policier. Le soir, j'ai invité mon copain à passer la soirée chez moi.

3 Avez-vous un emploi? Qu'est-ce que vous faites avec l'argent que vous gagnez (ou avec votre argent de poche)?

Je travaille dans un supermarché le jeudi et le vendredi soir. Je commence à cinq heures, et à huit heures, c'est fini. Ce n'est pas très amusant. Avec l'argent que je gagne j'achète des disques, et je fais des économies pour acheter une chaîne stéréo.

HOME TOWN, VILLAGE OR AREA

1 Où se trouve votre ville (village) exactement en Angleterre?

Banbury se trouve au centre de l'Angleterre. C'est à 200 km de Londres, et c'est assez près d'Oxford.

2 Quelles facilités y a-t-il pour les jeunes?

A Banbury il y a un complex sportif avec piscine, gymnase, etc. Il y a aussi une maison de la culture, où il y a aussi un foyer des jeunes. Au collège il y a beaucoup d'activités – des sports, des orchestres, un group de théâtre, etc. Et les jeunes participent souvent aux activités du jumelage avec Ermont, près de Paris, et Hennef, près de Bonn, en Allemagne. Comme distractions il y a un cinéma, beaucoup de cafés, et une discothèque en ville.

3 Quelles sont les industries principales?

Les industries principales sont l'alimentation – la production de café et de desserts – et il y a des laboratoires qui se concernent avec la technologie de l'aliminium. Il y a aussi un grand marché de bétail et beaucoup d'artisans.

4 Quelles attractions touristiques y a-t-il?

Il y a la croix célèbre – qui forme un rond-point au centre de la ville. La place du marché est très pittoresque, et on y trouve beaucoup de tavernes traditionnelles. L'église du 19e siècle est remarquable pour ses dimensions et sa tour.

5 Si on voulait faire une excursion dans la région, qu'est-ce qu'on pourrait faire?

On pourrait visiter Oxford – ville universitaire, et très pittoresque. Ou on pourrait faire une belle promenade en voiture dans les Cotswolds – c'est le nom d'une région vraiment jolie qui est à une demi-heure d'ici en voiture.

8 > **PRACTICE EXERCISES**

In its 'Extended Level' Speaking test, SEG includes the same written or visual stimulus with the same five set questions as at Basic level. In addition, there are other suggested questions which you will be asked. The examiners are interested in the quality of your answers, that is, the correctness of your French. As you will see from the sample given below, the extra questions are designed to discover whether you know certain grammatical features such as venir de and whether you know a wider range of vocabulary, for example words and expressions concerned with feelings and emotions.

EXAMINER'S SHEET – NOT TO BE SEEN BY THE CANDIDATE

   1   Le monsieur à droite, qu'est-ce qu'il donne à la femme?
   2   Pourquoi?
   3   Que fait la dame à côté de lui?
* 4   Qu'est-ce qu'elle vient de faire?
   5   Que fait la dame à gauche?
* 6   Alors, qu'est-ce que le charcutier a fait?
* 7   Qu'est-ce qu'il fera maintenant?
   8   Le monsieur au centre, qu'est-ce qu'il veut faire?
* 9   Pourquoi le chien ne peut-il pas entrer?
*10 Comment savez-vous que les chiens ne sont pas admis?
*11 Quelle est la réaction du monsieur?

Questions marked * are for Extended Level only – all those not so marked MUST be asked, and most of the remainder, or similar questions of appropriate relevance and level of difficulty, SHOULD be asked.   (SEG)

SEG and MEG also have a **picture or text** as a stimulus to a longer account by you. You need to be prepared to use your imagination to say as much as you can about it. Read the instructions carefully to see whether you need to use past or future tenses to tell the story (or a mixture – for example if a week's diary is given and you are told it is Thursday).

Don't forget that you can always mention the contents of a meal or the description of a person to give you a little more to say. If vocabulary or phrases are given, remember that these may be in the infinitive and will need to be put into the correct form. So the phrase 'tomber en panne' will need to be developed to, for example, 'Nous sommes tombé(e)s en panne. La voiture s'est arrêtée tout à coup, et elle ne voulait plus marcher du tout.'

Below is a sample of the sort of thing MEG sets for its Higher Part 2 Narrator. The MEG Narrator stimulus may not have any drawings at all, but consist entirely of text in note form. The SEG exercise is essentially similar, but will be purely pictorial. Your teacher may well have stocks of CSE and O Level picture essays which would make good practice for this sort of exercise.

        (MEG)

SPEAKING : CANDIDATE AS NARRATOR   *(20 marks)*

HIGHER LEVEL PART 2

CANDIDATE'S SHEET

The plan printed below gives an outline of a trip to France last summer.

Tell the examiner about the journey and what happened on it. You need not mention every detail of the outline on the page and you can, for example, decide whether it was you who made the trip or someone you know.

Be prepared to respond to any questions or observations the examiner might make,

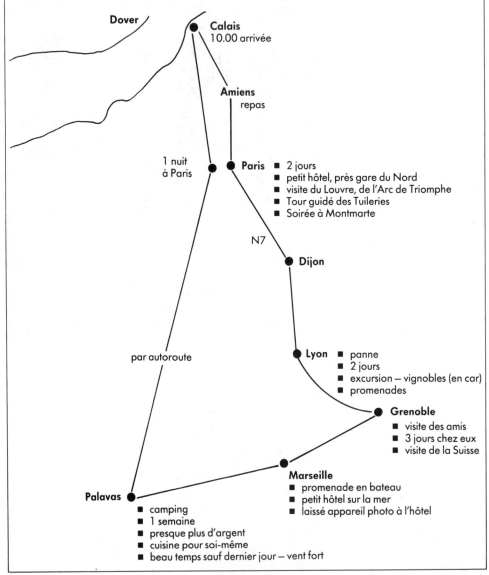

Dover

Calais
10.00 arrivée

Amiens
repas

1 nuit
à Paris   **Paris** ■ 2 jours
                    ■ petit hôtel, près gare du Nord
                    ■ visite du Louvre, de l'Arc de Triomphe
                    ■ Tour guidé des Tuileries
                    ■ Soirée à Montmarte

N7   **Dijon**

par autoroute   **Lyon** ■ panne
                            ■ 2 jours
                            ■ excursion – vignobles (en car)
                            ■ promenades

                                    Grenoble
                                     ■ visite des amis
                                     ■ 3 jours chez eux
                                     ■ visite de la Suisse

                        Marseille
                         ■ promenade en bateau
                         ■ petit hôtel sur la mer
Palavas   ■ laissé appareil photo à l'hôtel
    ■ camping
    ■ 1 semaine
    ■ presque plus d'argent
    ■ cuisine pour soi-même
    ■ beau temps sauf dernier jour – vent fort

(MEG)

A STEP FURTHER

Practice and preparation lead to proficiency. But knowledge of what is to come is very useful, too. Reproduced below are the two sides of an appointment sheet given to candidates at a school which uses the MEG syllabus. If you do a different one, amend it to suit your circumstances. And follow the advice it gives!

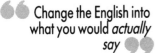

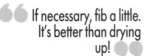

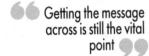

e) Because there's blood on her (1)
    She thinks it may be serious (1)   *(2)*
f) To call the police   *(1)*

EXTRACT 19

Q5 a) The table is too near (1) the stairs (1), there is a draught (1) which is
        not at all pleasant (1)   *(4)*
    b) To move to the corner   *(1)*
Q6 a) He's got the wrong table   *(1)*
    b) Medium   *(1)*
    c) He'll bring it to you (1) in a few minutes (1)   *(2)*
Q7 a) You are dining in France (1), so it's custom/usual he pays (1) *(2)*
        He has a part-time job (1), and earns lots of money (1)   *(2)*
    b) You would pay the bill   *(1)*

EXTRACT 20

Q3 a) iv)   *(1)*
    b) He was standing on the prison wall   *(1)*
    c) They didn't believe her   *(1)*
    d) Tunisian (1) aged 19 (1)   *(2)*

EXTRACT 21

Q20 1½ hours   *(1)*
Q21 Present – 9000 people (1)   *(2)*
     Past   – wine (1)   *(2)*
Q22 Both frequented by the rich   *(1)*
Q23 Previous building burnt down   *(1)*
Q24 a) Past link – gave bridge to Paris in 1604 (1)
     b) Present link – statue of King on or by bridge (1)   *(2)*

EXTRACT 22

Q1 a) Vineyards (1)
    b) Châteaux (1)   *(2)*
Q2 Any four of: imposing towers (1)   owned by wine co-op (1)
                  medieval appearance (1)   20km of vines (1)
                  built 16th century (1)   good white, red & rosé (1) *(4)*
Q3 a) 40km from Bordeaux (1)
    b) on hill (½) overlooks Garonne (½)
    c) 12th century (1)
    d) concerts (1), excellent white wine (1)   *(5)*
Q4 Famous French writer (Montesquieu) (1) born and lived there (1)   *(2)*
Q5 a) 7km from Bordeaux centre (1)
    b) no roof (1) because of recent fire (1)
    c) 14th century (1)
    d) Good white (1) and red (1) wine   *(6)*
Q6 Informative   *(1)*

A STEP FURTHER

It is as well to be able to understand common abbreviations such as HLM, SNCF, TFI, P et T, RER, ZUP, and so on. Keep a list of them here.

The ability to understand spellings given in French is also important. It is a good idea to be able to spell out such things as your own name, address and place of birth for the Speaking test. The French alphabet is therefore recorded on the tape as Extract 23. Use it to make sure you can spell fluently and can write down from others' spelling in French.

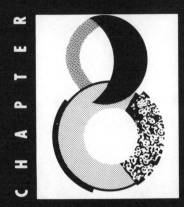

CHAPTER 8

BASIC READING

EXAM GROUP REQUIREMENTS

EFFECTIVE ANSWERS

WHICH VOCABULARY TOPICS?

PUBLIC SIGNS AND NOTICES

'FALSE FRIENDS'

NORMAL PERFORMANCE

GETTING STARTED

Basic Reading is one of the tests which everyone has to do, so it's as well to make sure you know what to expect and how to go about it. Good candidates often don't perform as well as they should in this skill because they have not learned the necessary vocabulary or because they don't understand the principles according to which the papers are set. This means that they are throwing away easy marks.

Yet Reading is a skill which is relatively easy to practise, which doesn't require special equipment, and which can be conveniently done in long or short sessions and in virtually any place. So don't neglect it!

ESSENTIAL PRINCIPLES

1 > **EXAM GROUP REQUIREMENTS**

There are many common features between the Examining Groups in their Basic Reading tests. The only matter on which they differ is *how long* the tests should take, so check the table below to see how long your Examining Group allows for this part of the GCSE.

Examining Group	LEAG	MEG	NEA	NISEC	SEG*	WJEC
Time in minutes	30	25	25	45	30	30
* General Level						

So much for the major difference between the Examining Groups – time. Let us look at what all the Groups *do* require of their candidates.

1   First the bad news. No dictionaries are allowed. Nor is there any choice of questions.
2   And now the good news. You are not tested on the full range of vocabulary topics, but only on the more straightforward ones.
3   For each piece of French you have to read, you are given a setting in English and a task in English. Do not forget to read these – they will often give you valuable help.
4   All questions will be in English. Most of them should be answered using short phrases or sentences in English (Welsh is an option with WJEC). There may be some multiple-choice questions in English. With these, you should make your choice clearly.
5   You are required to read French which was *intended* to be read (not, for example, a transcript of a conversation), from the point of view of a British 16-year-old who is typically supposed to be:

    a) in France
or b) reading a letter from a French person
or c) interpreting for someone who does not speak French
or d) reading published material in French

This really means that you should not have to pretend to be someone other than yourself (e.g. a French person or the Prime Minister), or be required to read texts which are beyond what is assumed to be the experience of the average 16-year-old.

6   You are required to find specific facts and information from short texts. The Examining Groups list many sorts of text, including the following:

    — public signs and notices
    — road signs
    — tickets, town plans, road maps
    — simple instructions (e.g. how to use a telephone)
    — menus, labels on food and drink
    — timetables (school and public transport)
    — notes left by other people
    — advertisements and special offers; handbills
    — guides and brochures concerning entertainment, sport and tourist attractions, etc.
    — informal letters from a French-speaking correspondent; invitations
    — formal letters (e.g. confirming reservations, making job applications)
    — newspaper and magazine articles likely to be ready by a 16-year-old.
    — imaginative writing likely to be read by a 16-year-old

This list is roughly graded with the easiest sorts of text first. The Examining Groups will usually start with straightforward texts – often only a few words – and work up to harder ones.

2 > EFFECTIVE ANSWERS

Let us now look at how to answer the questions most effectively. First of all, as everywhere in this examination, you must read the question carefully. This includes the setting given with each text, which will give you valuable clues as to what to expect. The importance of reading the setting cannot be stressed too much. Too many candidates don't even look at it and make silly mistakes as a result.

> 66 Read the question, carefully, including the setting 99

It seems likely that all Examining Groups will print a booklet for you to write your answers under the question. This has the advantage that you are less likely to miss out a question.

The answers need not be in full sentences – so don't waste time writing pretty sentences in English. For example, if the question is 'What does the hotel cost per night?', there is no need to write 'According to the text the cost of the hotel per night is 35 francs.' Your primary and first and second year secondary teachers may have insisted on that sort of answer. You can forget that now! The ideal GCSE French answer to the above question is '35 francs'. Go for short answers, although not so short that they don't fully answer the question!

> 66 Answers need not be in full sentences 99

Some students worry enormously about their English. GCSE French tests your understanding of French. There will therefore be no penalty if you make slight errors (such as spelling) in English, as long as your meaning is clear. So you can heave a sigh of relief!

It is worth knowing that questions on longer texts are usually set in sequence. So the third question on a text, for example, will refer to a point later in the text than the second, and so on. This knowledge is particularly helpful if you are struggling with a text and understand only some of it!

Another point worth knowing is that, if there is more than one mark allocated for a question, it is highly likely that there is more than one piece of information or detail required. Look for extra things to say – as long as you can find them in the text! On the other hand, the two marks may be given for saying that there is a big (1 mark) house (1 mark) – so make sure you include all the details.

Some Examining Groups have set questions where there are, say, two marks, but three possible answers. Generally speaking, two correct answers will be credited if you have given three including one wrong one, as long as the wrong one doesn't contradict a correct answer.

3 > WHICH VOCABULARY TOPICS?

Many of the questions will be seeking an answer about:

Who?	How long?
What?	How many?
Where?	How much?
When	Why?

A moment's thought will point you towards the vocabulary topics which are most likely to be covered by each of those questions.

Who? — family and friends, professions (under Education and future career), descriptions: physical appearance, size, age, etc.

What? — covers virtually all objects, prices, instructions and activities. Check out food and drink and free time and entertainment.

Where? — positions and prepositions, location of buildings in town and country, countries, directions and distances.

When? — time – by the 12- and 24-hour clock, and in relation to other events. Telling the time is in the Grammar chapter.

How long? — time, especially duration.

How many? — numbers (in the Grammar chapter)

How much? — quantity, numbers

Why? — reasons

A little time spent in directed preparation will not go amiss.

4 > PUBLIC SIGNS AND NOTICES

Public signs and notices have a language all of their own. Given below is a list – by no means exhaustive – of common ones which may well be tested in GCSE. Of course, you may find it very daunting to learn them all. If that is the case, learn some of the most obvious ones from each setting.

GENERAL PUBLIC NOTICES

Appuyer	Press	Ne pas . . .	Don't . . .
Appuyez	Press	Ouvert	Open
Défense de . . .	It is forbidden to . . .	Pousser	Push
Entrée	Entrance	Poussez	Push
Fermé	Closed	SVP (S'il vous plaît)	Please
Hors service	Out of order	Sortie	Exit
Interdit	Prohibited	Tirer	Pull
Interdiction de . . .	Prohibited to . . .	Tirez	Pull

HOME

Attention au chien	Beware of the dog	Libre	Vacant (on the loo door)
Chien dangereux/méchant	Dangerous dog	Occupé	Engaged

TOWN

Attendez	Wait (at pelican crossing)
Centre commercial	Shopping centre
Côté de stationnement	Parking on this side of the street only
Défense de stationner	No parking
Déviation obligatoire	Compulsory diversion
Pour poids lourds	Lorry route
Fin de zone bleue	End of disc parking zone
Parking gratuit	Free parking
Parking souterrain	Underground parking
Passez piétons	Cross now
Péage	Toll
Priorité à droite	Priority from the right
Privé	Private
Roulez au pas	Dead slow
Sens unique	One-way
Serrez à droite	Keep to the right
Sortie de camions	Lorry exit
Stationnement interdit	No parking
Zone bleue – disque obligatoire	Disc parking zone
Zone piétonne	Pedestrian zone

+ names of shops and buildings

PUBLIC TOILETS

Dames	Ladies	Messieurs	Gents
Femmes	Women	Toilettes	Toilets
Hommes	Men	WC Publics	Public toilets

SCHOOL

CES	Secondary school	Directeur	Headmaster
Bibliothèque	Library	Laboratoire	Laboratory
Bureau d'administration	School office	Réfectoire	Canteen
Cantine	Canteen	Salle des professeurs	Staffroom
Censeur	Head of discipline	Surveillants	Room for
Concierge	Caretaker		supervisors

PLACES OF ENTERTAINMENT

Caisse	Cash desk	Heures d'ouverture	Opening hours
Défense de fumer	No smoking	Vestiaires	Cloakrooms

PUBLIC TRANSPORT

Accès aux quais	To the platforms	Départs	Departures
Arrêt	Bus stop	Douane	Customs
Arrivées	Arrivals	Facultatif	Request stop
Autocars	Coaches	Horaires	Timetables
Banlieue	Suburbs	RATP	Paris suburban rail network
Billets	Tickets	Renseignements	Information
Consigne	Left luggage	SNCF	French railways
Consigne Automatique	Luggage lockers	Vol	Flight
Correspondances	Connections	Voyageurs	Passengers

SHOPS

Alimentation Générale	Grocer's	la pièce	each
Bricolage	DIY	Prière de ne pas toucher	Please don't touch
Caisse	Cash desk/pay here	Prêt-à-porter	Ready-to-wear
la dixaine	per ten	Prix chocs	Amazing prices
la douzaine	per dozen	Prix réduits	Reduced prices
à l'intérieur	inside	Servez-vous	Help yourself
jour de marché	market day	Soldes	Sales
Maison de la presse	Newsagent's	Sous-sol	Basement
Mode feminine	Women's clothes	TVA	VAT
Ne pas toucher	Don't touch	à vendre	for sale
du pays	local	en vente ici	on sale here

CAFÉS AND RESTAURANTS

TTC	Taxes included	Service non compris	Service not included
Service compris	Service included		

HOTELS

Accueil	Reception	Chambres libres	Rooms available/for rent
S'adresser à la réception	Ask at the reception desk	Complet	Full
		Prise-rasoir	Shaver socket
Ascenseur	Lift		

CAMPSITES

Bloc sanitaire	Washrooms	Emplacement	Pitch
Eau potable	Drinking water	Pour ordures	For rubbish
Eau non potable	Not drinking water		

GARAGE

Dépannage	Breakdown service	Pose pare-brise	Windscreen replacement service
Lavage	Car wash		
Libre-service	Self-service	Prix au litre	Price per litre

POST OFFICE

P et T	Post office	Heures de levées	Collection times
Autres destinations	Other destinations (for letters)	Timbres-poste	Postage stamps
		Cabine téléphonique	Phone cubicle
Imprimés	Printed matter		

There are many words in French which look like English ones, but which have different meanings. Make sure you are aware of them! Check the list below:

French word	English meaning
le car	coach (NOT car)
la cave	cellar (NOT cave)
complet	full, no vacancies (NOT complete)
la correspondance	place to change trains (NOT letters)
un hôtel de ville	town hall (NOT hotel)
la journée	day (NOT journey)
large	wide (NOT large)
la monnaie	change (NOT money)
le parfum	flavour (NOT always perfume)
passer	spend time (NOT to pass an exam)
la pension	board in hotel (NOT pension)
la place	square (NOT place)
le quai	platform (NOT *always* quay)

There are others. Add them to the list as you come across them.

Candidates who succeed in the Basic Reading test will have shown that they can extract concrete facts from a passage of French based on a limited (but nevertheless large) part of the syllabus. They will have written down clearly what they know, but not necessarily in complete sentences.

STUDENT'S ANSWERS – EXAMINER COMMENTS

1 ▷ SHORT ITEMS

QUESTION

While you are in a souvenir shop, you see the following notice.

> **DÉFENSE DE TOUCHER**

What are you asked not to do? *You are asked not to touch* _____ *(1)*

ANSWER

Examiner comment: Correct. But what a waste of time and ink. It would have been OK to write 'touch'.

FURTHER QUESTIONS

1 What does the notice above this petrol pump mean?

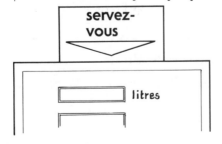

servez-
vous

litres

Answer _____ *(1)*

2   You are looking for somewhere to park. What restriction on parking is indicated by this sign?

Answer _____ *(2)*

3   You see this in the rear window of a car in France. What warning does it give?

Answer _____ *(1)*

4   What are you **not** allowed to do where you see this sign?

Answer _____ *(1)*

5   You see this sign in the Zoo

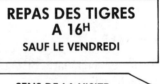

a) What happens at 4.00 p.m.?

   Answer _____ *(1)*

b) Except for which day?

   Answer _____ *(1)*

6 You are looking for somewhere to eat. At the roadside you see this sign.

```
┌─ EN FACE ─────────────┐
│                       │
│   CAFE BAL            │
│   ON PEUT            │
│   APPORTER          │
│   SON REPAS         │
│                       │
└───────────────────────┘
```

a) Where is the café?

   Answer ————————————————————————————— (1)

b) What does it tell you about food?

   Answer ————————————————————————————— (1)

                                                          (NISEC)

7 You have been handed a card advertising 'Luna-Park', a local tourist attraction. What special offer does the card entitle you to? On which days?

Answer ————————————————————————————————

——

————————————————————————————————— (5)

STUDENT'S ANSWER WITH EXAMINER'S COMMENTS

1 Serve you (Wrong. This is the command of a reflexive verb, se servir. Look up how they work!)

2 Reserved for 70 metres (OK for one mark. But this student should have realized that another piece of information was needed – it's reserved for lorries!)

3 Don't drive to close (Correct. And here it wouldn't really have been appropriate to use notes as it wouldn't have been clear enough. Wrong use of 'to' is tolerated.)

4 No Smoking (Correct. Défense de is confusing if you don't know it.)

5 a) tigers (not enough for a mark.)
   b)   (If you can't remember something like the days of the week in the heat of the exam, you should guess. You have a 1 in 7 chance of being right!)

6 a)   (Not surprising you didn't notice 'en face' (opposite) stuck up rather insignificantly at the top of the picture. If your Examining Group uses photos of signs, they may not always be very clear. Look at them carefully!)
   b) Bring your own. (Good use of note form.)

7 Half-price on all the attractions on Tuesdays and Thursdays (A fairly good answer. 4/5 It's really very straightforward to pick out '½' and 'attractions' from the text. So don't be put off if it seems simple – it may be simple! The skill in this question is sorting out what you do wish to know from the 50 words you don't want! Note that days of the week crop up again. This time there were three given – so why put only two in the answer?)

**2 ⟩   LONGER
           TEXTS**

QUESTION

You have found the following advert for the Hotel Fimotel on board the ferry you are travelling on.

a) Name two types of visitor this hotel is recommended for.

    i) _____

    ii) _____ *(2)*

b) Tick which **two** facilities this hotel offers

    i) very close to the Le Havre ferry port   ☐

    ii) a few kilometres from Caen ferry port   ☐

    iii) rooms with toilet but no showers   ☐

    iv) rooms with private TV   ☐

    v) a TV lounge   ☐

    vi) a shop on the premises   ☐

    vii) a hypermarket nearby   ☐

HOTEL RESTAURANT ∗ ∗ NN

**42 Chambres
tout confort**

repas à partir de 55f

Parking commun avec hypermarché Continent
Centre Commercial Supermonde

Un hôtel agréable et confortable pour touristes et
voyageurs. A 90 minutes du car-ferry au Havre, à 20
minutes du car-ferry Caen-Ouistreham.
Sans être de grand luxe, l'hôtel Fimotel vous offre de
très belles chambres (douche, WC privé, télévision). Prix
de la nuitée 110 F. Ce n'est vraiment pas cher.

Et pour nos amis britanniques, l'hypermarché Continent
est en face pour rendre plus facile leurs achats.

STUDENT'S ANSWER WITH EXAMINER'S COMMENTS

a) i) tourists (Good)
    ii) voyageurs (No credit – written in French)
b) vii) ☑ Why tick only one box? Read the question and follow the instructions!!!!)

QUESTION

Rouen, le 15 avril.

Chère Barbara,

Eh bien, je vais arriver à l'aéroport de Belfast le 1er juin – je te ferai savoir l'heure exacte de mon arrivée aussitôt que possible.

En attendant, peux-tu me donner des renseignements sur les vêtements nécessaires? Maman dit qu'il faut apporter un manteau de fourrure et des bottes en caoutchouc parce qu'elle a entendu dire qu'il fait très froid en Irlande et qu'il pleut sans cesse. Et comme je vais t'accompagner à l'école, faut-il que j'achète un uniforme?

J'attends ta réponse avec impatience.

Grosses bises,
Chantal.

a) When does Chantal expect to arrive?

_____ (1)

b) Where will she be arriving?

_____ (1)

c) What advice does Chantal want?

_____ (2)

d) What two things has Chantal's mother suggested she take?

_____

_____ (4)

e) Why has she suggested this?

_____ (2)

f) Why does Chantal want to know if she will have to buy a school uniform?

_____ (2)

(NISEC)

STUDENT'S ANSWER WITH EXAMINER'S COMMENTS

a) 1st June

b) She will arrive at Belfast Airport.   This is wasting your time!

c) What to wear

d) coat   Only 2 marks out of 4.
   boots   Add *details*, for extra
                                                 marks – *fur* coat, *rubber*
                                                 boots/wellies.

e) It's cold and rainy in Ireland.

f) because she's going to school

                                                 Only 1 mark out of 2 – omits Barbara.

P R A C T I C E   Q U E S T I O N S

The questions have been laid out so that you can write the answers in the book. Test yourself! The answers are given at the end of the chapter. An example is provided of each type of text which could be set in Basic Reading, except imaginative writing, as none of the Examining Groups has included that sort of text in its sample papers. But that is the one sort of text that is well represented in old CSE text-books – so ask your teacher!

PUBLIC SIGNS AND NOTICES

1 Printed below are some signs and short notices you may meet in France. Study each one carefully and answer the questions that follow.

a)
> **POUSSEZ**

You see this sign on a door. What should you do in order to open it?

_____ *(1)*

b)
> **COMPLET**

You see this notice on the door of a hotel. What does it tell you about that hotel?

_____ *(1)*

c)
> **ENTRÉE INTERDITE**

You see this sign on another door. What does it tell you?

_____ *(1)*

d)
> **DÉFENSE DE FUMER**

What should you **not** do where you see this sign?

_____ *(1)*

e)

> VERIFIEZ IMMEDIATEMENT
> VOTRE MONNAIE

You pay at the cash desk to visit a museum in Paris and you see this sign. What does it tell you to do?

_____ (2)

f)

> **HEURES D'OUVERTURE**
> mardi, mercredi, jeudi; 9h. à 18h.30
> vendredi, samedi; 9h. à 20.00
> Fermé: dimanche, lundi

You see this notice on the door of a shop. On which days of the week will you be able to buy things there at 7 p.m.?

_____ (2)

g)

> **ATTENTION!**
> LA PORTE D'ENTRÉE EST FERMÉE DE 1H À 7H. SI VOUS PENSEZ
> RENTRER TARD, N'HÉSITEZ PAS À DEMANDER UNE
> CLÉ DE LA PORTE DE SERVICE À LA RÉCEPTION.
> MERCI

You see this notice as you go out of a hotel for the evening. What does it tell you to do if you are going to be late back?

_____ (2)

(WJEC)

ROAD SIGNS   2

Who is not allowed to use this road?

_____ (1)

(MEG)

3   Near a sports stadium you see a sign pointing to a free car park.

> PARKING GRATUIT
> 2eme RUE A DROITE

Where is the free car park?

_____ (2)

(NISEC)

TICKETS, TOWN PLANS, ROAD MAPS

4 You are reading this brochure from the Hôtel de Noailles.

Pour faciliter votre arrivée à l'Hôtel, la Direction vous conseille d'emprunter le parking sous terrain de la place de la Comédie. Entrée face aux magasins MONOPRIX.

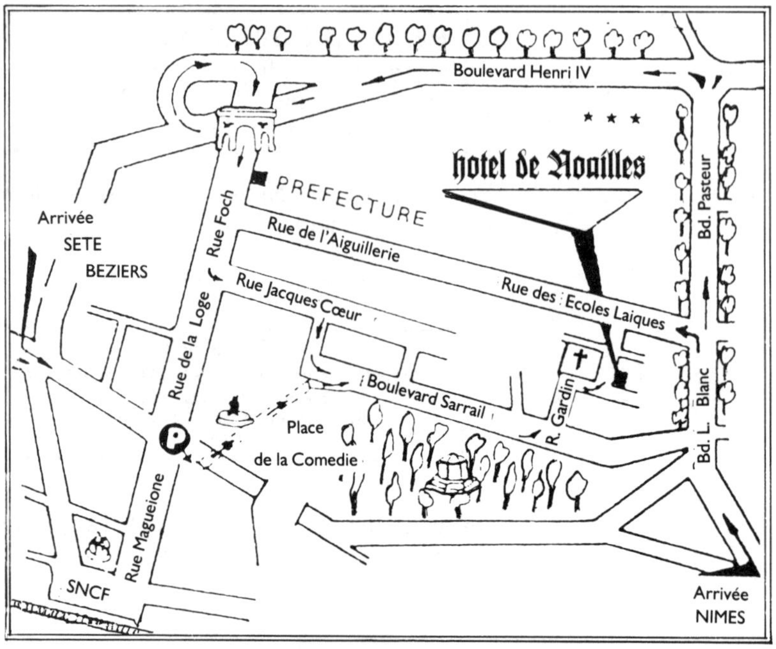

A 4 Km. de l'autoroute A9
A 7 Km. de l'aéroport de Montpellier Fréjorgues
A 500 m. de la gare SNCF
et aussi à 10 km. de la Méditerranée

---

a) What type of car park is recommended by the hotel?

_____ (2)

b) Where is the entrance to the car park?

_____ (2)

c) How far away from the hotel is the motorway?

_____ (1)

(NISEC)

SIMPLE INSTRUCTIONS

5 While queueing for a meal in a French motorway restaurant you see this notice alongside the bread.

Par mesure d'hygiène
on est prié
de choisir son pain
sans toucher aux autres
Merci

a) What are they inviting you to do? _____ (1)

b) What are you asked to take care **not** to do? _____ (1)

c) Why? _____ (1)

(NEA 16+ 1987)

MENUS, LABELS ON FOOD AND DRINK

6 You are invited out for a meal in a restaurant while on holiday in France. When you get home, you write home to your parents telling them what you ate. The menu is printed overleaf/on the opposite page.

a) Write down, in English, the 5 dishes you ordered (one from each section). Do not include coffee. (5)

b) What was included in the price of the meal? (1)

c) What was **not** included in this price? (1)

(LEAG)

Le Relais vous présente pour **79F.** + ¼ vin compris

Hors d'oeuvre variés
Salade de tomates
Sardines beurre
Saucisson beurre
Oeuf au plat
Melon Suppl 2F
Jambon de Paris
Pâté de campagne
Escargots de Bourgogne (les six) Suppl 4F

★ ★ ★

Sole frite
Haddock beurre
Colin froid mayonnaise

★ ★ ★

Steack grillé
Escalope de veau
Poulet rôti
Assiette anglaise
¼ de poulet froid mayonnaise

★ ★ ★

Légumes au choix: ★ Haricots verts ★ Petits pois ★ Riz ★ Frites
Salade de saison

★ ★ ★

Fromages: Camembert ★ Petits Suisses ★ Chèvre ★ Yaourt
Pâtisseries: Tarte maison ★ Gâteau au chocolat
Fruits: Pêche ★ Poire ★ Banane
Glaces: Pêche Melba ★ Cassate aux fruits
Café express 2F

Couvert compris   Service non compris   Consultez notre carte des vins

TIMETABLES (SCHOOL AND PUBLIC TRANSPORT)

7 This is the timetable of a 15-year-old French boy, Joël.
Read it and then answer the questions.

emploi du temps: 3ème B   **Collège**
34150 GIGNAC

	lundi	mardi	jeudi	vendredi	samedi
8.30 – 9.25	français	maths	anglais	maths	français
9.25 – 10.20	dessin	géographie	français	géographie	anglais
	récréation				
10.35 – 11.30	éducation physique	sciences physiques	maths	histoire	éducation physique
11.30 – 12.25	anglais		anglais renforcé	étude	
	déjeuner				
13.30 – 14.25	maths	travaux pratiques	travaux pratiques	français	
14.25 – 15.20	étude	biologie		anglais	
	récréation				
15.35 – 16.30	musique	français	histoire	anglais reinforcé	

What does Joël have

a) each day between 12.25–13.30?

_____ (1)

b) second period on Monday?

_____ (2)

c) fourth period on Friday?

_____ (2)

(NISEC)

NOTES LEFT BY OTHER PEOPLE

8　You are staying with your penfriend in France. You return to the house one day to find these messages written on a pad near the telephone.

MESSAGES TÉLÉPHONIQUES

1° Marc a téléphoné – veut savoir si tu veux jouer au tennis ce soir. Si oui – va chez lui à 8 h. Jean-Pierre vient aussi ? Si non – samedi au jardin public à 10 h. N'oublie pas ta raquette.

2° Julie demande – Tu veux rencontrer sa correspondante espagnole qui est arrivée de Bilbao? Elle sera au club à 17 h 30 avec elle et après au Bar de la Poste (en face du commissariat)

3° M. Jourdain dit – tes photos sont prêtes. Va les chercher cet après-midi Ouvert à 14 h 15. Coût 59,30 F.

Read the messages carefully then answer **in English** the following questions.

a) If you want to play tennis this evening, where should you meet?

_____ (1)

b) Why is Julie inviting you to the club?

_____ (1)

c) What does Monsieur Jourdain want you to do?

_____ (1)

(NEA 16+ 1987)

ADVERTISEMENTS AND SPECIAL OFFERS; HANDBILLS

9　You are on holiday at the seaside resort of Maubuisson. At the tourist office, you are given the following map which also advertises some local shops and restaurants.
　　For each question, the correct answer is one of the letters **A** to **E**. Match the advertisement to the question and write your answer in the space provided.

Where would you go if:

a) your bike needs some new brakes? _____

b) you want to buy a windsurfer? _____

c) you want to buy a fishing rod? _____

d) you need some more tent pegs? _____

e) you want to eat the local specialities? _____ (5)

(MEG)

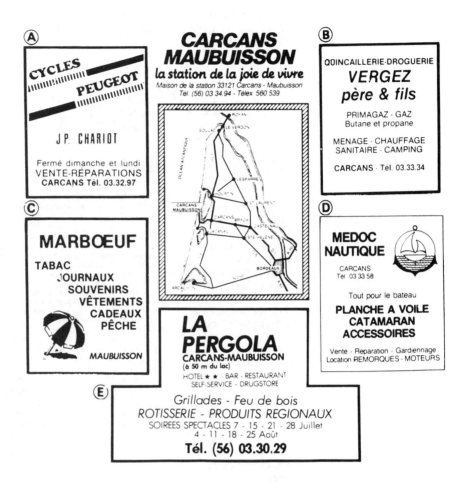

GUIDES AND BROCHURES

10 You are on holiday in Brittany and are considering a boat trip. Look at the following advertisement.

ROSMEUR

Pêche en mer à bord du Rosmeur *Photo Le Brusq*

Pêche en Mer

Juin et Septembre : sur réservations
    Juillet et Août :
Tous les jours : Départ. 7 h précises – Retour : 11 h Prix : 82.00 F
Vedette touristique de 60 passagers maximum.
Tarif réduit pour les enfants au-dessous de 12 ans.

Les réservations de groupes étant nombreuses, il est utile de retenir ses places.

a) What sporting activity is offered on board the Rosmeur?   (1)
b) In which **two** months does the Rosmeur offer this activity?   (2)
c) For what category of people is a price reduction offered?   (2)

(WJEC)

11 You have been given a leaflet containing information on motorway driving in France. Read this section of the leaflet carefully, and then answer the questions.

l'autoroute pratique A10

les services

Sur l'autorou-te, vous pouvez vous arrêter tous les 10 à 15 km sur des aires de repos (dotées de points d'eau et de sanitaires), et tous les 30 à 40 km sur des aires de service où vous trouverez des stations de pétroliers (avec boutiques), cer-taines étant équipées de ca-fétérias ou de restaurants.

Des télépho-nes publics, re-liés au réseau gé-néral, sont instal-lés sur les aires de service et de repos.

la sécurité

L'autoroute est 4 à 5 fois plus sûre que la route. A chacun de la rendre encore plus sûre, en appliquant quelques règles faciles à respecter.

Où s'arrêter ?
En cas de nécessité absolue, vous pou-vez vous arrêter sur la bande d'arrêt d'urgence. Prenez le maximum de pré-cautions car vous serez frôlé par les vé-hicules en circulation. stationnez-donc le plus à droite possible, faites fonction-ner votre système clignotant «alarme» et n'hésitez pas à utiliser en plus le triangle de présignalisation.

En cas de crevaison
Choisissez autant que possible, un en-droit où vous pourrez éloigner au maxi-mum votre véhicule de la voie de circu-lation. (Si vous êtes arrêté contre une glissière latérale, roulez quelques dizai-nes de mètres au ralenti et vous trouve-rez une interruption de la glissière) Si vous réparez vous-même, vous ne devez pas rester immobilisé sur la ban-de d'arrêt d'urgence plus d'une demi-heure.

Attention à la fatigue
La conduite sur autoroute tend à vous endormir. Deux secondes d'inattention à 130 km/h et vous parcourez 72 mè-tres incontrôlés. Evitez ce risque en cassant la monotonie de votre rythme de conduite en modifiant
• votre vitesse
• la température intérieure de votre voiture
N'hésitez pas à vous arrêter sur les par-kings et les aires de repos.

Vérifiez vos pneus
Un pneu sous gonflé finit par éclater si vous roulez vite et longtemps. Car ce sont les flancs du pneu qui travaillent et la bande de roulement risque de se dé-couper (même sur les pneus neufs). Pour ne pas compromettre votre sécu-rité, faites gonfler vos pneumatiques 200 grammes au-dessus de la pression préconisée.

a) *Services*
   i) What would you find in a rest area?

   Answer _____ (2)
   ii) What would you find in a service area?

   Answer _____ (3)

b) *Safety*
   i) According to the article, where can you stop in an emergency?

   Answer _____ (1)

   ii) What precaution should you take when parking?

   Answer _____ (2)

   iii) What other two pieces of 'safety equipment' are you asked to use?

   Answer _____
   _____ (4)

   iv) According to the article, what is the maximum length of time you can stay on the hard shoulder?

   Answer _____ (1)

   v) Apart from temperature, what else should you adjust to avoid tiredness?

   Answer _____ (1)

(NISEC)

INVITATIONS AND LETTERS

12

Paris, le 4 Décembre 1985

Ma Chère Trudy,

J'ai de bonnes nouvelles à t'annoncer. Enfin, j'ai trouvé un nouvel emploi. Je viens de terminer mon stage d'informatique. Que c'était dur ! Chaque semaine pendant toute une année, j'ai dû faire trois jours dans un bureau, plus deux jours d'études. Je ne gagne pas beaucoup en ce moment, mais j'ai eu la chance de trouver quelque chose. Je fais les mêmes heures que ma soeur qui travaille dans un bureau pas loin de là où je suis. On rentre ensemble en métro.

J'ai passé de très bonnes vacances à Méyère. Nous ne sommes partis qu'à quatre cette année, car mon frère voulait rester à Paris avec ses copains. C'était bien, pas de neige mais beaucoup de soleil.

Quand viens-tu à Paris? Tu sais, il y a bien longtemps que je ne t'ai pas vue. Lors de ton dernier séjour chez moi, on s'est bien amusé, n'est-ce pas? Qu'est-ce que tu fais pendant les vacances de février? Tu ne pourrais pas venir du 22 février au 1er Mars, par exemple? J'ai quelques jours de congé.

Donne-moi vite de tes nouvelles!
Grosses Bises,

Magali

Your sister Trudy has received a letter from a French girl she met while on holiday in Paris. She has asked you to help her check out what Magali is saying in her letter.
    Read the letter above and then answer these questions in English.

a) What is the news Magali has to tell Trudy?
b) How was Magali's working week divided up while she was on her course?
c) Where did Magali's family go on holiday?
d) Why was her brother not there?
e) What was the weather like on holiday?
f) Why is Magali so keen to see Trudy?
g) What is the importance of the dates 22nd February – 1st March?
h) Why did Magali suggest these dates?

(LEAG)

FORMAL LETTERS

13 Because you know some French, the manager of a lost property office asks you to help him with a letter in French which he has received.

Read the letter below and then fill in the information requested in English.

Aline Bontemps
3, rue Legendre

69 000 LYON

Monsieur,

Le 22 avril, j'ai pris le train de Londres à Folkestone et j'ai laissé mon sac à main dans le train ou dans la gare de Folkestone. C'est un grand sac en cuir vert, qui contient mon porte-monnaie.

Je vous serais reconnaissante de bien vouloir faire les recherches nécessaires et de me contacter chez moi.

Je vous prie d'agréer mes sentiments les plus distingués.

Aline Bontemps —

a) item lost: _____ (1)

b) description: _____

_____ (3)

c) where lost: _____ (2)

d) date lost: _____ (1)

e) any request: _____ (2)

(MEG)

NEWSPAPER AND MAGAZINE ARTICLES

14 While you are staying in France, a French friend shows you this item in a newspaper.

Le maître mord son chien

Bristol – Un homme a avoué au tribunal qu'il avait mordu son chien après que celui-ci eut mis la maison sens dessus dessous.

Stuart Smale, 19 ans, de Bristol a raconté aux magistrats qu'il s'était mis en colère après la mauvaise conduite de son chien, Jade, qu'il avait mordu à l'oreille avant de le jeter dehors.

Le jeune homme s'est vu interdire d'avoir un chien pendant un an et a été condamné à payer les frais de vétérinaire se montant à 23 livres.

a) What did this man do to his dog first? _____ (1)

b) What did he do to it then? _____ (1)

c) Why was he cross with the dog? _____ (1)

d) For how long has he now been banned from keeping a dog? _____ (1)

e) How much did he have to pay? _____ (1)

(SEG)

KEY TO PRACTICE QUESTIONS

PUBLIC SIGNS AND NOTICES

1 a) Push (1)
   b) It's full (1)
   c) Entry forbidden (1)
   d) Smoke (1)
   e) Check your change (1) immediately (1) (2)
   f) Friday and Saturday (2)
   g) Ask for a key to the side door (1) at the reception (1) (2)

ROAD SIGNS

2 Pedestrians (1)
3 Second road (1) on right (1) (2)

TICKETS, TOWN PLANS, ROAD MAPS

4 a) The underground car park (1) at the place de la Comédie (1) (2)
   b) Opposite (1) Monoprix/department store (1) (2)
   c) 4 kilometres (1)

SIMPLE INSTRUCTIONS

5 a) Choose your loaf of bread (1)
   b) Touch the others (1)
   c) For hygenic reasons (1)

MENUS, LABELS ON FOOD AND DRINK

6 a) Any five items. $(2 = \frac{1}{2}, 3 = 1, 4 = 1\frac{1}{2}, 5 = 2)$
   b) Place-setting (1)
   c) Service (1)

TIMETABLES

7 a) Lunch (1)
   b) Art or drawing (2)
   c) Study period or private study (2)

NOTES LEFT BY OTHER PEOPLE

8 a) At Marc's house (1)
   b) To meet her Spanish pen-friend (1)
   c) Fetch your photos (1)

ADVERTISEMENTS AND SPECIAL OFFERS; HANDBILLS

9 a) A (1)
   b) D (1)
   c) C (1)
   d) B (1)
   e) E (1)

GUIDES AND BROCHURES

10 a) Fishing (1)
    b) July and August (2)
    c) Children (1) under 12 (1) (2)

11 a) Services
    i) Water or taps (1), toilets (1)   *(2)*
    ii) Petrol stations (1), shops (1), cafés or restaurants (1)   *(3)*
   b) Safety
    i) Hard shoulder   *(1)*
    ii) Park as far as possible (1) to the right (1)   *(2)*
    iii) Hazard (1) indicators/lights (1), warning (1) triangle (1)   *(4)*
    iv) ½ hour   *(1)*
    v) Speed   *(1)*

INFORMAL LETTERS

12 a) Magali has a new job   *(1)*
   b) Three days in an office (½), two days studying (½)   *(1)*
   c) Mégève   *(1)*
   d) Wanted to stay in Paris (½) with his friends (½)   *(1)*
   e) No snow (½), lots of sunshine (½)   *(1)*
   f) They haven't seen each other for a long time   *(1)*
   g) They are the dates of the February or the half-term holiday   *(1)*
   h) Magali has a few days' holiday   *(1)*

FORMAL LETTERS

13 a) Handbag   *(1)*
   b) Big (1), green (1), leather (1)   *(3)*
   c) Train (1) or in Folkestone station (1)   *(2)*
   d) 22nd April   *(1)*
   e) Contact (1) at home address above (1), make necessary search (1)   *(Any 2 for 2)*

NEWSPAPER AND MAGAZINE ARTICLES

14 a) Bit it   *(1)*
   b) Threw it out   *(1)*
   c) Made the house a mess   *(1)*
   d) A year   *(1)*
   e) £23   *(1)*

A STEP FURTHER

Further hints for improving your performance in Reading include the following:

1 Make sure you get plenty of practice in reading the handwriting of native speakers of French, using your textbook, letters from pen-friends (your own and other people's) and the French Assistant(e) in your school.
2 Learn common abbreviations such as SNCF, TF1, P et T and so on.
3 Learn to take clues from the context given you in English, and from other parts of the passage. Use your common sense. Speakers of French are just as logical as you are. It sometimes pays to remind yourself of that!
4 Learn to use strategies for converting from French into English. These include the following:
   a) adverbs changing from '-ment' to '-ly' in English, e.g. complètement, rarement
   b) verbs removing the final 'r' to give the English, e.g. admirer, completer, arriver
   c) verbs ending in '-er' changing to '-ate' in English, e.g. décorer
   d) words ending in '-el' changing to '-al' in English, e.g. officiel, individuel
   e) words ending in '-aire' changing to '-ar' or '-ary', e.g. populaire, militaire
   f) words ending in '-e, -é or -ée' changing to '-y', e'g. economie, liberté, armée
   g) words ending in '-e' losing it in English, e.g. branche, signe, vaste, uniforme
   h) words gaining an '-e' in English, e.g. pur, futur, feminin
   i) present participles ending in '-ant' changing to '-ing' in English, e.g. arrivant, décidant, visitant

HIGHER READING

EXAM GROUP REQUIREMENTS

EFFECTIVE ANSWERS

WHICH VOCABULARY TOPICS?

'FALSE FRIENDS'

NORMAL PERFORMANCE

A STEP FURTHER

GETTING STARTED

Like all the Higher skills, Higher Reading is not compulsory in GCSE. However, if you are aiming at a high grade, you certainly ought seriously to consider attempting it. It's probably the most painless Higher test, although, of course it isn't actually any easier than the other three Higher tests.

If you do take Higher Reading, you also have to do Basic Reading, as we have seen. Take Basic seriously, even if it does seem straightforward. It counts just as much towards your final grade.

Finally, don't forget that getting practice in reading isn't difficult. Use spare moments wisely!

ESSENTIAL PRINCIPLES

1 › EXAM GROUP REQUIREMENTS

As in the Basic, the six Examining Groups agree very much over what should be tested in Higher Reading. However, once again they do set different *lengths of time* for the test. Check what your Examining Group does from the table below.

Examining Group	LEAG	MEG	NEA	NISEC	SEG*	WJEC
Time in minutes	30	Part 1: 25 Part 2: 25	40	40	30	40
* Extended Level						

Let us look at what the Examining Groups *agree* they are testing. The items for Higher Reading fall into two categories.

1   Some questions will be testing the same sort of skills as the Basic Reading, but over the full range of topics set for GCSE, as opposed to the restricted range set for Basic level. They will be mainly concerned with:

■ extracting facts

■ checking knowledge of vocabulary.

There will be only a few of these on the paper.

2   Some questions will be seeking to test skills which require a little more thought on your part. The Examining Groups will set questions which test:

■ whether you can find the **main points and themes** of a text

■ whether you can come to conclusions about it.

The Examiners will be interested in seeing whether you can:

■ spot the **attitudes and emotions** expressed in the texts

■ **infer** (work things out) correctly from the facts given.

This sort of question will make up at least 40% of the paper and may well be more than 50%.

> **Make sure you read the scenario**

As in the Basic, you do not have to pretend to be someone other than yourself when reading texts. The Examining Groups will give a short *scenario* giving the context and reason why you should be reading a particular text.

There is also agreement between the Examining Groups about what sort of texts the questions will be based on. There is a long list of possible authentic French material in the Basic Reading chapter. It will apply broadly to the Higher Reading, too, except that there will be a much greater amount of the following sorts of text:

— newspaper and magazine articles likely to be read by a 16-year-old; these may well include comparisons and articles contrasting different people's views on a subject
— informal letters from French people
— formal letters (e.g. confirming travel arrangements, dealing with exchanges, and in reply to job applications)
— brochures and guide books
— advertisements, including small ads
— imaginative writing

The texts that are set will very often be between 150 and 250 words long. There will not be questions on every detail of the text, but there may well be sentences or even the odd paragraph on which you are not asked anything specific at all. This is intentional, and is meant to test your ability to *skim* through the text looking for certain things only.

> **Be familiar with the various *styles* of French handwriting**

Some of the texts will be hand-written, so it is as well to familiarize yourself with the various French handwriting styles. You can do this by asking to see letters which your friends have received from pen-friends, and by consulting the examples in your text-book.

All Examining Groups except the IGCSE will set all their questions in English to be answered in English in the answer booklet they provide (Welsh is an option with WJEC). There may be a few multiple-choice questions, and some questions where you have to complete a grid or table.

EFFECTIVE ANSWERS

Let us now look at how best to answer the questions. As always in the GCSE, you should read the scene-setting carefully. It is often written with the intention of clearing up one or two of the difficulties of the text, and may therefore save you some puzzlement!

As with the Basic, there is *no requirement* to write your answers in full sentences, although you must express yourself clearly. Again, there is no penalty for errors in the English as long as the meaning is quite clear. So by all means **write in note form**.

If there is more than one mark allocated for a question, it is highly likely that there is more than one piece of information or detail required. Look for extra things to say, but be sure you can find them in the text!

Some Examining Groups have set questions where there are, say, two marks, but three possible answers. Generally speaking, two correct answers will be credited if you have given three including a wrong one, as long as the wrong one doesn't contradict a correct answer.

Under the rules for GCSE French laid down by the Secondary Examinations Council (which supervises GCSE for the government), Examining Groups may include words which do not appear in their Defined Content. They may not, however, include more than 5% of such words and may not ask questions which depend on knowing those words.

Experience of setting the papers suggests that the area where the '5% rule' is most likely to apply is Higher Reading. This means that you need to develop *strategies* for dealing with unfamiliar words. The application of common sense is the most useful one, but the section at the end of this chapter about prefixes and suffixes may help. If faced with an unfamiliar word, don't forget to consider the possibility that it could be a place name or a person's name.

Questions which are testing attitudes, emotions and ideas and which ask you to infer things will nevertheless have a logical basis. So you do need to use common sense coupled with the French to deal with these. And if you don't know a word, you should make a sensible guess as to what might come in the gap in your understanding. Many candidates seem to think that, because it's French, the normal rules of logic no longer apply! Examiners at GCSE have tried very much not to set 'trick' questions – they are more interested in French for practical communication.

As in the Basic test, questions will normally be in sequence. However, the first or last question or two may refer to the whole text if, for example, there is a question about the 'attitude of the author of the text' in general, or a question like 'what is the text about?'

WHICH VOCABULARY TOPICS?

Higher Reading tests the whole range of vocabulary prescribed for GCSE. However, adjectives and adverbs describing emotions, feelings and appearance would be worth some special attention. They are under Personal identification in the Vocabulary topics section.

Equally, in each vocabulary topic you will find the vocabulary listed separately for Higher Level. These are normally the more difficult words, and serious Higher Level candidates will make sure they know many of them.

If you have not already done so, look at the section in the Basic Reading which corresponds to this one. Likely targets for the examiners who set Reading papers are laid out there.

Topics which might be found more frequently at Higher Level in Reading include:

— current affairs
— more complicated instructions and adverts
— longer notices from shops, banks and post offices.

'FALSE FRIENDS'

Some simple 'false friends' have already been given in the Basic Reading chapter. Here are some more difficult ones.

French word	*English meaning*	
assister à	to be present at	(NOT to assist)
causer	to chat	(NOT to cause)
la chance	good luck	(NOT chance)
le courrier	letters, mail	(NOT courier)
doubler	to overtake	(NOT double)
se dresser	to rise up	(NOT to get dressed)
la figure	face	(NOT figure)
la lecture	reading	(NOT lecture)

la librairie	bookshop	(NOT library)
la licence	university degree	(NOT licence)
la location	hiring	(NOT location)
le médecin	doctor	(NOT medicine)
le mouton	sheep	(NOT only mutton)
la note	bill	(NOT note)
un omnibus	stopping train	(NOT bus)
le pétrole	crude oil	(NOT petrol)
le plat	culinary dish	(NOT plate)
la promotion	special offer	(NOT promotion)
la prune	plum	(NOT prune)
rester	to stay	(NOT to rest)
sensible	sensitive	(NOT sensible)
le stage	course of instruction	(NOT stage)
le wagon	railway coach	(NOT waggon)

5 › NORMAL PERFORMANCE

Candidates who do well in this part of the GCSE will have shown that they have a command of the full range of GCSE topics, that they can infer more than the bare facts from a passage where appropriate, and that they have a command of the full range of vocabulary set by their Examining Group. They should be capable of reading relatively straightforward French easily.

STUDENT'S ANSWERS – EXAMINER'S COMMENTS

Let us look at two typical texts, with sample student answers and examiner comments.

QUESTION

You have just received a letter from your French pen-friend, Sabine. This is one page of her letter – read it, and then answer the questions.

> Pour cet été, j'ai beaucoup d'idées. Je vais d'abord travailler chez un fermier. Je vais cueillir les cerises en juin, pendant les week-ends et en juillet, je vais ramasser les pêches. C'est un travail crevant, mais c'est assez bien payé. Avec cet argent, je vais aller à Cannes tout le mois d'août avec deux autres amies. On va camper au bord de la mer. Je vais nager et me faire bronzer tout le mois. J'adore la chaleur et le soleil. Mes parents vont nous rejoindre en septembre et je vais repartir avec eux juste avant la rentrée. Cette année, je suis en première et je vais passer mon bac de français. Ça me fait un peu peur!

1	How exactly is Sabine going to earn money a) in June? b) in July?	(2)
2	What does she say about this work?	(2)
3	What is she going to do with the money?	(2)
4	What class will she be in when she goes back to school?	(1)
5	Why does this frighten her a little?	(1)
		(NISEC)

STUDENT'S ANSWER WITH EXAMINER'S COMMENTS

1) a) June – eat cherries

How could that be right? Nobody earns money for eating cherries! So even if you didn't know cueillir the only possible earnings in connection with cherries would have to be picking them.

b) July – pick peaches

Correct!

2) It's quite well paid.

Missed out 'crevant' (= shattering) so only one mark.

3) Going camping by the sea at Cannes with friends.

Good.

4) Premieve.

No credit given for anything written in French. In this sort of case, explain, or give an equivalent, e.g. Upper Sixth, or: Final year of school.

5) She's going to pass her French exam.

'passer' means take, not pass. Common sense might have made you suspicious – few people are frightened of *passing* an exam!

QUESTION

Jean Ferrat raccroche sa guitare

Paris n'a pas su retenir Jean Ferrat. Est-ce le besoin de solitude et de vie calme, ou l'agitation de la capitale? Toujours est-il que le créateur de «La montagne» a raccroché sa guitare pour un retour au pays.

«Comme prévu!» s'etonne-t-il auprès de ceux qui regrettent son absence.

Malgré le million d'exemplaires vendus de son disque en quelques semaines, malgré les multiples interviews et reportages organisés par la presse, Jean Ferrat n'a pas cédé. Il ne rechantera pas sur scène.

«Je n'en ai plus envie», dit-il en souriant sous sa grande moustache gauloise.

Si l'on insiste un peu, Ferrat ajoute, énigmatique: «Mais, si un jour l'envie me prend, alors peut-être...»

A Entraigues où il vient de se réinstaller pour terminer l'hiver dans sa maison, Jean Ferrat est resté bloqué et coupé du monde plus de trois jours comme tous les habitants de la région d'Ardèche, pour cause de neige. C'est donc à la bougie que Ferrat et sa compagne Colette ont vécu quelques jours.

Ferrat s'amuse toujours de la curiosité de ses admirateurs à son égard. Il ne se rend pas vraiment compte que ceux qui l'aiment et suivent ses chansons depuis si longtemps ont envie de mieux connaître encore l'homme que se cache derrière sa musique.

C'est un peu pour cette raison que Jean Ferrat a accepté en novembre et décembre derniers à la télévision, les deux invitations faites par Bernard Pivot et Pascal Sevran. Face à la star de «Apostrophes» et au producteur de «La chance aux chansons», Ferrat simple et tranquille avec la distance que donne la province, s'est expliqué à cœur ouvert.

Les indices d'écoute, exceptionnels, prouvent s'il en est besoin la fidélité du public pour celui qui avoue en chantant: «Je ne suis qu'un cri».

Pas de rentrée donc pour Jean Ferrat, mais quand même quelques aller-retour Entraigues-Paris ou plutôt Ivry, où le chanteur possède toujours le petit appartement de sa jeunesse quand, avec sa femme Christine Sèvres, récemment disparue, il tentait sa chance chaque soir dans les petits cabarets rive gauche. C'était il y a vingt-cinq ans et il n'imaginait pas à l'époque qu'un jour sa gloire serait assez grande pour lui permettre de refuser les contrats mirifiques qu'on lui purpose.

Above is an article from a French newspaper about a famous guitarist who has surprised everyone by leaving Paris and going back to live in his home village in the country. Read the article and then answer the questions.

1   Give *two* reasons suggested by the writer for why Jean Ferrat has decided to leave Paris. _____

_____

2   What does Jean Ferrat say about whether he will come back to Paris or not? _____

_____

3   What happened to Jean Ferrat soon after his return to Entraigues? _____

_____

4   What surprises Jean Ferrat about the attitude of his admirers towards him? _____

_____

5   What are we told that he never imagined when he came to Paris twenty-five years ago?

_____

_____

(WJEC)

STUDENT'S ANSWER WITH EXAMINER'S COMMENTS

1) needs solitude

   capital too (agitated) ——————— Not clear if the student knows this means busy.

2) He won't ←————— Unless he feels like it one day. Doesn't want to
                     sing on stage. This is an insufficient answer,
                     as it stands.

3) caught by snow

   had to live by candlelight

4) that they want to know details ——— Full answer – good.

   about him, the man behind the music. ←

5) he would be in a position to refuse contracts

   OK, but could have said more about him singing in cabaret clubs on the Left Bank.

PRACTICE QUESTIONS

The questions here have been laid out so that you can write the answers in the book. Test
yourself! The answers are given later in the chapter. There are examples of each type of
text which could be set in Higher Reading, except Imaginative Writing, as none of the
Examining Groups has included that sort of text in its sample papers. Once again, that is
the one sort of text which is easy to find in old CSE and O Level text-books. Ask your
teacher to help you find some.

**1 ▷ NEWSPAPER
AND MAGAZINE
ARTICLES**

1   The views of six French pop-stars about the proposed Channel Tunnel are expressed
    in the following article from a French teenagers' magazine. The name of each one is
    given before what he or she says. Read the article carefully and answer the questions
    which follow.

INDOCHINE:

Sur le plan géographique, ça ne changer
pas grand chose. Même si certains
prétendent que l'Angletere ne sera plus une
ile. C'est surtout les Anglais qui vont peut
être se sentir dépossédés de leur chère
indépendance. J'espère que la facilité
d'acces entre les deux pays générera aussi
un meilleur contact et que, sur le plan
musical, les influences de part et d'autres
nous seront à tous bénéfiques!

SANDRA:

Ça fait partie de l'évolution des choses, en
un mot, du progrès. Mais je ne pense pas
que cela transforme pour autant
radicalement la vie de nos deuc pays.
Chacun conservera jalousement son entité
et son identité. Mais c'est quand même bien
ce changement, dans le sens où on a
l'impression d'une sorte de rapprochement
des peuples même si celui-ci n'est que fictif
et imaginaire.

MICHAEL JONES:

Je n'en vois pas le réel intetrèt, dans la
measure où l'avion pour se rendre d'un
point à l'autre restera la voie d'accès la plus
facile et la plus rapide.

RENAUD:

C'est Madame Thatcher qui va être
contente!...

SERGE GAINSBOURG:

Pour les Français, ça donne l'impression de
se rapprocher de l'Angleterre, et pour les
Anglais, ça doit donner l'impression de la
perte d'une certaine indépendance. De
toute façon, les deux se trompent
probablement...

NOE WILLER:

Personnellment, je pense que le projet du
pont était de loin préférable à celui du
tunnel. Au moins, on aurait pu y aller en
voiture. Mais considérant le fait que nous
devons faire des économies à tous les
niveaux, on n'avait pas trop le choix.

a) What idea about the tunnel is shared by Indochine and Serge Gainsbourg?

_____

_____ *(1)*

b) Which of the following do you consider best sums up the attitude of Sandra
towards the tunnel? (Tick the appropriate box). *(1)*

   i) That it is something everyone has been waiting for for a long time. ☐

   ii) That it will make a big difference to both France and England. ☐

   iii) That it will make a big difference to England, but not to France. ☐

   iv) That it is inevitable. ☐

   v) That it ought not to be built. ☐

c) What is Michael Jones' opinion of the tunnel? Why does he feel this way about it?

_____

_____ *(2)*

d) What is Serge Gainsbourg's opinion of the impressions of the tunnel
held by the French and by the English?

_____

_____ *(2)*

e) What would Noe Willer have preferred to a tunnel? What reason does he
give to support this preference?

_____

_____ *(2)*

f) What indication is there in the text that the tunnel will be cheaper
than other possibilities considered?

_____

_____ *(1)*

g) Which of the following best sums up the general attitude of these six people
towards the Channel Tunnel? (Tick the appropriate box). *(1)*

   i) They are very much in favour of it. ☐

   ii) They are very much against it. ☐

   iii) They think it will make very little difference. ☐

   iv) They think it will bring Britain and France closer together. ☐

   v) They think it will bring about better contacts between the two countries
as far as music is concerned. ☐

(WJEC)

2 Your French pen-friend sends you an article from *Phosphore*, a magazine for French
lycéens, about six teenagers who have won a trip to New York and are being
interviewed on their views on money.

    Read the article printed on the next page and answer these questions in English.

a) What false impressions is the reporter trying to dispel in this article?

_____ *(2)*

b) What question was put to both the French and American teenagers?

_____ *(2)*

c) What is the essential difference between what the French and American
teenagers would do?

_____ *(2)*

d) Explain why American teenagers find it unnecessary to look outside the home for entertainment.
(Give **two** examples from the text)

_____ (2)

e) How do American teenagers generally help to pay for their studies?
(Give **two** examples from the article)

_____ (2)

(LEAG)

MONEY

L'ARGENT DES JEUNES EN FRANCE ET AUX USA

New York

A ma droite, six jeunes Français. Ils ont de 15 à 20 ans, et ils sont à New York pour une semaine. A ma gauche, six jeunes Américaines, âges — rapport. Sujet de la discussion : l'argent. Comment on le gagne, comment on le dépense. Observateurs attentifs : des banquiers, des deux rives de l'Atlantique.

AUX USA, ÉTUDIER EST UN LUXE

Question : vous gagnez 1000 $ (environ 9 000 F) à une loterie. Vous en faites quoi? Côté français, l'imagination ne fait pas défaut : entre Dominique qui s'achèterait une planche à voile (s'il n'en avait déjà une...), Valérie qui partirait en voyage, et les autres qui s'offriraient des tonnes de disques ou une débauche de concerts, le pactole serait vite dilapidé. Côté américain, surprise : «Tepaierais mes études» cons ponse unanime. Les filles qui sont là n'ont pourtant pas l'air de premières de la classe polarisées et boutonneuses. Mais voilà : aux États-Unis, étudier est un luxe. Les universités sont toutes payantes, et les plus cotées d'entre elles, généralement privées, pratiquent des tarifs rédhibitoires : la scolarité coûte parfois jusqu'à

Les clichés ont la peau dure. Nous imaginons volontiers les jeunes Américains insouciants, pleins aux as, et menant une vie idyllique sur d'immenses campus verdoyants. A y regarder de plus près, la réalité est bien différente. Et entre les jeunes Français et les jeunes Américains, les plus fortunés ne sont pas forcément ceux qu'on pense...

25 000 $ par an (plus de 20 millions d'anciens francs)! A ce prix-là, même quand papa et maman ignorent les problèmes de fins demois, il ne reste généralement pas grand-chose pour les loisirs. De plus, le coût des études est supporté par les étudiants eux-mêmes, rarement par les parents, contrairement à ce qui se passe souvent chez nous.

A l'évidence, l'argent des jeunes Français sert principalement à financer leurs

loisirs, celui des jeunes Américains à payer la fac. Parce que les Américains sont plus sérieux? Pas exactement : »Côté loisirs, les jeunes Américains ont tout à la maison, observe Sheila Horowitz, qui enseigne le français dans le New Jersey. Pourquoi économiser pour acheter une chaîne stéréo, quand celle des parents est disponible? Aller au cinéma? Certes, mais on peut tout aussi bien regarder des cassettes sur le magnétoscope familial...«.

Du coup, cet argent dépensé différemment est aussi gagné différemment ici ou là-bas. Les jobs à temps partiel, du style cours particuliers, qui sont relativement rares chez les Français, sont élevés au rang d'institution par les Américains : il s'agit pour eux d'une condition sine qua non pour faire des études. Il est fréquent de rencontrer des étudiants qui travaillent jusqu'à 20 ou 30 heures par semaine, tout en étudiant! Autre source de revenus : le système »work and study« : les étudiants paient une partie de leur scolarité en s'engageant à effectuer régulièrement de menus travaux pour l'université (standard, entretien, etc). Mais cela ne couvre pas tout... Alors, dès la high school, les lycéens mettent des sous de côté pour l'avenir...

3 Read this French magazine article, then answer the questions.

L'épidémie est venue du Canada, mais très vite elle a frappé le monde entier. Partout elle donne lieu à de folles soirées au cours desquelles des gens complètement hystériques hurlent, gesticulent et... éclatent de rire. Les premiers Français touchés par Trivial Pursuit – baptisé un temps Remue-méninges – : Agnès Montenay et Danial Leclercq, les auteurs de la version française «Nous avons dû réinventer 90% des 6 000 questions de géographie, histoire, politique, ciné, sport, etc. etc., la culture américaine n'étant pas la même que le nôtre.»
Quel est le canard le plus riche du monde? Quelle maladie est-on sûr de ne pas attraper au Pôle Nord? Dans quel film Francis Blanche découvrait-il qu'il est difficile de faire avouer à un Japonais qu'il est Juif? A vous de jouer. En plus Trivial Pursuit fait des petits, une version junior et en avril une version Baby-boom sur la culture de 48 à aujord'hui. (Vendu 300 F environ). S.T.

a) What is the article about? *(1)*
b) According to the article, how widespread has the success of the game been? *(1)*
c) What changes had to be made to produce a French version? *(1)*
d) Why were changes felt to be necessary? *(1)*
e) In what way does this article suggest that the name of the game is an appropriate one? *(1)*
f) What further evidence is given of the game's commercial success? *(1))*

(SEG)

2 > INFORMAL LETTERS

4 You have arrived at a farmhouse in France for a self-catering holiday and have found a letter from some French friends. Your family does not understand French very well and wants to know what is in the letter.

Read the letter, which is on the next page, and then answer **in English** the following questions.

a) What are the **two** hopes your friends express at the beginning of the letter?

1 _____

2 _____ *(2)*

b) What has the weather been like and for how long?

_____ *(2)*

c) When are you invited to stay with your friends?

_____ *(1)*

d) What will prove no problem?

_____ *(1)*

e) Name **one** thing your friends suggest you bring for John

_____ *(1)*

f) When will the 'Onion Festival' take place?

_____ *(1)*

g) What **two** things can be done in the evening? – and where?

1 _____

2 _____ *(3)*

h) What do your friends suggest you do on Monday?

_____ *(1)*

i) How much would a child's ticket cost?

_____ *(1)*

j) What does Marie-Anne say the brochure advises you to do?

_____ *(1)*

k) When should you telephone your friends?

_____ *(1)*

l) What **two** things are you asked to tell them?

1 _____

2 _____ *(2)*

(NEA 16+ 1987)

Saint-Gilles Croix-de-Vie

Dimanche 18 août

Chers Amis,

Nous espérons que vous êtes bien arrivés et que l'endroit vous plaît. Vous aurez certainement le beau temps puisqu'il fait mauvais depuis la fin juillet. Ce temps couvert ne pourrait durer tout le mois d'août!

Je vous écris pour vous inviter à venir passer le weekend prochain chez nous. Aucun problème par coucher quatre personnes. Si donc vous avez un lit de camp ou un sac de couchage pour John, apportez-le, sinon il peut toujours dormir sur des coussins

Nous vous proposons vendredi 23 août car le jour suivant aura lieu la «foire aux oignons». L'après-midi défilent, majorettes, groupes folkloriques, fanfares, etc ... Le soir on peut manger la soupe aux oignons et danser sur la place publique. Jacques et moi avons pensé que le lundi vous pourriez faire une excursion en bateau à l'Île d'Yeu. Cela vaut vraiment la peine. En une journée on peut aisément visiter toute l'île en vélo. J'ai demandé les tarifs et les horaires. Les voici.

Adultes 90 F   (Enfants demi-tarif)
Départ St-Gilles 8 h   Départ Île d'Yeu 17 h

Vous trouvez peut-être que c'est cher mais s'il fait beau vous ne regretterez pas. Sur le prospectus que j'ai, il vaut mieux reserver à l'avance. Voici ce que je vous propose : téléphonez-nous quand vous aurez pris votre décision. Dites-nous – si vous êtes d'accord pour arriver chez nous vers 18 h vendredi 23 août – si nous devons réserver des places pour vous (vous louerez les vélos en arrivant sur l'île)

Bonne première semaine de vacances

A bientôt

Amitiés

Marie-Anne

5   Read this letter from a French boy, Marc, and then answer the questions.

Calais, le 4 Mars

Cher David,

J'écris à la hâte pour t'annoncer une triste nouvelle – je ne peux pas venir te rendre visite à Pâques. Je sais que tout est arrangé – je suis désolé – et je suis très ennuyé d'être forcé de refuser ton invitation.

Ma mère s'est cassé la jambe, et elle doit se reposer pendant quelques semaines. J'ai deux frères et deux sœurs, comme tu sais, et grand-maman habite chez nous aussi. Il y a donc beaucoup à faire, et mon père ne peut pas se débrouiller tout seul.

Si tu voyais ce que j'apprends à faire! Je ne savais pas qu'il y avait tout à faire. Je fais la vaisselle, je fais la lessive, je fais les courses, je fais la cuisine même.

Est-ce qu'il serait possible de venir au mois de juillet? J'aimerais beaucoup te revoir.

Rappelle-moi au bon souvenir de tes parents. et dis leur que je suis très déçu. J'espère les revoir en été.

Ton ami,
Marc

a) What is the sad news?

Answer _____ (2)

b) What has happened to Marc's mother?

Answer _____ (2)

c) What must she do?

Answer _____ (1)

d) Why can father not cope alone?

Answer _____ (4)

e) Name **two** of the things Marc is now learning to do.

Answer _____ (2)

f) What message does he want to be passed on to David's parents?

Answer _____ (2)

(NISEC)

6   A friend has received this letter and, as you know French, asks you to help her to
    understand it.
        Read the letter and then answer questions (a) to (e).

> Avignon, le 6 juin 1984
>
> Ma chère Michelle,
>
>   Aujourd'hui je me sens horriblement seule
> J'ai le cafard, mes copines ne viennent plus à l'école
> et je m'ennuie à mourir
>
>   Hier, je me suis encore disputée avec mes parents
> (tu vois l'ambiance) tout ça parce que mon petit
> copain m'a ramenée en moto et évidemment maman
> est arrivée à ce moment-là. Je n'ai rien pu lui
> expliquer elle s'est tout de suite imaginé des histoires
> invraisemblables. Le soir, quand papa est arrivé, elle
> s'est empressée de tout lui raconter. Quelle histoire !!
> En plus, mon frère est venu m'accuser de lui avoir
> volé son argent de poche (5 minutes plus tard, il
> l'avait retrouvé sur son lit).
>
>   L'incident s'est mal terminé pour moi : on m'a
> envoyée au lit sans manger et je dois aller à l'école
> jusqu'au dernier jour du trimestre (alors là c'est trop !!!).
> Je suis partie en claquant la porte et je me suis
> enfermée dans ma chambre. D'ailleurs, je suis bien
> décidée à y rester jusqu'à ce que mes parents
> renoncent à leur décision.
>
>   Qu'est-ce qu'il faut endurer quand on est jeune !
> Si seulement j'étais majeure ! Voilà qu'ils frappent
> à la porte maintenant !..
>
>   Souhaite-moi bonne chance quand même au lieu
> de rire...   Merci, tu es drôlement sympa !
>
>   Je t'embrasse très fort
>
>   Marilyne

a) From your reading of the letter, what can you say about Marilyne's mood?

    _____

    _____ (1)

b) What had Marilyne done to make her mother angry with her?

    _____

    _____ (1)

c) How did her parents punish Marilyne?

_____

_____ _(1)_

d) How did Marilyne show her feelings on being punished?

_____

_____ _(1)_

e) What is Marilyne looking forward to?

_____

_____ _(1)_

(MEG)

3 ▷ **FORMAL LETTERS**

7 You are helping your local twinning committee with the arrangements for a forthcoming visit. The following letter has arrived and you have been asked about certain details. Read the letter below and fill in the information for questions a) to h) by writing brief answers.

Hôtel de Ville,   Tonville, le 4 mai 1985
Tonville
86-94-07

Chers Mesdames et Messieurs,

Nous sommes très heureux de vous rendre visite bientôt à
l'occasion du jumelage de nos 2 villes. Notre délégation
arrivera le 1er juin, comme prévu, à 12h.30 à Douvres. Quelqu'un
peut-il venir nous chercher au port? Si cela est possible,
pouvez-vous me dire qui viendra nous accueillir? En cas
d'urgence vous pouvez me contacter au numéro qui figure en haut
de la page.

Nous sommes huit - M. le Maire, le Maire-adjoint, trois
conseillers, le Directeur du Lycee et M. le Président du Comité
de Jumelage et son épouse.

Pourriez-vous nous donner des renseignements sur le programme de
la visite? En particulier, quand est-ce que les discours auront
lieu? Pouvons-nous aussi avoir une liste des personnes qui nous
accueilleront pour nous permettre d'apporter un cadeau à chacun?

Nous vous prions de laisser un peu de temps libre pour nous
permetter de faire des courses. Madame Blanchard désirerait
rendre visite à un ami à Londres l'après-midi du 3 juin - est-ce
que cela serait possible?

Nous serons très heureux de .vous acceuillir en France en novembre
ou en janvier prochain. Nous aimerions recevoir rapidement une
réponse à cause des élections municipales qui se tiennent en fin
d'anée. Nous vous proposons donc ou du 7 au 10 novembre ou du 28
au 31 janvier.

Je vous prie d'agréer, Mesdames et Messieurs, l'expression de mes
sentiments les meilleurs.

          D. Rigouneau

Maire-adjoint

a) Object of the visit: _____ (2)

b) Date of arrival: _____ (1)

c) Time of arrival: _____ (1)

d) Number of persons coming: _____ (1)

e) Requests from French delegation: _____

_____

(5)

f) What does the writer say about Madame Blanchard on 3rd June?

_____ (3)

g) What is proposed for early November or the end of January?

_____ (2)

h) What needs to be done about this proposal and why? _____

_____ (4)

(MEG)

---

4 >	**BROCHURES AND GUIDE BOOKS**

8

Prenom ..*Jacques*......

Nom ..*LEGRAND*..........

Né(e) le ..*15/05/1962*....

Valable du ..*01.06.82*....

Jusqu au: ..*30.09.82*......

Signature *Jacques Legrand*

Cet été pour 100 F*, avec la carte Jeune,

50%

de réduction sur vos voyages en train en période bleue.

A qui s'adresse la carte Jeune?

La carte Jeune s'adresse à *tous les jeunes de 12 à 25 ans inclus*★.

Elle est utilisable du *1*er juin au *30 septembre 1982* sur toutes les lignes de la SNCF à l'exclusion des trains de la banlieue parisienne.

Quels sont les avantages de la carte Jeune?

Elle offre 50% de réduction sur le prix du billet dans tous les trains à l'intérieur de la France y compris le TGV. Il suffit que chaque trajet commence en période bleue, c'est-à-dire environ 5 jours par semaine.

Elle est utilisable en 1re comme en 2e classe,

même sur des allers simples.

Elle donne droit à une *couchette gratuite* à utiliser en *période bleue* entre le Ier juin et le 30 septembre 1982.

Les autocars touristiques associés à la SNCF accordent une réduction de 10%.

Son prix est de 100 F★. Elle est donc amortie en quelques centaines de km.

Comment obtenir la carte Jeune?

La carte Jeune est délivrée sur simple demande dans les gares et agences de voyages jusqu'à fin septembre.

Il suffit de présenter une pièce d'identité et une photo et d'acquitter la somme de 100 F quelle que soit la date de délivrance.

Période bleue

en général du samedi 12 h au dimanche 15 h, du lundi 12h au vendredi 15 h.

Période blanche

en général du vendredi 15 h au samedi 12 h, du dimanche 15 h au lundi 12 h et quelques jours de fêtes.

★Prix au 1/06/82.

Look at the leaflet on the opposite page.
Answer the questions below in English.

a) Who is allowed to use the Carte Jeune?

_____ *(2)*

b) Where, in France, **can't** the Carte Jeune be used?

_____ *(2)*

c) If you want to use your Carte Jeune for a journey on a Friday, by what time

must you catch your train? _____*(1)*

d) Apart from the 50% reduction on all trains, what two other advantages does
the Carte Jeune give?

1 _____

2 _____*(2)*

e) How and when do you apply for a Carte Jeune and where do you need to go?

_____

_____ *(6)*

(MEG)

9   You are on holiday in France, and you have been given this leaflet about a sailing school.
Read the leaflet, and then answer the questions.

ÉCOLE DE VOILE
DE BARNEVILLE-CARTERET
1983

L'école de voile de Barneville-Carteret est une école de voile municipale,
homologuée par la Fédération Française de Voile. Placée sous la
responsabilité d'un moniteur diplômé d'état, elle a pour principal objectif de
vous faire découvrir le monde de la mer et des voiliers

Nous naviguons sur des CARAVELLES et des VAURIENS : ce sont des
bateaux simples sûrs et marins. Véritables 2 CV de la mer, ils font maintenant
partie intégrante du paysage maritime de nos côtes et permettent un
apprentissage sérieux de la mer et des principales manoeuvres.

ORGANISATION INTERNE DE L'ÉCOLE

L'école est ouverte du Lundi 4 Juillet au Samedi 27 Août. Stage d'une
semaine complète, du lundi au samedi inclus. Chaque séance dure environ 4
heures. Les horaires sont fonction des heures de marée.

Enseignment:
2 niveaux différents
a) niveau débutant
b) niveau perfectionnement

Conditions d'Inscription:
- savoir nager
- être reconnu médicalement apte à la pratique de la voile
- âge minimum : 10 ans

Prix:
300 f pour un stage d'une semaine
250 f pour un 2ème stage
Réduction de 10% pour 2 inscriptions dans la même famille.
Durant les deux premières semaines de juillet, une réduction de 50% est
accordée aux stagiaires dont la résidence principale est à Barneville-
Carteret.

Inscriptions:
en saison, elles se font au local de l'école de voile, situé sur le port, tous les
dimanches matin entre 11h. et midi. Hors-saison, elles se font à la mairie.

MAIRIE - 50270 BARNEVILLE-CARTERET - ☎ (33) 54.8

a) The sailing dinghies used by the school are 'CARAVELLES' and 'VAURIENS'. What are you told about these dinghies?

_____ (2)

b) Each session during the training course lasts about 4 hours – how is the timetable decided?

_____ (1)

c) Apart from being at least ten years old, what two conditions must be fulfilled by people wishing to enrol?

_____ (2)

d) On what condition is a reduction of 10% offered?

_____ (1)

e) During the season, where and when do you enrol?

_____ (2)

(NISEC)

5 〉 SMALL ADS   10 Look at this section of the letters page of the pop magazine 'OK', then answer **in English** the questions which follow.

Vos suggestions, vos avis, et même vos critiques nous sont précieux... Voici notre adresse: «Cher OK!», B.P. 56-08, 75362 Paris Cedex 08.

—— CHER OK! ——

A VENDRE
Je vends des livres de la collection Harlequin. 5.20 F pièce. Et j'échange aussi des livres Harlequin contre des posters de Madonna. Si vous êtes intéressés, écrivex à Yolande Calvez, 6, avenue Joseph-Bedier, 75013 Paris.

CORRESPONDANCE
Je trouve votre magazine super. Je le lis depuis deux ans et j'en ai quatorze. Je lis les problèmes de certaines filles ou garçons, ils m'amusent ou me choquent. Voici le mien : depuis quelque temps, je me trouve seule et je recherche des correspondantes françaises

de 14 à 16 ans qui aiment la mode, la musique, la lecture, les journaux, OK! et la radio. Voici mon adresse : Angèle Nguekan. s/c Capitaine Moumi Anselme, CEM/Rqg, B.P. 1162, Yaoundé, Cameroun.

COLLECTION A ECHANGER
Je suis une de vos fidèles lectrices et je trouve OK! extra et, sans me décourager, je vous écris pour la troisième fois en vous demandant de publier ma petite annonce. Voilà, je fais collection de feuilles de papier à lettres (vierges bien sûr) et je suis prête à en échanger avec ceux qui m'en enverront des nouvelles. Merci d'avance. Ecrivez-moi. Corinne Foulon, 541, rue des Trannois-Dorignies, 59500 Douai.

AVIS DE RECHERCHE.
Je recherche tout ce qui concerne le joueur de tennis Henri Leconte (photos, posters...). Alors, si vous possédez ces documents, n'hésitez pas! merci de me rèpondre. Géraldine Hugou, Le Château, 83860 Nans-les-Pins.

---

a) What do the editors of the magazine find valuable? (Mention **three** things.)

1 _____

2 _____

3 _____ (3)

b) What interests does Yolande Calvez have?

_____

_____ (2)

c) What is Angèle Nguekan's problem?

_____ (1)

d) Give **four** interests she wants to share.

1 _____

2 _____

3 _____

4 _____ *(4)*

e) What suggests that Corinne Foulon is not a person to give up easily?

_____ *(1)*

(NEA 16+ 1987)

6 ⟩ INSTRUCTIONS

11 You have got some salt-water stains on your best clothes. Fortunately you come across this little article in a French magazine, and with any luck you will be able to remove the stains before your mother notices!

> ■ **ENLEVEZ LES TACHES D'EAU DE MER SANS TROP DE PROBLÈMES**
> Sur le tissu : faites tremper le vêtement dans de l'eau chaude et, en cas de besoin, mettez sur la tache une goutte d'alcool à brûler puis lavez. Sur le cuir : frottez avec un mélange d'une cuillerée de lait pour deux d'alcool à brûler, laissez sécher puis cirez.

a) How exactly should you remove stains from material?

Answer _____ *(4)*

b) How should you remove stains from leather?

Answer _____ *(4)*

(NISEC)

KEY TO PRACTICE QUESTIONS

1 CHANNEL TUNNEL

a) British will lose their feeling of independence *(1)*

b) (iv) *(1)*

c) Sees no point in it (1)
   Quicker by plane (1) *(2)*

d) French feel nearer England (1)
   English lose their feeling of independence (1) *(2)*

e) Would have preferred a bridge (1)
   Could have driven over (1) *(2)*

f) Noe Willer mentions saving money as the reason for choosing a tunnel instead of a bridge *(1)*

g) (iii) *(1)*

2 MONEY

a) That all American students are rich (1)
   That further education is provided free by the state (1) *(2)*

b) If you won $1000 (9,000F) in a lottery (1), what would you do with it? (1) *(2)*

c) French students would spend the money on leisure interests (1)
   American students would use the money to pay for their studies (1) *(2)*

d) Everything is provided in the home (1), e.g. stereo unit (½),
   video-recorder (½) *(2)*

e) By doing part-time jobs (1), e.g. any two of: private lessons (½),
   work and study' system (½), helping on switchboard (½), helping with
   cleaning and maintenance (½) *(2)*

3 TRIVIAL PURSUIT

a) The spread of Trivial Pursuit   *(1)*
b) World-wide   *(1)*
c) 90% of the questions had to be re-invented   *(1)*
d) American culture differs from French culture   *(1)*
e) By giving examples of trivial questions   *(1)*
f) New versions keep coming out   *(1)*

4 LETTER FROM MARIE-ANNE

a) You've arrived safely (1), you like the place (1)   *(2)*
b) Bad (1), since end of July (1)   *(2)*
c) Next weekend   *(1)*
d) Putting up four people   *(1)*
e) Either camp bed or sleeping bag   *(1)*
f) Saturday or 24th August   *(1)*
g) Eat onion soup (1), dance (1), in the square (1)   *(3)*
h) Take a boat trip   *(1)*
i) 45F   *(1)*
j) Reserve tickets in advance   *(1)*
k) When you've decided what to do   *(1)*
l) If you are going to arrive on 23rd August at 18.00 (1), if you want them
   to reserve boat tickets for you (1)   *(2)*

5 LETTER FROM MARC

a) He can't come to visit (1) at Easter (1)   *(2)*
b) Broken (1) her leg (1)   *(2)*
c) Rest   *(1)*
d) There is a large (1) family (1), lots (1) of housework/to do, etc. (1) *(4)*
e) Any two from: doing dishes, washing, shopping, cooking   *(2)*
f) Any two of: very disappointed, hopes to see them in the summer, he's
   asking about them   *(2)*

6 LETTER FROM MARILYNE

a) Miserable or bored   *(1)*
b) Ridden on a motorbike   *(1)*
c) Sent her to bed   *(1)*
d) Either Locked herself in her room, or Slammed the door   *(1)*
e) Being old enough to do what she likes   *(1)*

7 FORMAL LETTER

a) Celebrate the twinning (1) of the two towns (1)   *(2)*
b) 1st June   *(1)*
c) 12.30   *(1)*
d) 8   *(1)*
e) Any five of: programme of the visit (1), timing (1) of speeches (1),
   list of persons (1) to welcome the delegation (1), leave free time (1)   *(5)*
f) She wants to visit (1) a friend in London (1) in the afternoon (1)   *(3)*
g) Return visit (1) to France (1)   *(2)*
h) Answer (1) quickly (1) because of municipal elections (1) at end of year (1) *(4)*

8 CARTE DES JEUNES

a) Young people (1) aged 12–25 (1)   *(2)*
b) Paris (1), suburban trains (1)   *(2)*
c) Before 3 p.m. (15.00)   *(1)*
d) Any two of: free sleeper (1), 10% off on coaches (1), 1st or 2nd class
   on single journeys (1)   *(2)*
e) identification (1), photo (1), 100F (1), travel agency (1), station (1),
   before end of September (1)   *(6)*

9 SAILING SCHOOL

    a) Any two of: simple (1), safe (1), seaworthy (1)   *(2)*
    b) According to the tide   *(1)*
    c) Able to swim (1), medically fit to go sailing (1)   *(2)*
    d) If two members of one family enrol   *(1)*
    e) At the sailing school premises (1), on Sundays between 11 a.m. and noon (1) *(2)*

10 SMALL ADS

    a) Suggestions (1), advice (1), criticisms (1)   *(3)*
    b) Harlequin books (1), posters of Madonna (1)   *(2)*
    c) She's lonely   *(1)*
    d) Any four of: fashion (1), music (1), reading (1), newspapers (1), radio (1) *(4)*
    e) She has tried to get her advert published twice before   *(1)*

11 STAIN REMOVAL

    a) Soak (1) in hot water (1), put a drop of meths or alcohol on the stain (1),
       then wash (1)   *(4)*
    b) Rub (1) with a mixture of milk and meths or alcohol (1), dry (1), then polish (1)
                                                       (4)

A STEP FURTHER

You should first of all make sure you know the advice given in the chapter on Basic Reading under this heading.

❝Revise the endings of verbs❞

At Higher Level, it is also important to revise carefully the **endings of verbs,** the 'tense markers'. There is a vital difference in meaning between:

    j'aimerai (I will like . . .)

    j'aimerais (I would like . . .)

    j'aimais (I used to like or I was liking . . .)

The same is true of most verbs, and you can be certain that the examiners will be interested in discovering whether you can tell the difference between them. So **make sure of those tenses**!

A common problem at this level is failure of students to distinguish between the pluperfect and the perfect tenses. Yet the difference between 'j'étais allé' and 'je suis allé' could well give the clue to the order events happened in, for example. Be aware!

❝Check whether words are singular or plural❞

Another matter worth being extra sure about is knowing all the variations of French plurals, and making a point of looking to see **whether words are singular or plural**. This, too, will help the finer understanding of detail in texts.

As English and French are historically related to each other (1066 and all that . . .), there are many patterns of similarity which English speakers can exploit when reading French. Some of them are outlined in the Basic Reading chapter, but there are more. In particular, there are many clues to the meaning to be found in prefixes (which are added to the beginning of words) and suffixes (which are found at the ends of words).

Look at the examples below and add your own.

1 ⟩ PREFIXES	*French*	*English*	*Examples*
	dé-	dis-	décourager (to discourage) découvrir (to discover) déçu (disappointed) dégoûtant (disgusting) déguiser (to disguise) détruire (to destroy)
	dé(s)-	de-, un-	déformé (damaged) démodé (unfashionable) se déshabiller (to get undressed)
	éc-	sc-, squ-	école (school) Écosse (Scotland) échelle (musical scale; ladder) écran (screen) écraser (squash; run over)
	ép-	sp-	épeler (to spell) épice (spice) éponge (sponge) époux, épouse (spouse)
	ét-	st-	établissement (establishment) état (state) s'étonner (to be astonished) étranger (stranger) étudiant (student)
	im-, in-	un-, in-	impoli (impolite) inconnu (unknown person; stranger) incroyable (unbelievable)
	pré-	fore-, pre-	prédire (to predict) prénom (first name) prévoir (to foresee)
	re-	re-, again	recommencer (to begin again) redevenir (to become again) rentrer (to return) reprendre (to take back) retrouver (to meet; find again) revenir (to come back)
	sou-, sous-	sub-, under-	souterrain (underground) sous-marin (submarine) sous-sol (basement)

2 > SUFFIXES	*French*	*English*	*Examples*
	-aine	about	dixaine (about 10)
			douzaine (dozen)
			centaine (about 100)
	-é	-ed	enlevé (removed)
			fatigué (tired)
			situé (situated)
	-er, -ier	profession/ classification	boucher (butcher)
			patissier (pastry-cook; confectioner)
			vacancier (holidaymaker)
			voilier (sailing boat)
	-ier	tree	bananier (banana tree)
			cerisier (cherry tree)
			oranger (orange tree)
			pommier (apple tree)
	-eur	-er, -or	acteur (actor)
			chanteur (singer)
			directeur (director)
			mineur (miner)
	-eur	-ness	blancheur (whiteness)
			douceur (sweetness)
			hauteur (highness; height)
	-eux	-ous	curieux (curious)
			désastreux (disastrous)
			ingénieux (ingenious)
			merveilleux (marvellous)
			précieux (precious)
	-ir	-ish	abolir (abolish)
			finir (finish)
			punir (punish)
	-oire	-ory	gloire (glory)
			laboratoire (laboratory)
			réfectoire (refectory; canteen)
	-té	-ty	beauté (beauty)
			cité (housing estate/student hall of residence)
			difficulté (difficulty)
			facilité (facility)

Finally, it may be worth noting that where there is a circumflex in French, there is often an s in English. For example:

août	August
coûter	to cost
dégoûtant	disgusting
forêt	forest
hôtel	hotel (compare: hostel)
île	isle, island
intérêt	interest
pâte	pasta, paste
prêtre	priest
rôti	roast

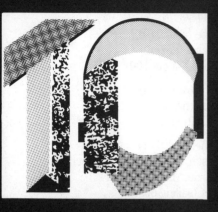

BASIC WRITING

EXAM GROUP REQUIREMENTS

MARK SCHEMES

INFORMAL LETTERS

FORMAL LETTERS

NORMAL PERFORMANCE

GETTING STARTED

Basic Writing is important because you cannot be awarded a grade C in GCSE unless you have done it. This means that many candidates would do well to look carefully at the contents of this chapter. There is a considerable variation amongst GCSE Examining Groups about what should be set for Basic Writing, and it pays to know what to expect! What doesn't vary much between Examining Groups is the way that they seek to reward 'getting the message across'. It's vitally important to do the tasks set in order to do well.

ESSENTIAL PRINCIPLES

1 > EXAM GROUP REQUIREMENTS

You cannot be awarded a grade C in GCSE French unless you have done the Basic Writing test, no matter how well you have done on the rest of your papers. But there is no need to panic, because the tasks have been selected to be reasonably straightforward, and well within the grasp of most candidates. Look at the table below to see what your Examining Group sets at this level.

> ❝You cannot get a grade C unless you do Basic Writing❞

Examining Group	LEAG	MEG	NEA	NISEC	SEG	WJEC
Time allowed in minutes	45	25	25	45	30	30
Lists of things	no	yes	no	yes	no	yes
Messages and notes	yes	yes	yes	yes	yes	yes
Postcards	yes	yes	yes	yes	yes	yes

Examining Group	LEAG	MEG	NEA	NISEC	SEG	WJEC
Completion of model letter	yes	no	no	no	no	no
Form-filling	yes	no	no	no	no	no
Diary entries	no	no	no	yes	no	yes
Reply to a stimulus in French	yes	yes	yes	yes	yes	yes
Letter with instructions in English	yes	no	yes	yes	yes	yes*
* Instructions optionally in Welsh						

LEAG

Length of paper: 45 minutes

There are two parts to the paper. Each one has two alternative questions to choose from. You have to do **two** questions.

Part 1 Alternative A

—Form-filling
—Completion of a model letter, filling in the blanks

One of these will be set each year.

Part 1 Alternative B

—Postcard in reply to one given in French
—Message

One of these will be set each year.

Part 2 Alternative A

—Informal letter in reply to a letter in French. Four items you have to mention out of six given. 60–70 words

Part 2 Alternative B

—Informal letter following instructions in English. Four items you have to mention out of six given. 60–70 words

MEG

Length of paper: 25 minutes

There are three questions, with no choice. The third question is worth half the marks. You have to do **all three** questions.

Question 1

—A list, e.g. for shopping, with ten items

Question 2

—Either a postcard to complete with five items you have to mention

or a message to write with five items you have to mention

Question 3

—Either a message to write with five items you have to mention

Or a postcard to complete with five items you have to mention

NEA

Length of paper: 25 minutes

Question 1

—A short message or postcard, possibly in reply to a similar item in French. Instructions about what to mention in English. Approximately 30 words

Question 2

—A letter either in reply to one given, or following instructions, or with a visual stimulus. Approximately 60 words

NISEC

Length of paper: 45 minutes

Question 1

—A short message, postcard, list, note, or diary entry

Question 2

—A reply to a letter in French. Seven tasks to complete. 50–60 words

SEG (General Level)

Length of paper: 30 minutes

Question 1

—A message in response to an English or French stimulus. Three tasks to complete. Approximately 20 words

Question 2

—Formal or informal letter. Seven tasks to complete. 70–100 words

WJEC

Length of paper: 30 minutes

Question 1

—One or more of: messages, postcards, diary entries, lists. Four tasks.

Question 2

—Formal or informal letter in response to English/Welsh stimulus, or French. Six tasks. 50–70 words

2 ▷ MARK SCHEMES

❝ Do *exactly* what the question asks you to ❞

The mark schemes which the Examining Groups will use are also designed to reward 'communication', that is 'getting the message across', much more than pure accuracy. So long as you can write French well enough to be understood by a 'sympathetic native speaker of French', you should be OK.

However, because the mark schemes reward communication, they also depend on you doing *exactly* what the question tells you to do. For example, the question may tell you to give the time and date of your arrival. Most of the marks will be for 'getting this message across'. Obviously, if you fail to mention the date of your arrival, you cannot get the marks allocated to that question. To put it another way: **if the question gives you tasks to complete, then complete them!**

❝ Get the *form* of the letter right ❞

In addition, for those boards (the majority) which set a letter for Basic Writing, there are marks to be gained for the **form** of the letter. So be sure you have put in, correctly, the address, the date, the salutation (Cher Monsieur, Chère Marie, etc.) and the closing formula (Amitiés, A bientôt, or, for a business letter, Je vous prie d'agréer, Monsieur, l'expression de mes sentiments distingués). Here is an opportunity to be sure of gaining marks in advance. Don't miss it.

3 ▷ INFORMAL LETTERS

GENERAL

Informal letters (to a friend) are usually written in the 'tu' form.

YOUR ADDRESS

This is usually written in full on the back of the envelope after Exp. (= Expéditeur). Inside, on the letter, you write the name of the town you are writing from, with the date, e.g. Scunthorpe, le 12 juin 1988.

OPENINGS

Cher Jean,
Chère Jeanne,
Chers amis,

DRAWING TO A CLOSE

Maintenant, je dois faire mes devoirs.
(Now I have to do my homework.)
Maintenant, je dois sortir avec ma mère.
(Now I have to go out with my mother.)
Maintenant je dois me coucher.
(Now it's time to go to bed.)
En attendant de tes nouvelles . . .
(Looking forward to hearing from you . . .)
Ecris-moi bientôt!
(Write soon!)
A bientôt!
(See you soon!)

SIGNING OFF

These are listed with increasing degrees of affection:

—Amicalement . . .
—Amitiés . . .
—Bien cordialement . . .
—Ton ami(e) . . .
—Ton/ta correspondant(e) . . .
—Grosses bises . . .

4 ▷ FORMAL LETTERS

GENERAL

Formal letters (to a business or an organization) are usually written in the 'vous' form.

YOUR ADDRESS

This is usually written in full on the back of the envelope after Exp (= Expéditeur). Inside, on the letter, you write your own name and address on the **top left-hand** corner of the page.

THE DATE

This is written in the top right-hand corner, together with the town you are writing from, e.g. Scunthorpe, le 12 juin 1988.

THE ADDRESS YOU ARE WRITING TO

This is written under the date in the top **right-hand corner** of the page.

OPENINGS

Monsieur,	(Dear Sir)
Madame,	(Dear Madam)
Messieurs,	(Dear Sirs)

SIGNING OFF

Business letters normally end with one of two 'formules', both meaning 'Yours sincerely' or 'Yours faithfully':

—Veuillez agréer, Monsieur, l'expression de mes sentiments distingués.

—Je vous prie d'agréer, Monsieur, l'expression de mes sentiments distingués.

> **Practise reading the handwriting of French native speakers**

If your Examining Group sets a letter or note in French for you to reply to, this may well be written in a French handwriting style. Use every opportunity to practise reading the handwriting of French native speakers. Your text-book should have examples in it, and you could also ask friends with pen-friends in France to show you their letters so that you get the hang of reading it.

NORMAL PERFORMANCE

The Basic Writing test is designed so that it is possible for candidates who obtain, overall, a maximum grade of D, to gain full marks in it. That should be reassuring. We have seen that getting the message across is the main source of marks and that absolute accuracy is of less interest to the examiners at this level, although what you write must, of course, be comprehensible.

STUDENT'S ANSWERS – EXAMINER'S COMMENTS

Let us now look at examples of the sort of question that you might find.

LIST OF THINGS

QUESTION

You and your French friend are arranging a picnic for some friends. Make a list in French of ten things for your French friend to buy. You could include items for making sandwiches, drinks, cakes, fruit and anything else you think suitable.

STUDENT'S ANSWER WITH EXAMINER'S COMMENTS

pain	OK
jamebon	Recognizable as ham – OK
chateau	Attempted for 'gâteau' but not good enough for credit
oranges	OK despite being identical to English

butter	No credit given for English here
chaises	Not likely to be bought for a picnic – no credit
eua gassy	Fizzy water? Might get some credit from the kind-hearted!
pommes	Ok

The candidate has only answered eight of the ten tasks, has one answer which was dubious, and two which were wrong. The mark would be about 5 out of 10.

Moral: answer the question!

2 ▷ MESSAGES/NOTES

QUESTION

Imagine that a French friend is coming to visit you by car. You write a short note for her, in French, to help her find where you live.

Using the map shown below to help you, tell her:

1 That you live at 34 Hall Street.
2 How to get there (Assume she is at the 30 mph sign shown on the map).
3 Where exactly she can park her car.   *(9)*
                                                                                         (SEG)

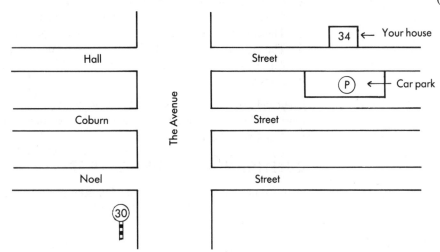

STUDENT'S ANSWER WITH EXAMINER'S COMMENTS

J'habite 34 Hall street.   Fine. 2 marks.

Prendre la 3e rue.   OK as far as it goes. But which way to turn? 1 out of 2.

Parking en face.   Simple and effective – 2 marks.

A good answer to a straightforward question, marred only by missing out a simple piece of information. 5 out of 6.

3 ▷ POSTCARDS

QUESTION WITH INSTRUCTIONS IN ENGLISH

On the blank postcard send a message of between 25 and 30 words to your friend. Mention the following five points:

—the weather
—the place you are staying at
—the food
—**two** things you have done

Now go back and check your work.

STUDENT'S ANSWER WITH EXAMINER'S COMMENTS

> Salut !
> Il fait isi. (1) Nous sommes
> au camping Beau Rivage. (2)
> Je mange des cockles. (3) C'est
> très bien. (4) Nous allons à
> la plage toutes (5) les jours. (6)
>
>   Mary

1 Spelling of 'ici' doesn't obstruct comprehension – OK at Basic Level.
2 Conveys point, and the lack of a capital letter on 'nous' is of no importance.
3 'Cockles' means absolutely nothing to a French person – no mark.
4 The combination of 'Je mange' and 'très bien' redeems (3) enough to award 1 out of 2.
5 The incorrect agreement of 'toutes' doesn't obstruct comprehension.
6 The candidate hasn't mentioned a second activity she has done, and throws away marks.

The candidate has only answered four of the five points, but did them reasonably well. The mark would be 7 out of 10. Once again, failing to answer the question fully reduces the final mark quite drastically.

QUESTION WITH A STIMULUS IN FRENCH

Your French friend is on holiday and has sent you this postcard.

> COULEURS ET LUMIÈRE DE FRANCE
> ANGERS (Maine-et-Loire)
> 115, La Cathédrale.
>
> Angers, le 3 Août.
> Arrivés ici à neuf heures.
> Il fait très chaud dans le
> Val-de-Loire. Angers est
> une grande ville située
> sur la Loire. D'ici on
> peut visiter les grands châ-
> teaux. Ce soir on va faire une
> promenade en vélo à la cam-
> pagne, au nord de la
> ville.   Claude
>
>   Mlle Gillian Evans
>   19 St Alban's Road
>   RIPON
>   North Yorkshire
>   ANGLETERRE

When you go on holiday to Brighton, you write a similar postcard, in **French**, telling your French friend that:

— you arrived at midday by coach
— it is raining in Brighton
— Brighton is on the coast in the South of England
— after dinner, you are going to a disco with a friend

You should write about 30 words on the postcard below. Try to avoid copying too much from the postcard above.

(NEA 16+ 1987)

STUDENT'S ANSWER WITH EXAMINER'S COMMENTS

Salut Claud! (1)

Je arrive midi by car. (2)

Il pleut à Brighton. (3)

Brighton est au sud d'Angleterre. (4)

Après dinner (5), je vais (6) discothèque

avec Martin

Angela.

1 Misspelling 'Claude' doesn't affect the mark. Nor does it give a good impression! Copy carefully.
2 Unclear whether Angela has already arrived or will arrive. 1 mark only out of 2. 'By' means nothing to a French person.
3 OK.
4 Slight error (should be 'de l'Angleterre'). But, more seriously, the coast hasn't been mentioned. 1 mark out of 2.
5 'Dinner' should be 'dîner' – but comprehensible, so no penalty.
6 'A la' has been left out, but probably doesn't prevent comprehension.

This attempt is worth 6 out of 8. Once again, missing things out has reduced the candidate's mark.

4 〉 FORM-FILLING   QUESTION

You have contacted an agency in France which organizes pen-friendships. They have sent you the following form to fill in:

Nom	Prénom(s) ....
Age .... ans	
Famille	

....

....

....

Nom du collège   ....

Matières préférées 1 ....

         2 ....

         3 ....

J'apprends le français depuis ....

Sports préférés   1 ....

         2 ....

Autres intérêts   1 ....

         2 ....

STUDENT'S ANSWER WITH EXAMINER'S COMMENTS

Nom .... John .... Prénom(s) ...... Smith ....

Age .... 16 .... ans

Famille ..... mère, ... père, ...frère...

....

....

Nom du collège ...... Banbury Technical College ...(2).

Matières préférées 1 .... English .... (3)

2 .... Maths .... (4)

3 .... Francais .... (5)

J'apprends le français depuis .... 5 ans .... (6)

Sports préférés 1 .... football ....

2 .... tennis ....

Autres intérêts 1 .... computers ...... (7)

2 .... (8)

1 'Nom' means surname! No marks.
2 'Collège' means secondary school. Unless you are a student at a Tech, beware!
3 No credit given for anything in English.
4 Maths – lucky there, I suspect – but GCSE examiners are kind-hearted!
5 Well copied. But why miss out the cedilla?
6 Well done.
7 If you didn't know the words 'l'informatique' or 'les ordinateurs', note them now. No credit given for anything written in English.
8 Why leave a blank? It earns no credit. Even if you do only have one interest in life, it will pay you to fib a little to be sure of having completed all the tasks set.

5 ▷ DIARY ENTRIES

QUESTION

Your pen-friend has asked you to enclose in your next letter a list of the things you would like to do on each day during your visit to his/her home. Start to prepare this list by writing out some of these activities in the spaces provided below.
(Activities for Monday have already been inserted.)

Dimanche	
Lundi	On va au collège
Mardi	
Mercredi	
Jeudi	
Vendredi	

(WJEC)

STUDENT'S ANSWER WITH EXAMINER'S COMMENTS

Dimanche	Se reposer (1)
Lundi	On va au collège (2)
Mardi	Sport – crown green bowling (3)
Mercredi	Visite à Londres (4)

1 OK.
2 OK, except for the fact that it is a copy of what is already on the paper, and therefore gets no marks.
3 'Sport' will gain 1 out of 2. 'Crown green bowling' means nothing to a French person without a lengthy explanation. It's a shame the candidate didn't write 'rugby'.
4 OK.

This fair attempt gains 5 out of 8.

QUESTION

Read the following entries in the pen-friends column of a teenage magazine; choose one and write a letter in French including the following details:

— your name
— your age
— where you live
— number in your family and their names and ages
— your interests

> J'ai 15 ans et je désire correspondre avec jeunes filles de 15 à 16 ans habitant Irlande du Nord.
> J'aime la musique et le cyclisme.
> Marie Legard, 13 chemin de Prés, 06770 Gattières.

> Jeune homme de 17 ans désire correspondre avec filles et garçons de tout âge et de tous pays.
> Réponse assurée. Intérêts: sport, cinéma.
> Alain Padonet, 33 rue des Frênes, 93100 Rosny.

> J'ai 16 ans et je désire correspondre avec des jeunes qui s'intéressent à la construction de modèles d'avions.
> Richard Cavaillé, 10 avenue du Maine, 33550 Largorian.

> Jeune fille de 16 ans désire correspondre avec des jeunes du même âge du monde entier. J'aime voyager et nager.
> Chantal Gaucher, 2 rue Echelle, 17000 La Rochelle.

Your letter should contain 50–60 words.

(NISEC)

STUDENT'S ANSWER WITH EXAMINER'S COMMENTS

Carlisle, le 23 juin (1)

Chère Chantal,

J'ai vu ton annonce dans un illustré.(2) Je m'appelle Brian Edgeware (3) et (4) j'habite à Carlisle, dans le nord de l'Angleterre.(5) Nous sommes cinq dans la famille. Il y a mon père Ian (45 ans), ma mère Joan (44 ans), mon frère Darren (13 ans) et ma soeur Teresa (11 ans). (6) J'aime la musique et le cyclisme et j'aime voyager et nager.(7)

Salut!

Brian (8)

There were seven tasks to complete: name, age, where you live, number in family, their names, their ages, and your interests.

In addition, many boards reward:

—date
—introduction of letter
—conclusion

1 Date correct.
2 Nice introduction.
3 Name given.
4 Age missed out.
5 Where he lives.
6 Number in family.
7 Hobbies mentioned. Candidate has very cunningly 'lifted' pieces from elsewhere on the question paper – and why not?
8 Almost exactly 60 words.

This student has managed all the tasks well, using very simple French. However, he has missed out his age, which is the only blot on an otherwise very good attempt. Answering the question carefully pays, no matter how good your French is!

7 ⟩ LETTER WITH INSTRUCTIONS IN ENGLISH

QUESTION

Write a letter of 75–85 words, in French, to a hotel, including the following points:

—Give the dates when you want to stay there.
—Say you want two double rooms.
—Say you want a shower.
—Ask the price of the room.
—Ask if the hotel is near the sea.
—Ask if the hotel has a restaurant.
—Ask if there is a garage.

Remember to start, date and end the letter correctly.

Below is a typical student's answer to the letter above. Even if your Examining Group does not set this particular sort of question at Basic level, the principles used in marking it still apply. You will note that the candidate who wrote this answer has not written it in correct French throughout. However, in most cases he has 'got the message across'.

STUDENT'S ANSWER WITH EXAMINER'S COMMENTS

> Birmingham, le cinq juin 1988
>
> Cher Monsieur,
>
> Je voudrais rester dans votre hotel avec mon famille. <u>Nous arriver</u> le 10 Juillet et partons le 12 Juillet 1988. Deux chambres à deux personnes, s'il vous plaît. Quel est le prix de la chambre?
> Est l'hôtel à côté de la mer? Il y a un restaurant dans votre ville? Vous avez un garage?
> Salut!
> John Smythe

This is quite a good attempt at the letter. The candidate gains the maximum 2 marks for the following items:

—Letter greeting
—Dates of stay (despite some errors in the French)
—Double rooms
—Price of room
—Enquiry if near sea
—Asking if there is a garage   (7 × 2 = 14 marks)

However, the candidate gets no marks for

—asking if there is a shower (he doesn't mention it at all);

and he only gains 1 of the possible 2 marks for

—asking about a restaurant (mentions restaurant in town and not in the hotel – some doubt as to whether he has 'got the message across')
—the correctness of the end of the letter – 'Salut' is probably OK in a letter to someone you know well, but it is not suitable for a business letter to a hotel.

So the total mark for that attempt was 14 + 2 = 16 out of 20.

Although not all Examining Groups set this sort of exercise, the principle is the same for all questions at Basic level: **make sure you do the task clearly**. Had the candidate missed out, say, two more of the points he had been asked to put in, he could seriously have affected his grade.

8 COMPLETION OF MODEL LETTER

QUESTION

The following letter contains several numbered spaces. Using the list below the letter, write out in French the words which would apply to your own circumstances.

> Birmingham, le .... (1)
>
> Monsieur,
>
> Je voudrais passer .... (2) dans votre auberge de jeunesse.
>
> Pouvez-vous me réserver (3) .... pour les nuits .... (4) .... jusqu'à .... (5) Nous voulons prendre .... (6) à l'auberge de jeunesse. Je voudrais savoir s'il est possible de .... (7) à l'auberge, et si l'auberge se trouve .... (8) .... Est-ce qu'il y a .... (9) ou .... (10) près de l'auberge?
>
> Je vous prie d'agréer, Monsieur, l'assurance de mes sentiments distingués.
>
> .... (Signature)

1   Today's date.
2   How long?
3   Number of beds.
4   Date of arrival.
5   Last night of stay.

6   Name of meal.
7   Some extra facility.
8   Location?
9   Some facility.
10 Some facility.

STUDENT'S ANSWER WITH EXAMINER'S COMMENTS

> Birmingham, le ..*16 juin*. (1)
>
> Monsieur,
>
> Je voudrais passer *deux nuits* (2) dans votre auberge de jeunesse.
>
> Pouvez-vous me réserver (3) *deux lits* pour les nuits *du août* (4) *au 15 août*
> jusqu'à *au 13 août* (5) Nous voulons prendre *le petit déjeuner* (6) à l'auberge de jeunesse. Je
> voudrais savoir s'il est possible de *mourir* (7) à l'auberge, et si l'auberge se trouve
> *au centre de la ville*. Est-ce qu'il y a *un parc* (9) ou *au 15 août* (10) près de
> l'auberge?
>
> Je vous prie d'agréer, Monsieur, l'assurance de mes sentiments distingués.
>
> .... (Signature)

1   Figures acceptable. But make sure it is **today's** date.
4   Use your common sense. No one would stay in the same youth hostel for 363 days – so no credit.
7   Again, not a remotely likely question – so no credit. (It's not usual to ask if it is possible to die in a youth hostel!)
    Why the blank (signature)? No credit.

This attempt is worth 7 out of 10.

PRACTICE QUESTIONS

1 ▶ LIST OF THINGS

You have visited a Swiss hotel, and have left various items behind. Make a list in French of the items to help jog your memory as you make a phone call to the hotel asking them to send them on.

2 ▷ MESSAGES/ NOTES

Your French exchange partner is staying with you and wants to travel alone to the swimming baths by bus. Write directions in French on the notepad below. Give:

—the number of the bus
—where to catch it
—the cost
—the length of the journey
—how to get from the bus-stop to the swimming baths

3 ▷ POSTCARDS

WITH INSTRUCTIONS IN ENGLISH

Write a postcard in French to your pen-friend.
—say you are staying in Blackpool
—describe the weather
—say you go swimming every day
—give **two** things you have done on holiday

WITH A STIMULUS IN FRENCH

The following postcard has been re-addressed to you in Devon where you are on holiday. It is from your pen-friend who is on holiday on the Cote D'Azur.

LUMIERE ET BEAUTE DE LA COTE D'AZUR
LA CIOTAT
Une partie du port et perspective
sur la Mairie

La Côte d'Azur est formidable
Le Soleil brille continuellement
— Je baigne tous les jours.
C'est un hôtel trois étoiles, avec
une disco tous les soirs. Ma
soeur m'embête, comme
toujours. Dis bonjour à
tes parents.   Amitiés
                        Jean

Write a similar postcard **in French** to your pen-friend, from Torquay. Say that it is raining continuously but you go swimming every day in the swimming pool on the camp-site. Your brother is ill. Ask to be remembered to your pen-friend's sister.

(LEAG)

4 ▷ FORM-FILLING

Write your answer in French in the spaces provided.

You have sent your name and address to an agency in France which was advertising for English teenagers to write to French children of the same age, and they have sent you the following form to fill in. Answer each point **in French** giving details of your family, school subjects and interests as requested.

Nom .... Prénom ....
Age .... ans .... mois
Famille ....
....
....
Etudes
Matières étudiées à l'école ....
....
Langues parlées ....
Intérêts
Sports préférés ....
Autres intérêts ....
....
Date ....

(LEAG)

5 ▷ DIARY ENTRIES

Avril	**Avril**
Dimanche 3	Dimanche 10
Lun. 4	Lun. 11
Mar. 5	Mar. 12
Mer. 6	Mer. 13
Jeu. 7	Jeu. 14
Ven. 8	Ven. 15
Sam. 9	Sam. 16

You are to entertain a French boy or girl who is coming to spend a fortnight in England. You plan a diary showing the places you will visit and the things you will do. When the diary is complete you will send it to the French person to give an idea of what you have planned.

Obviously you will not fill in every moment of the time but you want to make the visit seem attractive.

Enter **five** different activities and the places you will visit in the diary opposite, spaced reasonably in the diary.

Remember that your diary entries must be in French.

(MEG)

6 ▷ **REPLY TO A STIMULUS IN FRENCH**

Write a reply to the following letter from your French pen-friend Robert. Try to answer all the questions. Your letter should contain 50–60 words.

Meaux
Le 10 mars

Salut

Tu me dis dans ta lettre que tu dois arriver à Paris le lundi 10 avril. C'est chouette! A quel aéroport arrives-tu? Orly ou Charles de Gaulle?

Sais tu à quelle heure tu arrives?

Tu vas facilement me reconnaître car je vais porter un pull orange et un pantalon orange! Et toi, qu'est-ce que tu vas porter?

Aimes-tu le camping? Tu préfères la montagne ou la mer?

Qu'est-ce que tu aimes manger? As-tu un plat préféré? Ma mère fait très bien la cuisine. Et toi, tu aimes faire la cuisine?

Réponds-moi vite et donne-moi ton numéro de telephone.

Amicalement
Robert

(NISEC)

7 ▷ **LETTER WITH INSTRUCTION IN ENGLISH**

Write a letter of 70–80 words, in French, to a hotel.

—Give the dates when you want to stay at the hotel (2 tasks).
—Say what rooms you want.
—Say whether you want a bathroom or a shower.
—Ask if the hotel is near the cathedral.
—Ask what items are included in the price.
—Ask what there is to do in the town.

Remember to start, date and end the letter correctly.

8 > COMPLETION OF MODEL LETTER

The following letter contains several numbered spaces. Using the list **below** the letter write out in French the words which would apply to your own circumstances.

Londres, _____(1)_____

Monsieur,

    Je voudrais passer _____(2)_____ avec _____(3)_____ dans votre hôtel.

    Pouvez-vous me réserver une chambre _____(4)_____ avec douche et une chambre à deux personnes avec _____(5)_____, pour les nuits _____(6)_____ . Est-ce qu'il y a _____(7)_____ dans toutes les chambres? Nous préférons être au _____(8)_____

    Je voudrais **savoir** aussi s'il est possible de _____(9)_____ à l'hôtel, et si l'hôtel se trouve _____(10)_____

    Je vous prie d'agréer, Monsieur, mes sentiments distingués.

_____ (Signature)

ANSWERS

1 (Today's date) _____

2 (How long?) _____

3 (Who is accompanying you?)_____

4 (What kind of room?) _____

5 (Washing facilities?) _____

6 (Dates?) _____

7 (Some extra facility) _____

8 (Which floor?) _____

9 (Eating arrangements) _____

10 (Situation?) _____

(LEAG)

A STEP FURTHER

The most obvious step is to make sure that you know those things for which there are definitely marks and which will almost certainly come up. These include beginnings and ends of letters, commands, such things as dates and times of arrival and departure, and activities you or a pen-friend would like to do during an exchange visit. All of these should be found readily in most text-books.

    The other activity which cannot be stressed enough is to make sure that, on the day of the examination, you **read the question** and **do what you are told to do.**

    And finally a word for those candidates who are going on to do Higher Writing papers. On the day you will probably find the Basic Writing straightforward. In some Examining Groups there will be a global time allocation for Basic and Higher Writing. Once you have finished the Basic Writing, you would be well advised to get on with the Higher Writing, as that does lay much more stress on accuracy. On the other hand, in calculating your final grade, there is just as much stress laid on the Basic result as on the Higher one. So don't skimp it.

GETTING STARTED

The Higher Writing test is important because you cannot be awarded grade A or B unless you have done it (Part 1 and Part 2 in MEG). The Examining Groups set a variety of exercises in Higher Writing, but the principles they use to mark them are the same. They look for

— 'getting the message across'
— the accuracy of your French
— the variety of expression in your French.

Higher Writing is not intended to be easy. However, if you know what you are supposed to be doing, and what the Examiners are looking for, you can avoid throwing marks away.

AIMS OF HIGHER
WRITING

EXAM GROUP
REQUIREMENTS

WORD COUNTS

MARK SCHEMES

INFORMAL AND FORMAL
LETTERS

PHRASES TO IMPROVE
ESSAYS

NORMAL PERFORMANCE

ESSENTIAL PRINCIPLES

You cannot get a grade A or B unless you do *Higher* Writing

The Higher Writing test is designed to suit the more able candidates, but nothing is lost by attempting it if you think you **might** reach the standard. Take your teacher's advice.

Examining Group	LEAG	MEG	NEA	NISEC	SEG‡	WJEC
Time allowed in minutes	60	65	50	50	60	70
Number of words per question	100	Q1:100 Q2:150	100	200	100	100–120
Formal letter		Q1*				Q1*
Informal letter		Q1*				Q1*
Picture composition	Q1*		Q2*	Q1*	Q2*	Q2
Narrative report	Q2*	Q2*	Q2*			
Expand French original					Q2*	
Authentic documents + tasks	Q3*				Q1	
Reply to letter in French			Q1	Q1*		

* Choice of questions. In all Examining Groups except NISEC you have to do two questions
‡ Extended Level

The requirements differ in the various Examining Groups, although most of them require you to do two questions of about 100–120 words each. Check the list below for the exact requirements of your exam, and for the length of time you will have. Some Examining Groups allow a global time allocation for Basic and Higher; if that is so for your exam, don't waste too much time on the Basic at the expense of the Higher. It may be that the Examining Groups have assumed candidates for the Higher Writing will complete the Basic more quickly than those who are only doing Basic, and have not given a very generous time allocation to the Higher paper.

You will notice that you usually have some *choice* of which questions to answer. Don't spend too long choosing. Make your decision and stick to it. It will usually be possible to know in advance what you are best at, and you could, for example, swot up the details of formal or informal letters before the exam with a view to doing one of them. Plan your strategy.

Here are the requirements of the various Examining Groups listed in detail.

LEAG

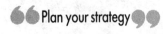

Plan your strategy

Length of paper: 60 minutes (global time allocation with Basic of 1¾ hours)
Number of questions: you have to do any two out of three questions set
Number of words per question: 100
Types of question: (a) Expansion of notes in the foreign language, with visuals and instructions in English
(b) Narrative or report with instructions in English, possibly with visuals such as maps, charts or diagrams
(c) Composition based on a series of pictures

MEG

Length of paper: Higher Part 1 – 30 minutes
Higher Part 2 – 35 minutes
(Global time allocation with Basic of 90 minutes)
Number of questions: Higher Part 1 – one out of the two set
Higher Part 2 – one out of the two set
Number of words per question: Higher Part 1 – 100 words
Higher Part 2 – 150 words
Types of question: Higher Part 1
—Either formal letter with instructions in English
—or informal letter with instructions in English
—or replying to formal or informal letter in French

Higher Part 2
—Either narrative/descriptive/personal experience
—or report of an event or incident for police, school magazine, etc.

NEA

Length of paper: 50 minutes (Global time allocation with Basic of 65 minutes)
Number of questions: two – no choice
Number of words per question: 100
Types of question: Question 1
—Letter in response to a letter in French with some instructions in English
Question 2
—Account with instructions in English and/or visual stimulus

NISEC

Length of paper: 50 minutes
Number of questions: one – choice of two
Number of words per question: 200
Types of question: Either answer to a letter in French
or composition with instructions in English
or composition based on a series of pictures
or composition based on a written stimulus in French

SEG

Length of paper: 60 minutes
Number of questions: two
—Question 1 has a choice of two options
—Question 2 has no choice
Number of words per question: 100
Types of question: Question 1
—Either composition based on a series of pictures
—or account with instructions in English or French, possibly based on a newspaper cutting
Question 2
—Task based on several documents in French with instructions in English

WJEC

Length of paper: 70 minutes
Number of questions: two
—Question 1 may have a choice of two options
—Question 2 has no choice
Number of words per question: 100–120
Types of question: Question 1
—Formal or informal letter with instructions in English or Welsh
Question 2
—Composition with written or visual instructions

3 WORD COUNTS

The Examining Groups are very specific about the number of words they want you to write. It is certainly foolish to write less than they require. But there is nothing to be gained from writing more than is needed. You would be better employed polishing the work that falls within the limits.

If you *have* written too much, it is far better to cut one or two complete sentences than to go through removing the adjectives and adverbs from what you have written. Under some of the mark schemes, adjectives and adverbs are very highly rewarded.

For word counts, the Examining Groups define a word as 'a group of letters with a space either side'. So 'Il y a' is three words, 'y a-t-il' is two. Abbreviations are deemed to be words, but figures (5) are not. In letters, the address and the date are not counted. Nor is your signature.

> **Physically count the number of words you have written**

It is actually worth taking the trouble to count the number of words you have written. If you write a marker every 20 or so, it's easier to make adjustments after additions and deletions from your work. Beware of just counting the words on one line and then multiplying by the number of lines. It's often inaccurate.

4 MARK SCHEMES

The mark schemes which the Examining Groups use have three main parts. There are marks for:

- **'Communication'** – getting the message across, as at Basic level
- **accuracy** of the French you have written – the more you get right, the higher the mark
- **the range and variety** of the expressions you use in your French

The 'communication' marks depend on you doing what the question tells you to, as at Basic level. So, once again, if you are given tasks to do, complete them!

> **Write answers on every *other* line**

The accuracy marks depend on you writing with as much of the French correct as possible. To help you to do this, you should write your answers on every other line. Then, if you need to change a word, you can write in what you think it should be, without making your script difficult to read. It is much better to cross out a word completely and re-write it than to go over letters to correct them. The other tip worth bearing in mind is to *check systematically* for errors. You could check using the list below:

- **Prepositions**
- **Adjectives**: correct agreement? position before or after noun?
- **Verbs**: correct ending? choice of tense?
- **Accents**: in place? pointing the right way? unambiguous?
- **Nouns**: correct gender? spelling?

This can be remembered as a mnemonic – PAVAN.

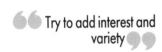

> **Try to add interest and variety**

The marks for 'range and variety of expression' reward just that. Examiners are looking for (correct and relevant) use of interesting adjectives, vocabulary and constructions. Apply the same guidelines to improving your French writing as you would when checking a draft for your English teacher. Remove repetition (especially of 'avoir' and 'être'), irrelevance and boring vocabulary, and add interest and variety. The sort of thing you might use is listed later in the chapter.

5 INFORMAL AND FORMAL LETTERS

INFORMAL LETTERS

Full details are given in Chapter 10 Basic Writing. But candidates for Higher Writing need to be doubly sure of being accurate.

FORMAL LETTERS

Basic details are given in Chapter 10 Basic Writing. However, the sorts of task you might find at Higher level will require some more complicated expressions. These are listed as follows:

ACKNOWLEDGING RECEIPT

J'accuse réception de votre lettre du 6 juin.
(I acknowledge receipt of your letter of 6th June.)
Je vous remercie de votre lettre du 6 juin.
(Thank you for your letter of 6th June.)

REQUESTING SOMETHING

Je vous prie de me réserver deux chambres.
(Please reserve two rooms for me.)
Veuillez m'envoyer un dépliant sur votre région.
(Please send me a brochure about your area.)
Je serais très reconnaissant(e) si vous pouviez me réserver . . .
(I would be very grateful if you could reserve me . . .)

ENCLOSING SOMETHING

Veuillez trouver ci-joint un eurochèque sur . . . F à titre d'arrhes.
(Please find enclosed a Eurocheque for . . . F as a deposit.)
Veuillez trouver ci-joint un mandat de réponse internationale.
(Please find attached an international reply coupon.)

APOLOGIZING

Je regrette de vous faire savoir que . . .
(I am sorry to have to tell you that . . .)
Veuillez accepter mes excuses.
(Please accept my apologies.)

6 ⟩ PHRASES TO IMPROVE ESSAYS

Writing with variety will be made much easier with a little work on learning suitable vocabulary to enrich your essays. The list given here is by no means exhaustive. Most text-books will contain a list of useful vocabulary and phrases for writing essays and stories, perhaps in a reference section at the back. Do take the opportunity to compare them with the ones given below. You will gain from doing so. Try them out in your homework before the examination so that you are sure how they 'really' work.

 Learn suitable vocabulary to enrich your essays

ENRICHING YOUR WRITING

à ce moment-là	at that moment
à sa grande surprise	to his/her astonishment
ainsi	thus
alors	then, so
après avoir fait cela	after having done that
après y être arrivé(e)(s)	after arriving there
cependant	but, however
c'est à dire	that is to say
complètement	completely
d'abord	first of all
déjà	already
de toute façon	anyway
donc	therefore, so
en effet	as a matter of fact
en fait	in fact
enfin	at last
ensuite	after that
en mangeant	while eating
finalement	finally
heùreusement	fortunately
malgré	despite
malheureusement	unfortunately
naturellement	naturally
parce que	because
peut-être	perhaps
puis	then

quand	when
quand même	all the same
simplement	simply
soudain	suddenly
tandis que	while, whilst
tout à coup,	suddenly
tout à fait	entirely, completely
tout de suite	immediately

There are many more. Add to this list as you meet them.

ALTERNATIVES FOR AVOIR AND ÊTRE

se trouver	to be situated
posséder	to possess

Examples:

—Manchester $\frac{\text{se trouve}}{\text{est}}$ dans le nord.

—Nous $\frac{\text{possédons}}{\text{avons}}$ une Peugot.

7 NORMAL PERFORMANCE

Normal performance in this GCSE test does not call for absolute accuracy. However, the more accurate, the better. Interest and variety are important too, and, once again, so is answering the question!

STUDENT'S ANSWERS – EXAMINER'S COMMENTS

1 FORMAL LETTER

QUESTION

Write a formal letter to a French hotel where you and your friend want to stay.

Give
—the dates of your stay
—the rooms you require

Then
—ask about facilities
—say why you have chosen the hotel
—enquire about excursions which are available.

You should write about 100 words in French.

STUDENT'S ANSWER WITH EXAMINER'S COMMENTS

> Leicester, le 13 avril 1989
>
> Monsier, (1)
>
> Je voudrais réserver deux chambres avec douche et WC dans votre hôtel du mardi 15 auot (2) au jeudi 17 auot (2). Je vous prie de confirmer la résenation, s'il te (3) plaît. Nous venons à votre hôtel parce que ma père (4) a visité votre hôtel en 1987 pendant trois semaines. (5)
>
> J'ai un frère Andrew qui a 15 ans. Il est tres aimable. (6) Il aime jouer au football. (6) Est-ce que vous aimez jouer au football? (6)
>
> Le votre sincèrement
>
> John McLaren
>
> P.S. Est-ce que vous avez des facilités? (8)

1 Spelt 'Monsieur' wrongly – a poor start.
2 Spelt 'août' wrongly – not a good sign.
3 S'il vous plaît – use 'vous' in formal letters throughout!
4 The gender of 'père' is not hard to learn – weak candidate here.
5 Good reason for choosing the hotel.
6 Irrelevant material, gains no credit.
7 This candidate has not prepared himself by learning a 'formule'.
8 PS a legitimate addition. But why not use some common sense by asking 'Est-ce que vous avez un restaurant/bar/parking?'

The candidate has not made a very good job of this.
Getting the message across: has fulfilled only three tasks of the five set. Has included a lot of irrelevant material more suited to an informal letter. The PS enquiry about 'facilities' doesn't really communicate anything. But the inclusion of a point you may have missed in a PS is allowable.
Accuracy: not good. Spells all sorts of things poorly, even elementary words like 'Monsieur' and 'août'. Mixes 'tu' and 'vous'.
Variety of expression: not good. Has little 'feel' for French, as shown by the attempt to translate 'Yours sincerely'.

2 INFORMAL LETTER

QUESTION

Write a letter in French, based on the outline below, of **not less than 100 and not more than 120 words** excluding your own address and the date.

You should not attempt to translate the instructions, but you are to include these points in your own words in your letter.

You have just received from your French pen-friend a birthday card and present. Write a letter in reply in which you cover the following points:

Thank your friend for the card and present. Say how pleased you were to receive them and say something about what you have done with the present or what use you propose to make of it.

Tell your friend how you spent your birthday. Give details of any party, special meal or other event with which you celebrated it. Say something about other presents which you received.

Tell your friend that you will soon be going on holiday. Say something about where you hope to go and what you hope to do in the course of this holiday.

(WJEC)

STUDENT'S ANSWER WITH EXAMINER'S COMMENTS

> Bangor, le 16 juin
>
> Chère Claudine
>
> Je te remercie de ta carte d'anniversaire. Merci aussi pour le cadeau. J'ai été (1) très heureuse de les recevoir. J'aime beaucoup les livres d'Astérix, et j'ai commencer (2) de (3) le lire.
>
> Pour mon anniversaire, je suis allé (4) à la discothèque avec mes amis. Nous avons danser (2) jusqu'à minuit. Mon copain George a donner (2) moi (5) un disque — c'est excellent. Mon père a donner moi 15 pounds. J'aime mon père.
>
> (cont)

> Nous allons à Bognor en vacances en juillet. Je vais nager (6), je vais rester au soleil (7), et je vais danser. Nous allons camper à Bognor.
>
>   Amitiés (8)
>   Helen

1 Imperfect needed here – j'étais.
2 Sounds right, but should be 'commencé', 'dansé', 'donné'.
3 Commencer **à**.
4 Agreement missing – girls need to remember the extra e.
5 Clumsy – 'm'a donné' is much better.
6 Good grasp of future time with 'aller' + infinitive.
7 Better would be: je vais me bronzer.
8 Suitable ending – good.

This is not a bad attempt. Helen has done everything she has been asked to do, and there is no irrelevant material. Her letter is the correct length. The letter does, however, show her weakness with the perfect tense and with one or two other language points.

3 > PICTURE COMPOSITION

QUESTION

Imagine that you are a member of the family in the incident shown in the pictures below, which takes place while you are on holiday in France. On your return home you write a letter to a French friend in which you tell him/her about this incident. Write in **not less than 100 and not more than 120 words** the account of this incident, which you include in the letter.

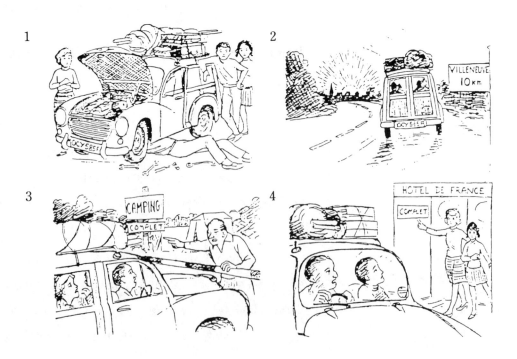

(WJEC)

STUDENT'S ANSWER WITH EXAMINER'S COMMENTS

Le deuxième jour de notre séjour en France (1) ne nous a pas amusés (2) Tu sais que mon père conduit une vieille (3) Morris. Vingt kilomètres avant Villeneuve nous sommes tombés en panne (4). Papa a mis trois heures pour réparer la voiture. C'était casse-pieds, je t'assure! (5) Nous sommes arrivés enfin à Villeneuve le soir, vers huit heures. Le camping était complet car (6) nous étions arrivés trop tard. Alors on a demandé à l'hôtel de France, mais malheureusement (7) il n'y avait plus de chambres libres. A ce moment-là maman commençait à devenir furieuse. Elle a annoncé son intention de vendre la Morris. A la station-service papa a raconté notre histoire au patron. (8) Il nous a offert un endroit pour camper dans son jardin. Enfin nous avions trouvé un endroit pour dormir. Tout est bien qui finit bien. (9)

1   Nice setting of the scene.
2   PDO agreement – good!
3   Irregular feminine form of the adjective and correct gender of car types.
4   Good idiom.
5   Nice and idiomatic.
6   Good conjunction.
7   Useful adverb.
8   Good knowledge of French terminology for owner.
9   Nice ending. Could be used elsewhere.

A very good attempt!

4 ▷ NARRATIVE/ REPORT

QUESTION

Write 100 words on the topic below.

You are writing a letter to your French pen-friend. Write a description of a trip your family made recently for inclusion in the letter. Do not write the whole letter. Say how you travelled, what you saw and did, what you ate, and give your opinion of the day out.
(100 words)

STUDENT'S ANSWER WITH EXAMINER'S COMMENTS

La semaine dernière mes parents ont décidé de faire une excursion. Nous nous sommes levés de bonne heure et après avoir pris notre petit déjeuner, nous sommes montés dans la voiture et nous nous sommes misen route pour la côte

Une fois arrivé, nous avons visité le musée, que, j'ai trouvé très intéressant, et puis, vers midi, nous nous sommes baignés à la mer.

A une heure nous avons déjeuné. Maman avait apporté un pique-nique magnifique du poulet rôti du jambon fumé, et de la salade.

L'après-midi, nous sommes restés au soleil sur la plage. C'était une journée vraiment agréable!

(101 Words)

This is as good an answer as could be expected from a GCSE candidate. I have ringed the features which enhance its quality – the variety of vocabulary, the use of adjectives, the varied sentence structure. It also has almost exactly 100 words.

5 ▷ EXPANDING FRENCH ORIGINAL

QUESTION

La voiture était toujours là mais les pneus avaient disparu

En retrouvant l'autre matin sa voiture qu'il avait garée dans le boulevard Saint Michel, M. Andrew Anderson, vacancier britannique, a eu la désagréable surprise de constater que les quatre pneus de sa voiture avaient tout simplement disparu!

Read this cutting from a French newspaper. Imagine you are one of Mr Anderson's children and were there when the incident happened. Later you write to a French friend, enclosing this newspaper cutting. Write the section of the letter in which you deal with this incident. **Do not write the whole letter.** Write about 100 words.

STUDENT'S ANSWER WITH EXAMINER'S COMMENTS

> En vacances en France, quelque chose de très choquant est arrivé. Papa avait garée (1) la voiture dans le boulevard Saint Michel. Quand il est aller (2) chercher la voiture le prochain matin (3) il avait (4) une surprise désagréable. Les quatres pneus avaient tout simplement disparu! (5) Quelqu'un les avait volé. (6) 'Merde!' a-t-il dit. (7) 'On ne peut pas rouler sans pneus!' Il a appelé la police. Après être arrivés (8) les policiers ont cherché les pneus, mais ils ne les ont (9) pas trouvés Papa n'était pas content. (10) Il était obligé d'acheter de nouveaux pneus!

1   PDO doesn't apply here, so no extra e on 'gare' – one of the dangers of 'lifting material' from the stimulus.
2   Careless use of incorrect past participle.
3   le prochain matin – should be 'le lendemain matin'.
4   Wrong tense – should be perfect as in the cutting.
5   A successful piece of 'lifting' from the stimulus.
6   PDO missing here – should be 'les avait volés'.
7   Good inversion after speech. Direct speech can sometimes improve a banal essay if it's not overdone.
8   Good use of stock 'essay phrase' – agreement right!
9   Correct position of object pronoun with negative – good.
10 Chance for linking two short sentences with 'parce que' missed.

This is a fair attempt at dealing with quite a difficult stimulus. Fairly intelligent use has been made of the French text, although this answer shows some of the pitfalls which can result from 'lifting' text. However, good candidates could probably be expected to improve on some of the grammatical niceties which have defeated this candidate.

6 AUTHENTIC DOCUMENTS AND TASK

QUESTION

A youth orchestra from Nantes is planning to visit the district in which you live and give some performances. You have been asked by the organizers to help by writing in French to confirm some of the arrangements.

Read the three documents on the next page as a starting point, and write a letter of approximately 100 words with the following content:

1   Acknowledge Mme Gravrand's letter and telegram.
2   Confirm that the group is now expected on Thursday 23rd June at 8 p.m.
3   Say you are enclosing a programme.
4   Give more details of the three activities printed in **bold** in the programme (document 3).
5   Wish them a pleasant journey.

DOCUMENT 1

> Nantes, le 28 mai 1989
>
> Siège social
> 4, Rue des Irlandais,
> 44000 Nantes
>
> Chers amis,
>
> Je suis heureuse de vous annoncer que les préparatifs pour la visite de nos jeunes musiciens en Angleterre sont maintenant complets.
>
> Nous espérons arriver (en car) le mercredi 22 juin vers cinq heures. Je vous ferai savoir l'heure précise de notre arrivée dans quelques jours.
>
> Nous attendons avec impatience d'être parmi vous, et de faire la connaissance des familles qui ont gentiment proposé de nous héberger.
>
> En attendant le vingt-deux, je vous remercie de tous les soins que vous avez pris pour assurer le succès de cette visite.
>
> Gervaise Gravrand (Mme)

DOCUMENT 2

> REGRETTONS CHANGEMENT DE PLAN.
> ORCHESTRE ARRIVE JEUDI 23 JUIN 20.00 H.
> GRAVRAND.

DOCUMENT 3

Visit of youth orchestra from Nantes – programme

Thursday	23 June	20.00 Arrival bus station Evening with families
Friday	24 June	Morning – Reception at town hall (11.00–12.00) Afternoon – Rehearsal, High School (14.00) Evening – Concert, Church Hall (19.30)
Saturday	25 June	Coach tour and picnic lunch (12.00–17.00) Evening – Youth club disco (20.30–23.45)
Sunday	26 June	Morning – Rehearsal, High School (10.00) Afternoon – Concert, Youth Centre (15.30)
Monday	27 June	Free for shopping, sightseeing etc. Evening – Farewell party for visitors and hosts (20.00)
Tuesday	28 June	Morning – Departure from bus station (10.15)

STUDENT'S ANSWER WITH EXAMINER'S COMMENTS

Chipping Norton, le 14 juin 1989

Chère Mme Gravrand,

J'accuse réception de votre lettre (1) du 28 mai et de votre télégramme du 8 juin.

Nous attendons votre groupe le jeudi 23 juin à 20.00 à la gare routière.

Veuillez trouver ci-joint (2) un programme pour votre visite. Il y a trois événements importants (3) (à part les concerts, naturellement).

La réception à la mairie commencera à 11.00. Les journalistes du 'Chipping Norton Advertiser' seront là avec un photographe. (4)

Le samedi après-midi il y a (5) une excursion en car à Oxford, avec pique-nique. J'espère qu'il fait (5) beau.

Le lundi est libre pour faire des achats. Votre groupe pourra aussi visiter (6) les attractions touristiques de Chipping Norton, par exemple le théâtre, le marché (7), et même le Macdonalds.

Je vous souhaite bon voyage!

Chris

1   Phrase learnt by heart – correctly used.
2   Phrase learnt by heart – correctly used.
3   Good link.
4   Sensible expansion of event.
5   Error – future time should have future tenses – il y aura, il fera beau.
6   Correct use of 'visiter' – to sightsee.
7   If your town is less picturesque than Chipping Norton (and most are, let's face it!) invent some attractions!

A good answer, in good French. Careful preparation of formal letters has paid off.

7 REPLY TO LETTER IN FRENCH

QUESTION

Write a letter in answer to the following letter from your French pen-friend. Your letter should contain about 200 words.

Salut

Le Tréport
Le 30 janvier.

Merci beaucoup pour ta carte qui m'a fait beaucoup rire. C'est toi qui l'a dessinée?

Je vais beaucoup mieux maintenant et on va enfin me retirer mon plâtre le 12 février (jour de mon anniversaire! C'est un beau cadeau n'est-ce pas?) – A propos, quelle est la date de ton anniversaire?

En trois mois, mon plâtre a changé de couleur car tous mes amis y ont mis leur signature.... On fait la même chose en Irlande du Nord?

J'ai passé une quinzaine de jours à l'hôpital, ce qui m'a donné l'occasion d'observer le travail des médecins et infirmières. Je crois que j'aimerais bien être médecin. Quand j'ai dit ça à ma mère, elle a éclaté de rire et m'a conseillé de travailler plus dur au collège.

Et toi, qu'est-ce que tu aimerais faire comme métier? C'est difficile de choisir n'est-ce pas?

As tu eu de bonnes notes à tes examens de fin de trimestre?

Quelle est ta matière préférée? Moi, j'aime beaucoup l'Anglais. J'aimerais cependant lire plus souvent des magazines anglais. Pourrais-tu m'en envoyer de temps en temps? Ça me ferait très plaisir!

Je viens de terminer "Maigret à New York" de Simenon. J'aime beaucoup ce genre de roman policier, et toi?

Qu'est-ce que tu as fait pendant les vacances de Noël? Ici, il a beaucoup neigé – C'était très chouette (pour ceux qui pouvaient marcher!)

Dis bonjour à tes parents de ma part
A bientôt,
Paul

(NISEC)

STUDENT'S ANSWER WITH EXAMINER'S COMMENTS

> Belfast, le 12 février
>
> Salut Paul (1)
>
> Merci de ta lettre – et bon anniversaire! (2) Moi, je suis né le 30 novembre. A propos, est-ce qu'on a retiré le plâtre de ta jambe aujourd'hui? (3) Et qu'est-ce que tu as reçu comme cadeaux d'anniversaire?
>
> L'année dernière ma sœur s'etait cassé une jambe et tout le monde ont (4) mis leur signature sur son plâtre. C'est une habitude universelle. (5)
>
> Comme métier, moi j'aimerais être professeur. Il y a beaucoup de vacances, et le travail finit à quatre heures. Moi aussi, je voudrais travailler au collège! (6) Si cela ne marche pas, je travaillerai comme facteur. J'aime les lettres.
>
> Dans les examens que je viens de passer, j'ai eu de bonnes notes en français et en anglais, mais mon professeur de biologie n'est pas content. Je ne suis pas fort en biologie. (7)
>
> Ma matière préférée est le français. Alors, comme toi, tu veux des magazines anglais, je te propose une échange mensuelle (8) de magazines. Veuillez trouver ci-joint 4. (9)
>
> Moi, je n'aime pas les romans policiers. Je préfère la science-fiction. Pendant les vacances de Noël (10) j'en ai lu six car chez nous aussi il a beaucoup neigé. Il a neigé pendant cinq jours – c'est très rare, ça, chez nous.
>
> Maintenant, je dois faire mes devoirs. (11)
> Amitiés
>
> William

1 Appropriate start – mirrors the question.
2 Shows good understanding of the situation – note the careful choice of the date of writing.
3 Responds well to stimulus – has made good use of language in the original in a specialized area.
4 Tout le monde is grammatically singular.
5 Nice comment – this candidate is in control!
6 A touch of humour to brighten the examiner's day – enfin!
7 Reasonable comment.
8 Good vocab – how many candidates know 'hebdomadaire' (weekly)?
9 Incorrect application of a phrase learned for business letters – should be 'Tu en trouveras quatre ci-joint'.
10 Nice combination of points asked.
11 'Closer' learned from the list in the Revise Guide – well done!

This candidate has managed very well with the rather long letter he had to read, and the number of questions that were asked. If you have to do this sort of question, make sure that you have found all the points the examiners might want you to respond to in the French original. Your teacher will know how many the Examining Group is looking for. (It's ten in the example given.) Make sure you have replied to them or made some comment about them in order to gain the 'getting the message across' marks. And remember that a command such as 'Décris-moi ta maison' requires a response from you just as much as a straight question such as 'Aimes-tu écouter des disques?'

PRACTICE QUESTIONS

1 FORMAL LETTER

You have been asked to help arrange the local music club's annual concert in your twin town. Write to the mayor of the town:
—Ask if you can come
—Give possible dates
—Say what accommodation you need
—Say how many there are in your party
—Ask about suitable excursions

Your letter should contain about 100 words.

2 INFORMAL LETTER

Your French friend is coming to visit you. Write a letter to him/her in French making arrangements (time, place etc.) about meeting him/her at the railway station and enquiring what (s)he would like to do during the visit, making your own suggestions.

Your letter should contain about 100 words.

(MEG)

3 PICTURE COMPOSITION

You have been on holiday at the camp-site in Brécey. Your French teacher at home has asked you to write an article on your stay for the school magazine. Base your essay on this brochure which you have brought home with you. Your essay should contain about 200 words.

BRECEY STATION VERTE DE VACANCES
COMMUNE DE 2000 HABITANTS

TOUS COMMERCES
MARCHE PITTORESQUE LE VENDREDI
TENNIS, PROMENADES

BRECEY

MANCHE – NORMANDIE

SOUS LES POMMIERS

A 1 KM DE BRECEY (ROUTE DE ST HILAIRE
LE CHATEAU DU LOGIS XVII s.

EXPOSITIONS PERMANENTES
TOUS LES JOURS DE 11^{30} A 11^{30}

INTERIEURS NORMANDS
PRESENTATION
EXCEPTIONNELLE
DE MILLIERS D'ETIQUETTES DE
CAMEMBERTS
MUSEE PERMANENT DE
PREHISTOIRE ETC...

DANS LE **CANTON DE BRECEY,**

VISITEZ:

LE VILLAGE FLEURI DE CUVES
LA BELLE EGLISE DE TIREPIED
LES BOIS DU PETIT ET DU
GRAND CELLAND
LE MAGNIFIQUE BOCAGE DE
ST GEORGES DE LIVOYE ETC...

A 800 M DU BOURG, ROUTE DE SOURDEVAL

**CAMPING MUNICIPAL ★★★
ET PISCINE DE PLEIN AIR**
RIVIERES A TRUITES ET A SAUMONS

(NISEC)

4 NARRATIVE/ REPORT

You are staying with your uncle and aunt in England. When they are out, you discover to your horror that the dog has disappeared.

Write an account of this episode, including how it ended, for inclusion in a letter to your French pen-friend.

(MEG)

5 ⟩ EXPANDING FRENCH ORIGINAL

> *Une cyclomotoriste blessée par une voiture dont le conducteur prend la fuite*
>
> Dans l'après-midi de dimanche, un accident a eu lieu à Gleizé, sur le C.D. 504 au lieu-dit «Les Bruyères».
> Une cyclomotoriste, Mlle Nathalie Chignier, demeurant à Villefranche, a été heurtée à l'arrière par un véhicule dont le conducteur a pris la fuite.
> Souffrant d'une fracture du bras gauche, Mlle Chignier a été conduite à l'hôpital d'Ouilly.

The above is a cutting from a French newspaper. Imagine that you were having a picnic by the roadside while on holiday in France when you witnessed the incident described in the newspaper, and it was your father who took Mademoiselle Chignier to hospital. Later you write to a French friend, enclosing the newspaper cutting, giving more details and saying how you felt and what happened afterwards. Write the section of the letter in which you deal with this incident. **Do not write the whole letter.** Write about 100 words.

(SEG)

6 ⟩ AUTHENTIC DOCUMENTS AND TASK

You are on a group visit to France. For a couple of days you stay at Beaubourg-sur-Loue. With the help of this page from the local guide book, you are asked by your teacher to write, in French, an account of your visit, saying where you stayed, the places you visited, the excursions and walks you enjoyed (100 words). Credit will be given for using a variety of words and expressions, but irrelevant material will earn no marks.

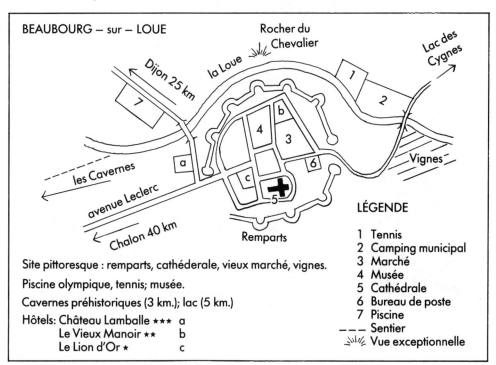

BEAUBOURG – sur – LOUE

Rocher du Chevalier
Lac des Cygnes
Dijon 25 km
la Loue
les Cavernes
avenue Leclerc
Chalon 40 km
Vignes
Remparts

Site pittoresque : remparts, cathédérale, vieux marché, vignes.

Piscine olympique, tennis; musée.

Cavernes préhistoriques (3 km.); lac (5 km.)

Hôtels: Château Lamballe ★★★ a
 Le Vieux Manoir ★★ b
 Le Lion d'Or ★ c

LÉGENDE

1 Tennis
2 Camping municipal
3 Marché
4 Musée
5 Cathédrale
6 Bureau de poste
7 Piscine
− − − Sentier
〰 Vue exceptionnelle

(LEAG)

7 ⟩ REPLY TO LETTER IN FRENCH

> ★ **URGENT** ★
>
> Recherche jeunes, 16 à 21, pour travail hôtelier, juin à septembre, 2 000F min: s'adresser Hôtel Provençal, St. Raphaël.

You have already seen the above advertisement in a French newspaper and have sent a letter to ask whether English students would be considered. You are delighted to have received the reply printed below from the hotel manager. Write, in French, a letter in reply to that of the hotel manager, using about 100 words.

Hôtel Provençal

197 rue Garonne
St. Raphaël
83700 Var

Tel. 95 01 52

le 22 mai 1987

Monsieur/Madame,

J'ai bien reçu votre letter du 15 mai où vous me demandez s'il vous serait possible de travailler dans notre hôtel. Je suis ravi de voir que vois avez trouvé notre petite annonce parue le 7 mai dans Le Figaro.

Avant de prendre une décision, je vous prie de bien vouloir me donner des renseignements sur vous-même. Je vous assure que nous cherchons des jeunes de n'importe quelle nationalité pour travailler dans notre hôtel. Quelle expérience avez-vous du travail? Et quand serez-vous libre pour travailler ici? Jll me faut absolument quelqu'un avant le 18 juin.

Je vous demande enfin de me dire si vous parlez bien le français.

Si vous voulez savoir autre chose sur ce travail, n'hésitez pas à me le demander dans votre prochaine letter.

En attendant le plaisir de vous lire, veuillez agréer, Monsieur/Madame, l'expression de mes sentiments le plus distingués.

F. Hervet
(Directeur)

(NEA 16+ 1987)

A STEP FURTHER

Look back over work which your teacher has corrected over the year. If you look at compositions and letters which you did early in the course you will now be able to see many ways of improving them.

You could also look at the list of vocabulary areas and put yourself in the examiner's shoes. What sort of question could you set about, say, schools? Quite likely it would be a description or comparison of an incident in class. There isn't really much further scope. So you could 'question-spot' to some extent and prepare topics in advance.

Another tip for improving your French is to write a diary and either get a convenient French-speaker to check it for you, or ask your teacher. It makes a concrete activity that you could do over a short holiday for say, half an hour a day.

Get yourself a pen-friend – and write often. You may well find that this improves your reading comprehension skills, too. If you are a little shy, you could either ask your pen-friend to write half and half English and French, or get them to correct at least some of your French in their next letter.

Finally, make absolutely sure from your teacher how many points you are expected to make in each written task. It really does pay to know what the Examining Groups are looking for and to give it to them! If your teacher is a little vague, ask him or her to show you the sample papers and mark schemes. Every school has had them!

VERB TABLE

Infinitive Present participle Imperative	Present	Perfect	Imperfect	Pluperfect	Future	Conditional	Past Historic
Regular verbs							
parler *to speak,* *talk* parlant	je parle tu parles il parle	j'ai parlé tu as parlé il a parlé	je parlais tu parlais il parlait	j'avais parlé tu avais parlé il avait parlé	je parlerai tu parleras il parlera	je parlerais tu parlerais il parlerait	je parlai tu parlas il parla
parle! parlons! parlez!	 nous parlons vous parlez ils parlent	 nous avons parlé vous avez parlé ils ont parlé	 nous parlions vous parliez ils parlaient	 nous avions parlé vous aviez parlé ils avaient parlé	 nous parlerons vous parlerez ils parleront	 nous parlerions vous parleriez ils parleraient	 nous parlâmes vous parlâtes ils parlèrent
finir *to finish* finissant	je finis tu finis il finit	j'ai fini tu as fini il a fini	je finissais tu finissais il finissait	j'avais fini tu avais fini il avait fini	je finirai tu finiras il finira	je finirais tu finirais il finirait	je finis tu finis il finit
finis! finissons! finissez!	 nous finissons vous finissez ils finissent	 nous avons fini vous avez fini ils ont fini	 nous finissions vous finissiez ils finissaient	 nous avions fini vous aviez fini ils avaient fini	 nous finirons vous finirez ils finiront	 nous finirions vous finiriez ils finiraient	 nous finîmes vous finîtes ils finirent
vendre *to sell* vendant	je vends tu vends il vend	j'ai vendu tu as vendu il a vendu	je vendais tu vendais il vendait	j'avais vendu tu avais vendu il avait vendu	je vendrai tu vendras il vendra	je vendrais tu vendrais il vendrait	je vendis tu vendis il vendit
vends! vendons! vendez!	 nous vendons vous vendez ils vendent	 nous avons vendu vous avez vendu ils ont vendu	 nous vendions vous vendiez ils vendaient	 nous avions vendu vous aviez vendu ils avaient vendu	 nous vendrons vous vendrez ils vendront	 nous vendrions vous vendriez ils vendraient	 nous vendîmes vous vendîtes ils vendirent
se laver *to wash* *oneself* se lavant	je me lave tu te laves il se lave	je me suis lavé(e) tu t'es lavé(e) il s'est lavé elle s'est lavée	je me lavais tu te lavais il se lavait	je m'étais lavé(e) tu t'étais lavé(e) il s'était lavé(e) elle s'était lavée	je me laverai tu te laveras il se lavera	je me laverais tu te laverais il se laverait	je me lavai tu te lava il se lava
lave-toi! lavons-nous! lavez-vous! 	 nous nous lavons vous vous lavez ils se lavent	 nous nous sommes lavé(e)s vous vous êtes lavé(e)(s) ils se sont lavés elles se sont lavées	 nous nous lavions vous vous laviez ils se lavaient	 nous nous étions lavé(e)s vous vous étiez lavé(e)(s) ils s'étaient lavés elles s'étaient lavées	 nous nous laverons vous vous laverez ils se laveront	 nous nous laverions vous vous laveriez ils se laveraient	 nous nous lavâmes vous vous lavâtes ils se lavèrent
Irregular verbs							
aller *to go* allant	je vais tu vas il va	je suis allé(e) tu es allé(e) il est allé elle est allée	j'allais tu allais il allait	j'étais allé(e) tu étais allé(e) il était allé elle était allée	j'irai tu iras il ira	j'irais tu irais il irait	j'allai tu allas il alla
va! allons! allez!	 nous allons vous allez ils vont	 nous sommes allé(e)s vous êtes allé(e)(s) ils sont allés elles sont allées	 nous allions vous alliez ils allaient	 nous étions allé(e)s vous étiez allé(e)(s) ils étaient allés elles étaient allées	 nous irons vous irez ils iront	 nour irions vous iriez ils iraient	 nous allâmes vous allâtes ils allèrent

apprendre *to learn* see **prendre**

s'asseoir *to sit down* s'asseyant	je m'assieds tu t'assieds il s'assied	je me suis assis(e) tu t'es assis(e) il s'est assis elle s'est assise	je m'asseyais tu t'asseyais il s'asseyait	je m'étais assis(e) tu t'étais assis(e) il s'étais assis elle s'était assise	je m'assiérai tu t'assiéras il s'assiéra	je m'assiérais tu t'assiérais il s'assiérait	je m'assis tu t'assis il s'assit
assieds-toi! asseyons- nous! asseyez- vous! 	 nous nous asseyons vous vous asseyez ils s'asseyent	 nous nous somes assis(e)s vous vous êtes assis(e)(es) ils se sont assis elles se sont assises	 nous nous asseyions vous vous asseyiez ils s'asseyaient	 nous nous étions assis(e)s vous vous étiez assis(e)(es) ils s'étaient assis elles s'étaient assises	 nous nous assiérons vous vous assiérez ils s'assiéront	 nous nous assiérions vous vous assiériez ils s'assiéraient	 nous nous assîmes vous vous assîtes ils s'assirent
avoir *to have* ayant	j'ai tu as il a	j'ai eu tu as eu il a eu	j'avais tu avais il avait	j'avais eu tu avais eu il avait eu	j'aurai tu auras il aura	j'aurais tu aurais il aurait	j'eus tu eus il eut
aie! ayons! ayez!	 nous avons vous avez ils ont	 nous avons eu vous avez eu ils ont eu	 nous avions vous aviez ils avaient	 nous avions eu vous aviez eu ils avaient eu	 nous aurons vous aurez ils auront	 nous aurions vous auriez ils auraient	 nous eûmes vous eûtes ils eurent
battre *to beat* battant	je batas tu bats il bat	j'ai battu tu as battu il a battu	je battais tu battais il battait	j'avais battu tu avais battu il avait battu	je battrai tu battras il battra	je battrais tu battrais il battrait	je battis tu battis il battit
bats! battons! battez!	 nous battons vous battez ils battent	 nous avons battu vous avez battu ils ont battu	 nous battions vous battiez ils battaient	 nous avions battu vous aviez battu ils avaient battu	 nous battrons vous battrez ils battront	 nous battrions vous battriez ils battraient	 nous battîmes vous battîtes ils battirent

Infinitive Present participle Imperative	Present	Perfect	Imperfect	Pluperfect	Future	Conditional	Past Historic
boire *to drink* buvant bois! buvons! buvez!	je bois tu bois il boit nous bovons vous buvez ils boivent	j'ai bu tu as bu il a bu nous avons bu vous avez bu ils ont bu	je buvais tu buvais il buvait nous buvions vous buviez ils buvaient	j'avais bu tu avais bu il avait bu nous avions bu vous aviez bu ils avaient bu	je boirai tu boiras il boira nous boirons vous boirez ils boiront	je boirais tu boirais il boirait nous boirions vous boiriez ils boiraient	je bus tu bus il but nous bûmes vous bûtes ils burent

comprendre *to understand* see **prendre**

conduire *to drive* conduiant conduis! conduisons! conduisez!	je conduis tu conduis il conduit nous conduisons vous conduisez ils conduisent	j'ai conduit tu as conduit il a conduit nous avons conduit vous avez conduit ils ont conduit	je conduisais tu conduisais il conduisait nous conduisions vous conduisiez ils conduisaient	j'avais conduit tu avais conduit il avait conduit nous avions conduit vous aviez conduit ils avaient condit	je conduirai tu conduiras il conduira nous conduirons vous conduirez ils conduiront	je conduirais tu conduirais il condduriait nous conduirions vous conduiriez ils conduiraient	je conduisis tu conduisis il conduisit nous conduisîmes vous conduisites ils conduisirent
connaître *to know* connaissant connais! connaissons! connaissez!	je connais tu connais il connait nous connaissons vous connaissez ils connaissent	j'ai connu tu as connu il a connu nous avons connu vous avez connu ils ont connu	je connaissais tu connaissais il connaissait nous connaissions vous connaissiez ils connaissient	j'avais connu tu avais connu il avait connu nous avions connu vous aviez connu ils avaient connu	je connaîtrai tu connaîtras il connaîtra nous connaîtrons vous connaîtrez ils connaîtront	je connaîtrais tu connaîtrais il connaîtrait nous connaîtrions vous connaîtriez ils connaîtraient	je connus tu connus il connut nous connûmes vous connûtes ils connurent

construire *to build* see **conduire**

contenir *to contain* see **tenir**

convenir *to suit* see **veniur**, but take avois in perfect and pluperfect tenses

coudre *to sew* cousant couds! cousons! cousez!	je couds tu couds il coud nous cousons vous cousez ils cousent	j'ai cousu tu as cousu il a consu nous avons cousu vous avez cousu ils ont cousu	je cousais tu cousais il cousait nous cousions vous cousiez ils cousaient	j'avais cousu tu avais cousu il avait cousu nous avions cousu vous aviez cousu ils avaient cousu	je coudrai tu coudras il coudra nous coudrons vous coudrez ils coudront	je coudrais tu coudrais il coudrait nous coundrions vous coudriez ils coudraient	je cousis tu cousis il cousit nous cousîmes vous cousîtes ils cousirent
courir *to run* courant cours! courons! courez!	je cours tu cours il court nous courons vous counrez ils courent	j'ai couru tu as couru il a couru nous avons couru vous avez couru ils ont couru	je courais tu courais il courait nous courions vous couriez ils couraient	j'avais couru tu avais couru il avait couru nous avions couru vous aviez couru ils avaient couru	je courrai tu courras il courra nous courrons vous courrez ils courront	je courrais tu courrais il courrait nous courrions vous courriez ils couraient	je courus tu courus il courut nous courûmes vous courûtes ils coururent
craindre *to fear* craignant crains! craignons! craigez!	je crains tu crains il craint nous craignons vous craignez ils craignent	j'ai craint tu as craint il a craint nous avons craint vous avez craint ils ont craint	je craignais tu craignais il craignait nous craignions vous craigniez ils craignaient	j'avais craint tu avais craint il avait craint nous avions craint vous aviez craint ils avaient craint	je craindrai tu craindras il craindra nous craindrons vous craindrez ils craindront	je craindrais tu craindrais il craindrait nous craindrions vous craindriez ils craindaient	je craignis tu craignis il craignit nous craignîmes vous craignîtes ils craignirent
croire *to believe* croyant crois! croyons! croyez!	je crois tu crois il croit nous croyons vous croyez ils croient	j'ai cru tu as cru il a cru nous avons cru vous avez cru ils ont cru	je croyais tu croyais il croyait nous croyions vous croyiez ils croyaient	j'avais cru tu avais cru il avait cru nous avions cru vous aviez cru ils avaient cru	je croirai tu croiras il criora nous croirons vous croirez ils croiront	je croirais tu croirais il croirait nous croirions vous croiriez ils croiraient	je crus tu crus il crut nous crûmes vous crûtes ils crurent

découvrir *to discover* see **ouvrir**

descendre *to go down* descendant descend! descendons! descendez!	je descends tu descends il descend nous descendons vous descendez ils descendent	je suis descendu(e) tu es descendu(e) il est descendu elle est descendue nous sommes descendu(e)s vous êtes descendu(e)(s) ils sont descendus elles sont decendues	je descendais tu descendais il descendait nous descendions vous descendiez ils descendaient	j'étais descendu(e) tu étais descendu(e) il était descendu elle était descendue nous étions descendu(e)s vous étiez descendu(e)(s) ils étaient descendus elles étaient descendues	je descendrai tu descentras il descendra nous descendrons vous descendrez ils descendront	je descendrais tu descendrais il descendrait nous descendrions vous descendriez ils descendraient	je descendis tu descendis il descendit nous descendîtes vous descendîtes ils descendirent

detruire *to destroy* see **conduire**

devenir *to become* see **venir**

Infinitive Present participle Imperative	Present	Perfect	Imperfect	Pluperfect	Future	Conditional	Past Historic
devoir *to have, to owe* devant dois! devons! devez!	je dois tu dois il doit nous devons vous devez ils doivent	j'ai dû tu as dû il a dû nous avons dû vous avez dû ils ont dû	je devais tu devais il devait nous devions vous deviez ils devaient	j'avais dû tu avais dû il avait dû nous avions dû vous aviez dû ils avaient dû	je devrai tu devras il devra nous devrons vous devrez ils devront	je devrais tu devrais il devrait nous devrions vous devriez ils devraient	je dus tu dus il dut nous dûmes vous dûtes ils durent
dire *to say* disant dis! disons! dites!	je dis tu dis il dit nous disons vous dites ils disent	j'ai dit tu as dit il a dit nous avons dit vous avez dit ils ont dit	je disais tu disais il disait nous disions vous disiez ils disaient	j'avais dit tu avais dit il avait dit nous avions dit vous aviez dit ils avaient dit	je dirai tu diras il dira nous dironsvous direz ils diront	je dirais tu dirais il dirait nous dirions vous diriez ils diraient	je dis tu dis il dit nous dîmes vous dîtes ils dirent

disparaître *to disappear* see **connaître**

dormir *to sleep* dormant dors! dormons! dormez!	je dors tu dors il dort nous dormons vous dormez ils dorment	j'ai dormi tu as dormi il a dormi nous avons dormi vous avez dormi ils ont dormi	je dormais tu dormais il dormait nous dormions vous dormiez ils dormaient	j'avais dormi tu avais dormi il avait dormi nous avions dormi vous aviez dormi ils avaient dormi	je dormirai tu dormiras il dormira nous dormirons vous dormirez ils dormiront	je dormirais tu dormirais il dormirait nous dormirions vous dormiriez ils dormiraient	je dormis tu dormis il dormit nous dormîmes vous dormîtes ils dormirent

s'endormir *to go to sleep* see **dormir**, but note reflexive verb taking être in perfect and pluperfect tenses.

écrire *to write* écrivant écris! écrivons! écrivez!	j'écris tu écris il écrit nous écrivons vous écrivez ils écrivent	j'ai écrit tu as écrit il a écrit nous avons écrit vous avez écrit ils ont écrit	j'écrivais tu écrivais il écrivait nous écrivions vous écriviez ils écrivaient	j'avais écrit tu avais écrit il avait écrit nous avions écrit vous aviez écrit ils avaient écrit	j'écrirai tu écriras il écrira nous écrirons vous écrirez ils écriront	j'écrirais tu écrirais il écrirait nous écririons vous écririez ils écriraient	j'écrivis tu écrivis il écrivit nous écrivîmes vous écrivîtes ils écrivirent
entendre *to hear* entendant entends! entendons! entendez!	j'entends tu entendsil entend nous entendons vous entendez ils entendent	j'ai entendu tu as entendu il a entendu nous avons entendu vous avez entendu ils ont entendu	j'entendais tu entendai il entendait nous entendions vous entendiez ils entendaient	j'avais entendu tu avais entendu il avait entendu nous avions entendu vous aviez entendu ils avaient entendu	j'entendrai tu entendras il entendra nous entendrons vous entendrez ils entendront	j'entendrais tu entendrais il entendrait nous entendrions vous entendriez ils entendraient	j'entendis tu entendis il entendit nous entendîmes vous entendîtes ils entendirent

entretenir *to maintain* see **tenir**

envoyer *to send* envoyant envoie! envoyons! envoyez!	j'envoie tu envoies il envoie nous envoyons vous envoyez ils envoient	j'ai envoyé tu as envoyĕ il a envoyé nous avons envoyé vous avez envoyé ils ont envoyé	j'envoyais tu envoyais il envoyait nous envoyions vous envoyiez ils envoyaient	j'avais envoyé tu avais envoyé il avait envoyé nous avions envoyé vous aviez envoyé ils avaient envoyé	j'enverrai tu enverras il enverra nous enverrons vous enverrez ils enverront	j'enverrais tu enverrais il enverrait nous enverrions vous enverriez ils enverraient	j'envoyai tu envoyas il envoya nous envoyâmes vous envoyâtes ils envoyèrent
éteindre *to put out, to switch off* éteignant éteins! éteignons! éteignez!	j'éteins tu éteins il éteint nous éteignons vous éteignez ils éteignent	j'ai éteint tu as éteint il a éteint nous avons éteint vous avez éteint ils ont éteint	j'éteignais tu éteignais il éteignait nous éteignions vous éteigniez ils éteignaient	j'avais éteint tu avais éteint il avait éteint nous avions éteint vous aviez éteint ils avaient éteint	j'éteindrai tu étendras il éteindra nous éteindrons vous éteindrez ils éteindront	j'éteindrais tu éteindrais il éteindrait nous éteindrions vous éteindriez ils éteindraient	j'éteignis tu éteignis il éteignit nous éteignîmes vous éteignîtes ils éteignirent
être *to be* étant sois! soyons! soyez!	je suis tu es il est nous sommes vous êtes ils sont	j'ai été tu as été il a été nous avaons été vous avez été ils ont été	j'étais tu étais il était nous étions vous étiez ils étaient	j'avais été tu avais été il avait été nous avions été vous aviez été ils avaient été	je serai tu seras il sera nous serons vous serez ils seront	je serais tu serais il serait nous serions vous seriez ils seraient	je fus tu fus il fut nous fûmesvoys fûtes ils furent
faire *to do, make* faisant fais! faisons! faites!	je fais tu fais il fait nous faisons vous faites ils font	j'ai fait tu as fait il a fait nous avaons fait vous avez fait ils ont fait	je faisais tu faisais il faisait nous faisions vous faisiez ils faisaient	j'avais fait tu avais fait il avait fait nous avions fait vous aviez fait ils avaient fait	je ferai tu feras il fera nous ferons vous ferez ils feront	je ferais tu ferais il ferait nous ferions vous feriez ils feraient	je fis tu fis il fit nous fîmes vous fîtes ils firent
falloir *must, is necessary*	il faut	il a fallu	il fallait	il avait fallu	il faudra	il faudrait	il fallut

Infinitive Present participle Imperative	Present	Perfect	Imperfect	Pluperfect	Future	Conditional	Past Historic
lire *to read* lisant	je lis tu lis il lit	j'ai lu tu as lu il a lu	je lisais tu lisais il lisait	j'avais lu tu avais lu il avait lu	je lirai tu liras il lira	je lirais tu lirais il lirait	je lus tu lus il lut
lis! lisons! lisez!	nous lisons vous lisez ils lisent	nous avons lu vous avez lu ils ont lu	nous lisions vous lisiez ils lisaient	nous avions lu vous aviez lu ils avaient lu	nous lirons vous lirez ils liront	nous lirions vous liriez ils liraient	nous lûmes vous lûtes ils lurent
mettre *to put (on)* mettant	je mets tu mets il met	j'ai mis tu as mis il a mis	je mettais tu mettais il mettait	j'avais mis tu avais mis il avait mis	je mettrai tu mettras il mettra	je mis tu mis il mit	
mets! mettons! mettez!	nous mettons vous mettez ils mettent	nous avons mis vous avez mis ils ont mis	nous mettions vous mettiez ils mettaient	nous avions mis vous aviez mis ils avaient mis	nous mettrions vous mettriez ils mettraient	nous mîmes vous mîtes ils mirent	
mourir *to die* mourant	je meurs tu meurs il meurt	je suis mort(e) tu es mort(e) il est mort elle est morte	je mourais tu mourais il mourait	j'étais mort(e) tu étais mort(e) il était mort elle était morte	je mourrai tu mourras il mourra	je mourrais tu mourrais il mourrait	je mourus tu mourus il mourut
meurs! mourons! mourez!	nous mourons vous mourez ils meurent	nous sommes mort(e)s vous êtes mort(e)s ils sont morts elles sont mortes	nous mourions vous mouriez ils mouraient	nous étions mort(e)s vous étiez mort(e)(s) ils étaient morts elles étaient mortes	nous mourrons vous mourrez ils mourront	nous mourrions vous mourriez ils mourraient	nous mourûmes vous mourûtes ils moururent
naître *to be born* naissant	je nais tu nais il naît	je suis né(e) tu es né(e) il est né elle est née	je naissais tu naissais tu naissait	j'étais né(e) tu étais né(e) il était né elle était née	je naîtrai tu naîtras il naîtra	je naîtrais tu naîtrais il naîtrait	je naquis tu naquis il naquit
	nous naissons vous naissez ils naissent	nous sommes né(e) vous êtes né(e)(s) ils sont nés elles sont nées	nous naissions vous naissiez ils naissaient	nous étions né(e)s vous étiez né(e)(s) ils étaient nés elles étaient nées	nous naîtrons vous naîtrez ils naîtront	nous naîtrions vous naîtriez ils naîtraient	nous naquîmes vous naquîtes ils naquirent

obtenir *to obtain* see **tenir**

offrir *to offer, give* see **ouvrir**

ouvrir *to open* ouvrant	j'ouvre tu ouvres il ouvre	j'ai ouvert tu as ouvert il a ouvert	j'ourais tu ouvrais il ouvrait	j'avais ouvert tu avais ouvert il avait ouvert	j'ouvrirai tu ouvriras il ouvrira	je ouvrirais tu ouvrirait il ouvrirait	j'ouvris tu ouvrit il ouvrit
ouvre! ouvrons! ouvrez!	nous ouvrons vous ouvrez ils ouvrent	nous avons ouvert vous avez ouvert ils ont ouvert	nous ouvrions vous ouvriez ils ouvraient	nous avions ouvert vous aviez ouvert ils avaient ouvert	nous ouvrirons vous ouvrirez ils ouvriront	nous ouvririons vous ouvririez ils ouriraient	nous ouvrîmes vous ouvrîtes ils ouvrirent

paraître *to appear* see **connaître**

partir *to leave* partant	je pars tu pars il part	je suis parti(e) tu es parti(e) il est parti elle est partie	je partais tu partais il partait	j'étais parti(e) tu étais parti(e) il était parti elle était partie	je partirai tu partiras il partira	je partirais tu partirais il partirait	je partis tu partis il partit
pars! partons! partez!	nous partons vous partez ils partent	nous sommes parti(e)s vous êtes parti(e)(s) ils sont partis elles sont parties	nous partions vous partiez ils partaient	nous étions parti(e)s vous étiez parti(e)(s) ils étaient partis elles étaient parties	nous partirons vous partirez ils partiront	nous partirions vous partiriez ils partiraient	nous partîmes vous partîtes ils partirent
pleuvoir *to rain* pleuvant	il pleut	il a plu	il pleuvait	il avait plu	il pleuvra	il pleuvrait	il plut
pouvoir *to be able,* *can*	je peux tu peux il peut	j'ai pu tu as pu il a pu	je pouvais tu pouvais il pouvait	j'avais pu tu avais pu il avait pu	je pourrai tu pourras il pourra	je pourrais tu pourrais il pourrait	je pus tu pus il put
	nous pouvons vous pouvez ils peuvent	nous avons pu vous avez pu ils ont pu	nous pouvions vous pouviez ils pouvaient	nous avions pu vous aviez pu ils avaient pu	nous pourrons vous pourrez ils pourront	nous pourrions vous pourriez ils pourraient	nous pûmes vous pûtes ils purent
prendre *to take* prenant	je prends tu prends il prend	j'ai pris tu as pris il a pris	je prenais tu prenais il prenait	j'avais pris tu avais pris il avait pris	je prendrai tu prendras il prendra	je prendrais tu prendrais il prendrait	je pris tu pris il prit
prends! prenons! prenez!	nous prenons vous prenez ils prennent	nous avons pris vous avez pris ils ont pris	nous prenions vous preniez ils prenaient	nous avions pris vous aviez pris ils avaient pris	nous prendrons vous prendrez ils prendront	nous prendrions vous prendriez ils prendraient	nous prîmes vous prîtes ils prirent

prévenir *to warn* see **venir**, but takes avoir in perfect and pluperfect tenses.

recevoir *to receive*	je reçois tu reçois	j'ai reçu tu as reçu	je recevais tu recevais	j'avais reçu tu avais reçu	je recevrai tu recevras	je recevrais tu recevrais	je reçus tu reçus

Infinitive Present participle Imperative	Present	Perfect	Imperfect	Pluperfect	Future	Conditional	Past Historic
recevant	il reçoit	il a reçu	il recevait	il avait reçu	il recevra	il recevrait	il reçut
reçois!							
recevons!	nous recevons	nous avons reçu	nous recevions	nous avions reçu	nous recevrons	nous recevrions	nous reçûmes
recevez!	vous recevez	vous avez reçu	vous receviez	vous aviez reçu	vous recevrez	vous recevriez	vous reçûtes
	ils reçoivent	ils ont reçu	ils recevaient	ils avaient reçu	ils recevront	ils recevraient	ils reçurent

reconnaître *to recognise* see **connaître**
repartir *to set out again, to go away again* see **partir**
reprendre *to take again, to resume* see **prendre**

retenir *to hold back, to retain* see **tenir**
revenir *to hold back, return* see **venir**

Infinitive Present participle Imperative	Present	Perfect	Imperfect	Pluperfect	Future	Conditional	Past Historic
rire	je ris	j'ai ri	je riais	j'avais ri	je rirai	je rirais	je ris
to laugh	tu ris	tu as ri	tu riais	tu avais ri	tu riras	tu rirais	tu ris
riant	il rit	il a ri	il riait	il avait ri	il rira	il rirait	il rit
ris!							
rions!	nous rions	nous avons ri	nous riions	nous avions ri	nous rirons	nous ririons	nous rîmes
riez!	vous riez	vous avez ri	vous riiez	vous aviez ri	vous rirez	vous ririez	vous rîtes
	ils rient	ils ont ri	ils riaient	ils avaient ri	ils riront	ils riraient	ils rirent
savoir	je sais	j'ai su	je savais	j'avais su	je saurai	je saurais	je sus
to know	tu sais	tu as su	tu savais	tu avais su	tu sauras	tu saurais	tu sus
sachant	il sait	il a su	il savait	il avait su	il saura	il saurait	il sut
sache!							
sachons!	nous savons	nous avons su	nous savions	nous avions su	nous saurons	nous saurions	nous sûmes
sachez!	vous savez	vous avez su	vous saviez	vous aviez su	vous saurez	vous sauriez	vous sûtes
	ils savent	ils ont su	ils savaient	ils avaient su	ils sauront	ils sauraient	ils surent

se sentir *to feel* see **partir**
servir *to serve* see **partir**, but takes avoir in perfect and pluperfect tenses

sortir *to go out* see **partir**

Infinitive Present participle Imperative	Present	Perfect	Imperfect	Pluperfect	Future	Conditional	Past Historic
suivre	je suis	j'ai suivi	je suivais	j'avais suivi	je suivrais	je suivrais	je suivis
to follow	tu suis	tu as suivi	tu suivais	tu avais suivi	tu suivrais	tu suivrais	tu suivis
suivant	il suit	il a suivi	il suivait	il avait suivi	il suivrait	il suivrait	il suivit
suis!							
suivons!	nous suivons	nous avons suivi	nous suivions	nous avions suivi	nous suivrions	nous suivîmes	
suivez!	vous suivez	vous avez suivi	vous suiviez	vous aviez suivi	vous suiriez	vous suivîtes	
	ils suivent	ils ont suivi	ils suivaient	ils avaient suivi	ils suivraient	ils suivirent	

surprendre *to surprise* see **prendre**

Infinitive Present participle Imperative	Present	Perfect	Imperfect	Pluperfect	Future	Conditional	Past Historic
tenir	je tiens	j'ai tenu	je tenais	j'avais tenu	je tiendrai	je tiendrais	je tins
to hold tenant	tu tiens	tu as tenu	tu tenais	tu avais tenu	tu tiendras	tu tiendrais	tu tins
	il tient	il a tenu	il tenait	il avait tenu	il tiendra	il tiendrait	il tint
tiens!							
tenons!							
tenez!	nous tenons	nous avons tenu	nous tenions	nous avions tenu	nous tiendrons	nous tiendrions	nous tînmes
	vous tenez	vous avez tenu	vous teniez	vous aviez tenu	vous tiendrez	vous tiendriez	vous tîntes
	ils tiennent	ils ont tenu	ilss tenaient	ils avaient tenu	ils tiendront	ils tiendraient	ils tinrent
venir	je viens	je suis venu(e)	je vanais	j'étais venu(e)	je viendrai	je viendrais	je vins
to come	tu viens	tu es venu(e)	tu venais	tu étais venu(e)	tu viendras	tu viendrais	tu vins
venant	il vient	il est venu	il venait	il était venu	il viendra	il viendrait	il vint
		elle est venue		elle était venue			
viens!							
venons!	nous venons	nous sommes venu(e)s	nous venions	nous étions venu(e)s	nous viendrons	nous viendrions	nous vînmes
venez!	vous venez	vous êtes venu(e)(s)	vous veniez	vous étiez venu(e)(s)	vous viendrez	vous viendriez	vous vîntes
	ils viennent	ils sont venus	ils venaient	ils étaient venus	ils viendront	ils viendraient	ils vinrent
		elles sont venues		elles étaient venues			
vivre	je vis	j'ai vécu	je vivais	j'avais vécu	je vivrai	je vivrais	je vécus
to live	tu vis	tu as vécu	tu vivais	tu avais vécu	tu vivras	tu vivrais	tu vécus
vivant	il vit	il a vécu	il vivait	il avait vécu	il vivra	il vivrait	il vécut
vis!							
vivons!	nous vivons	nous avons vécu	nous vivions	nous avions vécu	nous vivrons	nous vivrions	nous vécûmes
vivez!	vous vivez	vous avez vécu	vous viviez	vous aviez vécu	vous vivrez	vous vivriez	vous vécûtes
	ils vivent	ils ont vécu	ils vivaient	ils avaient vécu	ils vivraient	ils vivraient	ils vécurent
voir	je vois	j'ai vu	je voyais	j'avais vu	je verrai	je verrais	je vis
to see	tu vois	tu as vu	tu voyais	tu avais vu	tu verras	tu verrais	tu vis
voyant	il voit	il a vu	il voyait	il avait vu	il verra	il verrait	il vit
vois!							
voyons!	nous voyons	nous avaons vu	nous voyions	nous avions vu	nous verrons	nous verrions	nous vîmes
voyez!	vous voyez	vous avez vu	vous voyiez	vous aviez vu	vous verrez	vous verriez	vous vîtes
	ils voient	ils ont vu	ils voyaient	ils avaient vu	ils verront	ils verraient	ils virent
vouloir	je veux	j'ai voulu	je voulais	j'avais voulu	je voudrai	je voudrais	je voulus
to want, wish	tu veux	tu as voulu	tu voulais	tu avais voulu	tu voudras	tu voudrais	tu voulus
voulant	il veut	il a voulu	il voulait	il avait voulu	il voudra	il voudrait	il voulut
veuille!							
veuillons!	nous voulons	nous avons voulu	nous voulions	nous avions voulu	nous voudrons	nous voudrions	nous voulûmes
veuillez!	vous voulez	vous avez voulu	vous vouliez	vous aviez voulu	vous voudrez	vous voudriez	vous voulûtes
	ils veulent	ils ont voulu	ils voulaient	ils avaient voulu	ils voudront	ils voudraient	ils voulurent

GRAMMAR

VERBS

ADJECTIVES

ADVERBS

NOUNS

PRONOUNS

WORD ORDER

NUMBER AND TIME

CONJUNCTIONS

PREPOSITIONS

Grammar is often seen as boring and irrelevant. It isn't, as it allows you to generate sentences which you have not come across before, and helps your reading and listening comprehension. Find out how it works and you have the key to more French than you can possibly expect to learn by heart.

The grammar you need to know for GCSE French is laid down by the Examining Groups in their Defined Contents. They have divided what you need to know into four categories, two at each of the Basic and Higher levels.

At each level they list:

- **productive** skills (things you have to be able to say and write)
- **receptive** skills (things you need to understand, but are not necessarily able to say or write from memory)

This is just the same as in English, where you will understand many words and some items of grammar which you wouldn't necessarily use yourself.

We start by defining the terms which you will meet in your study of grammar.

GLOSSARY OF GRAMMATICAL TERMS

Not all teachers teach using formal grammar in their English or French lessons nowadays. There is nothing to be frightened of in the use of grammatical terms. After all, a mechanic wouldn't attempt to describe what a spanner is every time he wanted to have one passed to him. He just uses the technical term, which is 'spanner'. These grammatical terms are the technical 'jargon' of language-learning, and give you access to the patterns of French and other languages to enable you to learn them quicker.

The terms are defined simply, with examples. There are further examples and explanations given later in the chapter.

ADJECTIVES

These are words which describe a noun or pronoun. They give information about such things as colour, type, disposition, etc.

Example: le garçon **aimable**

ADVERBS

These are words which describe a verb (add to the verb). They give information about *how* something is done.

Example: Il court **vite**

Adverbs can also be used to add to adjectives or other adverbs.

Examples: le garçon **très** aimable
Il court **très** vite

AGREEMENT

Adjectives in French alter their spelling to agree with, or conform to, or 'match' the noun they describe.

Example: C'est un **beau** jardin et une **belle** maison avec de **beaux** arbres et de **belles** fleurs.
Past participles agree, too. Look up the rules.

CLAUSES

These are parts of a sentence which contain a subject and a verb which agrees with that subject. There are main clauses – which tell you most of the message of the sentence.

Example: **Il court très vite**
and subordinate clauses – which tell you something more about some other part of the sentence.

Example: Le garçon **qui habite à Lyon** court très vite

COMPARATIVES

A way of using adjectives and adverbs to, say, compare two people or things.

Examples: Je suis **plus fort** que toi.
(I am stronger than you.)
Il court **plus vite** que moi.
(He runs faster than me.)

CONJUGATION

The name given to the pattern that verbs follow. Regular verbs in French belong to the -er, -ir and -re conjugations. But there are unfortunately lots of exceptions!

IMPERATIVES

These are the command forms of verbs, and are used when telling people to do something. They include the 'Let's . . .' sort of command, which is a way of telling yourself and one or more other people to do something.

Example: Ecoute!   Listen!
            Ecoutez!   Listen!
            Ecoutons!   Let's listen!

INFINITIVE

The part of the verb you find when you look it up in a vocabulary list, and which means 'to . . .'. It doesn't agree with a subject. They may be found in combination with other verbs.

Example: manger

INTERROGATIVE PRONOUNS

These are question words. Their English equivalents mostly begin with 'wh'.

Examples: Qui? (Who?)
            Quoi? (What?)

IRREGULAR VERBS

Verbs which don't follow one of the set patterns. These verbs are written out for you in the verb table on page 203. They tend to be common verbs.

PRESENT PARTICIPLES

These are parts of the verb which are expressed by '. . ing' in English, and in French is usually found in combination with 'en'.

Example: en mangeant (while eating)

PAST PARTICIPLES

These are parts of the verb which are used with 'avoir' and 'être' to form the perfect and pluperfect tenses. Irregular verbs commonly have irregular past participles. Be careful about the agreement of past participles.

Examples: J'ai **dormi**
            Nous sommes **arrivés**
            Ils se sont **lavés**

PREPOSITIONS

These are words which are placed in front of nouns and pronouns to show position and other relationships.

Examples: Le bol est **dans** l'évier
             Marie vient **chez** moi

PRONOUNS

These are words which are used to avoid repeating a noun or proper name.

Examples: Je, il, me, etc.

REFLEXIVE VERBS

These are verbs where the person does the action to himself. There are rather more of them in French than in English, and you would do well to familiarize yourself with the list given in the grammar reference section.

Example: **se** laver – je **me** lave (I wash myself)

RELATIVE PRONOUNS

These introduce a relative clause, which is a clause which tells you something more about another part of the sentence. They can often be omitted in English, but never in French.

Examples: Voilà l'homme **que** je cherche
(There's the man I am looking for
There's the man that I am looking for
There's the man who I am looking for)
C'est un homme **qui** est très fort
(He's a man who is very strong)

SUPERLATIVES

A way of using adjectives and adverbs to say who is the best, the fastest, etc.

Examples: Je suis **le plus fort**
(I am the strongest)
Il court **le plus vite**
(He runs the fastest)

TENSES

These are the different forms of verbs which describe mainly **when** something takes place, took place, will take place, etc. There are some differences in the use of tenses between French and English, but future tenses refer to the future, present tenses refer to now or to regular events which are still going on, and past tenses refer to events which have already taken place. The conditional is used for conditions, while the French subjunctive has no direct equivalent in English. Look them up in the grammar.

G R A M M A R   L I S T S

To simplify matters, grammar will be listed under Basic and Higher levels. Anything which is listed with an (R) against it is for **receptive** use only. Items which have an (R) in the Basic lists will be used **productively** at Higher level.

Space does not allow many examples in the list. However, the correct grammatical terms for structures are given so that you can look them up in the grammar reference section of this chapter. If you do have to set a priority on the most important things to revise, go for the forms of verbs in the various tenses first, followed by the agreement of adjectives.

VERBS **BASIC LEVEL**

Present tense (je joue, je finis, je réponds etc.)
Perfect tense (also called passé composé) with avoir and être (j'ai joué, je suis arrivé, j'ai répondu, j'ai fini etc.)
Imperfect tense (je jouais, je finissais, je répondais etc.)
Future using aller + infinitive (je vais manger)
(R) Future tense (je jouerai, je finirai etc.)
Reflexive verbs (je m'appelle Anne, papa se lève, etc.)
Question forms
Command forms (imperative) (Joue! Jouez! Jouons!)
Infinitive (jouer, répòndre, finir, etc)
(R) Infinitive following pour, sans, avant de, il faut (il faut jouer. C'est pour manger)
(R) Common verb + à or de + infinitive (il a décidé de manger en ville, il demande à sortir)
(R) Perfect infinitive (après avoir fini, après être venu)
(R) Use of present tense with depuis (J'habite à Blackpool depuis deux ans)
Negatives (ne . . . pas, ne . . . jamais, ne . . . rien)
(R) Negatives (ne . . . aucun, ne . . . nulle part, ne . . . personne, ne . . . plus, ne . . . que, ne . . . ni . . . ni . . .)
(R) En + present participle (en jouant, en finissant, etc.)

HIGHER LEVEL

Pluperfect tense

Agreement of past participle with preceding direct object (je les ai achetées, les montres)

Venir de + infinitive (je viens d'arriver, je venais d'arriver, etc.)

Etre en train de + infinitive (je suis en train de manger)

Use of imperfect tense with depuis (j'habitais à Londres depuis cinq ans quand je me suis décidé à quitter la grande ville)

Conditional (j'aimerais voir tes dessins; si j'étais plus âgée, je conduirais une belle voiture)

(R) Passive (il a été mordu, etc.)

Agreement of past participle with être (elles sont arrivées)

(R) Present subjunctive of regular -er, -ir and -re verbs and of avoir, être, aller, faire, pouvoir, savoir, prendre, venir (il faut que je fasse mes devoirs, il faut qu'ils soient bien faits)

(R) Past historic (il regarda Napoléon, ils se regardèrent)

ADJECTIVES

BASIC AND HIGHER LEVELS

Form of adjective

Position

Agreement

(R) Certain masculine adjectives before a vowel (bel, nouvel, vieil)

Possessive adjectives (mon, ma, mes, etc.)

Comparative (je suis plus grand que toi)

Superlative (je suis la plus belle)

HIGHER LEVEL

As Basic Level plus:

Certain masculine adjectives before a vowel (bel, nouvel, vieil)

ADVERBS

BASIC AND HIGHER LEVELS

Bien, mal

Regular formation ending in -ment, -emment, -ément

Comparison of adverbs (il joue mieux que toi, il court plus vite que toi)

NOUNS

BASIC AND HIGHER LEVELS

Gender (le or la, un or une)

Number (singular or plural)

Plurals, including the irregular ones (le cheval – les chevaux)

PRONOUNS

BASIC LEVEL

Subject and object and emphatic pronouns – also known as stressed or disjunctive pronouns (je, me, moi, etc.)

Position of pronouns

(R) Order of pronouns (il me l'a donné)

Relative pronouns (qui, que)

(R) Relative pronouns (ce qui, ce que, dont)

Indefinite pronouns (quelque chose, quelqu'un, tout tous, tout le monde)

HIGHER LEVEL

As for Basic, plus (R) relative pronoun lequel, lesquels, etc.

WORD ORDER	**BASIC AND HIGHER LEVELS**

(R) Inversion after direct speech ('Je mange' a-t-elle dit)
(R) Inversion after peut-être (peut-être vient-il)
(R) Inversion in relative clauses (le collège où travaille mon cousin)
(R) Order of pronouns (il me l'a donné)

HIGHER LEVEL

As for Basic Level, but all for productive use.

NUMBER AND TIME	**BASIC AND HIGHER LEVELS**

Cardinal numbers (un, deux, trois, etc.)
Ordinal numbers (premier, deuxième, troisième, etc.)
Telling the time on 12-hour clock and on 24-hour clock
Dates (oral only – '1988' or '1066' acceptable in figures in the written examination)

USE OF CONJUNCTIONS	Basic and Higher Levels. Correct usage.

USE OF PREPOSITIONS	Basic and Higher Levels. Correct usage.

GRAMMAR REFERENCE

Use the grammar lists to find out which grammatical features you are expected to know at either Basic or Higher Level, and whether you should know them actively or passively. In practice, the more you know the better, and there is a strong case for ignoring the Examining Groups' rather arbitrary divisions and concentrating on mastering the fundamentals of French grammar outlined below.

VERBS	French verbs are notoriously difficult. Many of the common ones are irregular, i.e. they do not follow a rule. In all of them the spelling changes, depending on who is speaking, but the pronunciation does not always change to match. If you can master them, you have the key to success. So do make every attempt to get to grips with them. Take a few at a time. Make a point of checking the spelling, including the accents.

PRESENT TENSE

There is only one form of the present tense for each French verb. In English there are three: I eat, I am eating and I do eat. The French form 'je mange' is used as an equivalent for all three. (You will probably have noticed that French speakers often mix up the English forms.)

USE OF THE PRESENT TENSE

The present tense is used

- to describe events that happen regularly.
  Example: Je mange beaucoup de bonbons
        (I eat a lot of sweets)
- to describe what is happening now
  Example: Je lis un livre intéressant
        (I am reading an interesting book)
- after depuis (see below)

FORMATION OF THE PRESENT TENSE

Regular verbs are identified by the last two letters of their infinitive: -er, -ir and -re. They form the present tense in different ways.

– er verbs

Regular -er verbs in French follow this pattern:

parler   to talk or speak

je parle	I speak, I am speaking
tu parles	you (singular) speak, you are speaking
il parle	he speaks, he is speaking
elle parle	she speaks, she is speaking
on parle	we speak, we are speaking (one speaks, etc.)
nous parlons	we speak, we are speaking
vous parlez	you speak, you are speaking
ils parlent	they speak, they are speaking
elles parlent	they (feminine) speak, they are speaking

The endings for -er verbs are:

je	-e	nous	-ons
tu	-es	vous	-ez
il/elle/on	-e	ils/elles	-ent

These are added to the **stem** of the verb, that is the infinitive **parler** minus its **-er** ending.

Other common regular -er verbs include: aider, aimer, arriver,* casser, chercher, compter, danser, déjeuner, désirer, dessiner, détester, donner, durer, écouter, entrer,* fumer, gagner, inviter, jouer, laver, louer, marcher, monter,* montrer, oublier, penser, pleurer, porter, poser, pousser, quitter, préparer, regarder, rencontrer, rentrer,* réparer, réserver, rester,* retourner,* rouler, sauter, sonner, tomber,* toucher, tourner, travailler, traverser, trouver, visiter, voler.
Verbs marked * take être in the perfect tense.

Note: This list is by no means exhaustive. Add new verbs to it as you come across them.

Irregular -er verbs

The most irregular -er verb is aller (to go):

je vais	nous allons
tu vas	vous allez
il va	ils vont
elle va	elles vont
on va	

A number of common -er verbs have very slight irregularities.

1   Manger and other verbs ending in -ger have irregular 'nous' forms for phonetic reasons (to make the g soft by following it with an e). These verbs follow this pattern:

manger   to eat

je mange	nous mangeons
tu manges	vous mangez
il mange	ils mangent
elle mange	elles mangent
on mange	

Other verbs in this category include: changer, échanger, loger, nager, obliger, partager, ranger, voyager.

2   Commencer and other verbs ending in -cer have irregular 'nous' forms for phonetic reasons (to make the c soft by giving it a cedilla (̧). These verbs follow this pattern:

commencer   to begin

je commence	nous commençons
tu commences	vous commencez
il commence	ils commencent
elle commence	elles commencent
on commence	

Other verbs in this category include: avancer, lancer, menacer, placer, prononcer, remplacer.

3   Most verbs ending in -eler and -eter double the -l or the -t in some persons of the verb. The verbs follow this pattern:

s'appeler to be called		**jeter** to throw	
je m'appelle	nous nous appelons	je jette	nous jetons
tu t'appelles	vous vous appelez	tu jettes	vous jetez
il s'appelle	ils s'appellent	il jette	ils jettent
elle s'appelle	elles s'appellent	elle jette	elles jettent
on s'appelle		on jette	

Other verbs in this category include: appeler.

4   Verbs ending in -e-er follow this pattern:

lever to lift	
je lève	nous levons
tu lèves	vous levez
il lève	ils lèvent
elle lève	elles lèvent
on lève	

Other verbs in this category include: acheter, geler, mener, peser, se promener.

5   Verbs ending in -é-er follow this pattern:

considérer to consider	
je considère	nous considérons
tu considères	vous considérez
il considère	ils considèrent
elle considère	elles considèrent
on considère	

Other verbs in this category include: espérer, s'inquiéter, préférer, répéter, révéler.

6   Verbs ending in -yer change the y to an i where it is followed by an e. The verbs follow this pattern:

nettoyer to clean	
je nettoie	nous nettoyons
tu nettoies	vous nettoyez
il nettoie	ils nettoient
elle nettoie	elles nettoient
on nettoie	

Other verbs in this category include: appuyer, balayer, employer, ennuyer, envoyer, essayer, essuyer, payer.

-ir verbs
Regular -ir verbs in French follow this pattern:

finir to finish	
je finis	I finish, I am finishing
tu finis	you (singular) finish, you are finishing
il finit	he finishes, he is finishing
elle finit	she finishes, she is finishing
on finit	we finish, we are finishing (one finishes, etc.)

nous finissons	we finish, we are finishing
vous finissez	you finish, you are finishing
ils finissent	they finish, they are finishing
elles finissent	they (feminine) finish, they are finishing

The endings for -ir verbs are:

je	-is	nous	-issons
tu	-is	vous	-issez
il/elle/on	-it	ils/elles	-issent

These are added to the **stem** of the verb, that is the infinitive **finir** minus its **-ir** ending.

Other common regular -ir verbs include: agrandir, applaudir, atterrir, bâtir, choisir, démolir, remplir. This list is by no means exhaustive. Add new verbs to it as you come across them.

Irregular -ir verbs

Some common -ir verbs have a present tense just like an -er verb.

couvrir   to cover

je couvre	nous couvrons
tu couvres	vous couvrez
il couvre	ils couvrent
elle couvre	elles couvrent
on couvre	

Other verbs in this category include: découvrir, offrir, ouvrir, souffrir. Check the verb table for other tenses of these verbs.

There are many other irregular -ir verbs. The following are also included in the verb table: contenir, convenir, courir, devenir,* dormir, s'endormir, entretenir, mourir,* obtenir, partir,* prévenir, repartir, retenir, revenir,* se sentir,* servir, se servir,* sortir,* tenir, venir*.

Note: Verbs marked * take être in the perfect tense

-re verbs

Regular -re verbs in French follow this pattern:

vendre   to sell

je vends	I sell, I am selling
tu vends	you (singular) sell, you are selling
il vend	he sells, he is selling
elle vend	she sells, she is selling
on vend	we sell, we are selling (one sells, etc.)
nous vendons	we sell, we are selling
vous vendez	you sell, you are selling
ils vendent	they sell, they are selling
elles vendent	they (feminine) sell, they are selling

The endings for -re verbs are:

je	-s	nous	-ons
tu	-s	vous	-ez
il/elle/on	-	ils/elles	-ent

These are added to the **stem** of the verb, that is the infinitive **vendre** minus its **-re** ending.

Other common regular -re verbs include: attendre, descendre, entendre, perdre, rendre, répondre. This list is by no means exhaustive. Add new verbs to it as you come across them.

Irregular -re verbs

There are many irregular -re verbs. The following are included in the verb table: apprendre, battre, boire, comprendre, conduire, connaître, construire, coudre, craindre, croire, détruire, dire, disparaître, écrire, éteindre, être,* faire, lire, mettre, naître,* paraître, prendre, reconnaître, reprendre, rire, suivre, surprendre, vivre.

Note: Verbs marked * take être in the perfect tense

-oir verbs

There is a group of verbs ending in -oir which are all irregular. The following are included in the verb table: s'asseoir,* avoir, devoir, falloir, pleuvoir, pouvoir, recevoir, savoir, voir, vouloir.

Note: Verbs marked * take être in the perfect tense

Common errors with the present tense

- Spelling, especially with -er verbs with accents
- Failing to use any ending at all
  Example: je regarder
  Correct version: je regarde
- Using the wrong ending
  Example: il vends
  Correct version: il vend
- Trying to express 'I am drinking' by je suis boire
  Correct version: je bois
  Students who do this haven't appreciated that there is only one form of the present tense for each verb in French.
- Getting confused between present and perfect Je allé
  Example: Je allé au collège tous les jours
  Correct version: Je vais au collège tous les jours

PERFECT TENSE

The perfect tense is also known as the passé composé. In French, it is used to express the English 'have done' and 'did'. So j'ai mangé une pomme could mean

I ate an apple
or I have eaten an apple
or I did eat an apple

(You will probably have noticed that French speakers often mix up the English forms.)

Use of the perfect tense

The perfect tense is used in conversation and letters:

- to describe an action in the past which is completed and is no longer happening
- to describe an action in the past which happened once only

Formation of the perfect tense

The perfect tense is made up of two parts, the auxiliary verb, which is the present tense of either avoir or être, and the past participle. Most verbs have avoir as their auxiliary.

Perfect tense with avoir – regular verbs
The past participles of regular verbs (including those -er verbs with minor changes in spelling in the present tense) are formed by removing -er, -ir or -re from the infinitive and adding -e, -i, or -u.
Examples: parler   parlé
  finir   fini
  vendre   vendu
The past participles are then combined with the auxiliary, the present tense of avoir, as follows:

j'ai parlé	nous avons parlé
tu as parlé	vous avez parlé
il a parlé	ils ont parlé
elle a parlé	elles ont parlé
on a parlé	

j'ai fini	nous avons fini
tu as fini	vous avez fini
il a fini	ils ont fini
elle a fini	elles ont fini
on a fini	

j'ai vendu	nous avons vendu
tu as vendu	vous avez vendu
il a vendu	ils ont vendu
elle a vendu	elles ont vendu
on a vendu	

Perfect tense with avoir – irregular verbs

Many common verbs are irregular. The formation of the perfect tense follows the same principle as for regular verbs, i.e. there is an auxiliary, the present tense of avoir, and the past participle. The only problem is that the past participles have to be learned, as irregular verbs don't obey set rules.

Example: lire (past participle lu)

j'ai lu	nous avons lu
tu as lu	vous avez lu
il a lu	ils ont lu
elle a lu	elles ont lu
on a lu	

Here are 25 of the most commonly used verbs with their past participles. These and other irregular verbs can be checked in the verb table. If you don't know them already, make it a top priority to master them.

Infinitive	*Past participle*	*Infinitive*	*Past participle*
avoir	eu	lire	lu
boire	bu	mettre	mis
comprendre	compris	ouvrir	ouvert
conduire	conduit	pleuvoir	plu
connaître	connu	pouvoir	pu
courir	couru	prendre	pris
croire	cru	recevoir	reçu
devoir	dû	rire	ri
dire	dit	savoir	su
écrire	écrit	tenir	tenu
être	été	vivre	vécu
faire	fait	voir	vu
		vouloir	voulu

Perfect tense with être – reflexive verbs

All reflexive verbs have the present tense of être as their auxiliary. Their past participles may be either regular or irregular – check the verb table. The past participle agrees (like an adjective) with the subject, as in the following example.

se laver   to wash oneself

je me suis lavé(e)	nous nous sommes lavé(e)s
tu t'es lavé(e)	vous vous êtes lavé(e)s
il s'est lavé	ils se sont lavés
elle s'est lavée	elles se sont lavées
on s'est lavé(e)(s)	

If the (e) is in brackets, it is only added if the subject is feminine.
If the (s) is in brackets, it is only added if the subject is plural.
Where an irregular past participle ends in -s, (e.g. assis) no further s is required for the masculine plural agreement.
Example: Les garçons se sont assis

Perfect tense with être – 16 verbs

There are 16 common verbs which are **not** reflexive that also form the perfect tense with être as the auxiliary. Most of them can be remembered in six pairs which are (or are nearly) opposite in meaning. Make it a top priority to master them.

Infinitive	*Past participle*	*Infinitive*	*Past participle*
aller	allé	monter	monté
venir	venu	descendre	descendu
arriver	arrivé	rester	resté
partir	parti	tomber	tombé
entrer	entré	naître	né
sortir	sorti	mourir	mort

The others are:
retourner	retourné
revenir	revenu
devenir	devenu
rentrer	rentré

As with reflexive verbs, the past participles of these verbs have to agree with the subject, as in the following example.

retourner   to return

je suis retourné(e)	nous sommes retourné(e)s
tu es retourné(e)	vous êtes retourné(e)(s)
il est retourné	ils sont retournés
elle est retournée	elles sont retournées
on est retourné(e)(s)	

If the (e) is in brackets, it is only added if the subject is feminine.
If the (s) is in brackets, it is only added if the subject is plural.

Common errors with the perfect tense

- Using an incorrect form of the past participle, usually caused by not knowing which verbs are irregular. A big help is knowing that
    —all -er verbs except aller are regular
    —no -oir verbs are regular
    —most reflexive verbs are regular

- Using a verb form which sounds the same, but isn't perfect at all
    Example: j'ai regarder or j'ai regardez
    Correct version: j'ai regardé

- Using the wrong auxiliary verb
    Example: Il a venu
    Correct version: il est venu

- Getting confused between perfect and imperfect
    Example: Il a traversé la rue quand une voiture le tuait
    Correct version: Il traversait la rue quand une voiture l'a tué

- Failing to make the past participles of verbs which take être agree with the subject. This is particularly common with feminine and/or plural subjects
    Example: Elles sont allé à Paris
    Correct version: Elles sont allées à Paris

- Using the negative incorrectly (see page 228)

IMPERFECT TENSE

The imperfect tense refers to events in the past. It is usually found in combination with the perfect tense.

Use of the imperfect tense

The imperfect tense in French is used:

- to set the scene in the past (to say what **was happening** when something else happened)
    Example: Il traversait la rue quand une voiture l'a tué (He was crossing the road (imperfect tense) when a car killed him (perfect tense))

- for description in the past
    Example: Il faisait beau, le soleil brillait, Jeanne était contente
         (The weather was good, the sun was shining, Jeanne was happy)

- for something that happened frequently in the past, or used to happen
    Example: Quand j'habitais à Londres, j'allais acheter mes cadeaux chez Harrods
         (When I lived in London I used to buy my presents at Harrods)

- in reported speech (also known as indirect speech) to report the present tense
    Example: 'Je viens de l'Angleterre' (actual speech)
         (I come from England' (present tense))
         Il a dit qu'il venait de l'Angleterre (reported speech)
         (He said (perfect tense) he came (imperfect tense) from England)
         See also pluperfect tense – reported speech

Formation of the imperfect tense

1 Nearly all verbs, -er, -ir, -re and -oir, form the imperfect tense in the following way:

—First   find the 'nous' form of the present tense.
—Then   remove the -ons to leave the imperfect stem.
—Finally add the imperfect endings:

je -ais	nous -ions
tu -ais	vous -iez
il -ait	ils -aient
elle -ait	elles -aient
on -ait	

Example: faire (to make/do)
Nous form of present tense: faisons
Imperfect stem (faisons minus -ons): fais
Imperfect tense:

je faisais	nous faisions
tu faisais	vous faisiez
il faisait	ils faisaient
elle faisait	elles faisaient
on faisait	

2 There is one irregular verb in the imperfect tense, être.

j'étais	nous étions
tu étais	vous étiez
il était	ils étaient
elle était	elles étaient
on était	

If you look carefully, you will see that it is only the imperfect stem, ét-, which is irregular. The endings are what you would expect.

3 The -er verbs which have an extra e inserted into the nous form to soften a g don't need the extra e in the nous and vous forms in the imperfect because the g is softened by the i in the endings -ions and -iez. These verbs follow this pattern:

je mangeais	nous man**g**ions
tu mangeais	vous man**g**iez
il mangeait	ils mangeaient
elle mangeait	elles mangeaient
on mangeait	

Other verbs in this category include: changer, échanger, loger, nager, obliger, partager, ranger, voyager.

4 The -er verbs which have a cedilla (¸) inserted into the nous form to soften a c don't need one in the nous and vous forms in the imperfect because the c is softened by the i in the endings -ions and -iez. These verbs follow this pattern:

je commençais	nous commen**c**ions
tu commençais	vous commen**c**iez
il commençait	ils commençaient
elle commençait	elles commençaient
on commençait	

Other verbs in this category include: avancer, lancer, menacer, placer, prononcer, remplacer.

Common errors with the imperfect tense

■ spelling, especially of the -er verbs which have either the extra e or the cedilla
  Example: je nagais
  Correct version: je nageais

- Using an ending which sounds the same, but isn't imperfect at all
  Example: je regarder or je regardé
  Correct version: je regardais

- Using the wrong ending
  Example: il vendais
  Correct version: il vendait

- Getting confused between imperfect and perfect
  Example: Il a traversé la rue quand une voiture l'a tué
  Correct version: Il traversait la rue quand une voiture l'a tué

- Translating 'would' meaning 'used to' with the French conditional when in fact the imperfect is correct
  Example: Il viendrait chaque été à Paris
  (He would come to Paris each summer)
  Correct version: Il venait chaque été à Paris

FUTURE USING ALLER + INFINITIVE

This is the simplest way of talking about events in the future, and is similar to the English 'I am going to . . .'

Use of the future with aller + infinitive

Aller + infinitive is used:

- to talk about events in the immediate future
  Example: Je vais regarder la télévision ce soir
  (I am going to watch TV tonight)

Formation of the future with aller + infinitive

Take the present tense of aller and add the infinitive of any verb, regular or irregular, as in the following example.

je vais acheter	nous allons acheter
tu vas acheter	vous allez acheter
il va acheter	ils vont acheter
elle va acheter	elles vont acheter
on va acheter	

Common errors with aller + infinitive

- Using the wrong part of aller
  Example: Vous aller acheter des pommes
  Correct version: Vous allez acheter des pommes

FUTURE TENSE

The use of the future tense

The future tense in French is used:

- to express firm intention
  Example: Je regarderai la télé ce soir
  (I shall watch TV this evening)

- to refer to events further ahead than the short term
  Example: Dans cinq ans j'aurai 21 ans
  (I shall be 21 in five years' time)

Formation of the future tense

Regular -er grand -ir verbs
Add these endings to the infinitive, as in the following examples.

je -ai	nous -ons	je parlerai	nous parlerons
tu -as	vous -ez	tu parleras	vous parlerez
il -a	ils -ont	il parlera	ils parleront
elle -a	elles -ont	elle parlera	elles parleront
on -a		on parlera	

je finirai	nous finirons
tu finiras	vous finirez
il finira	ils finiront
elle finira	elles finiront
on finira	

Regular -re verbs

Remove the e from the infinitive. Add the same endings as for all other verbs, as in the following example.

je vendrai	nous vendrons
tu vendras	vous vendrez
il vendra	ils vendront
elle vendra	elles vendront
on vendra	

Irregular verbs

Irregular verbs have the same future endings as all other verbs. However, the future stem needs to be learnt. Listed below are the future tenses of 21 of the most common irregular future tenses. Note that this contains some -er verbs which are not irregular in other parts.

Infinitive	*Future tense*	*Infinitive*	*Future tense*
acheter	j' achèterai	falloir	il faudra
aller	j'irai	jeter	je jetterai
appeler	j'appellerai	mourir	je mourrai
s'asseoir	je m'assiérai	pleuvoir	il pleuvra
avoir	j'aurai	pouvoir	je pourrai
courir	je courrai	recevoir	je recevrai
devoir	je devrai	répéter	je répéterai
envoyer	j'enverrai	savoir	je saurai
être	je serai	tenir	je tiendrai
faire	je ferai	venir	je viendrai
		voir	je verrai

The future in French but not in English

The future must be used in French to refer to events in the future. This is not immediately obvious to an English-speaker, and needs to be watched out for.

Examples: Quand elle viendra, je lui donnerai ta lettre
(When she comes (present in English, future in French) I'll give her your letter)
Elle viendra quand l'émission sera finie
(She will come when the programme is over (present in English, future in French))

Common errors with the future tense

- Using the wrong endings
  Example: je serer là
  Correct version: je serai là

- Confusion with the conditional (see page 232) which sounds similar
  Example: je serais là
  Correct version: je serai là

REFLEXIVE VERBS

These verbs have se or s' in front of the infinitive when you look them up.

Use of reflexive verbs

Reflexive verbs in French are used:

- as part of the normal vocabulary of French. They can be used in any way a normal verb can be. There are many more in French than there are in English, and some of the meanings are, at first, confusing.

- often when referring to a part of the body
  Example: Je me suis coupé le doigt
  (I have cut my finger)
  Elle se lave les dents
  (She is cleaning her teeth)
  Elle s'est cassé la jambe
  (She has broken her leg)

Formation of reflexive verbs

1 Add the reflexive pronoun between the subject and the verb.
   This applies in all tenses, as in the following example. If in doubt, check the verb table.

je me lave	nous nous lavons
tu te laves	vous vous lavez
il se lave	ils se lavent
elle se lave	elles se lavent
on se lave	

2 Where the reflexive verb is used as an infinitive, the reflexive pronoun agrees with the subject of the verb.
   Example: **Je** suis obligé de **me** coucher à neuf heures
   Nous sommes obligés de **nous** coucher à neuf heures
   On est obligé de **se** coucher à neuf heures

3 In the perfect and pluperfect tenses:

   - all reflexive verbs have être as the auxiliary verb
   - the past participles of reflexive verbs agree with the subject
   - most reflexive verbs except s'asseoir (je me suis assis), se mettre à (je me suis mis à . . .) and se souvenir de (je me suis souvenu de . . .) have regular past participles.

se laver   to wash oneself

je me suis lavé(e)	nous nous sommes lavé(e)s
tu t'es lavé(e)	vous vous êtes lavé(e)(s)
il s'est lavé	ils se sont lavés
elle s'est lavée	elles se sont lavées
on s'est lavé(e)(s)	

If the (e) is in brackets, it is only added if the subject is feminine.
If the (s) is in brackets, it is only added if the subject is plural.

Where an irregular past participle ends in -s (e.g. assis) no further s is required for the masculine plural agreement.
Example: Les garçons se sont assis.

Common reflexive verbs

s'amuser	to enjoy oneself	s'entendre avec	to get on with
s'appeler	to be called	se fâcher	to get angry
s'approcher (de)	to approach	se faire mal	to hurt oneself
s'arrêter	to stop	s'habiller	to get dressed
se baigner	to bathe	s'inquiéter	to worry
se brosser	to brush (one's hair)	s'intéresser à	to be interested in
(les cheveux)		se laver	to get washed
se casser	to break	se lever	to get up
se coucher	to go to bed	se méfier	to mistrust
se débrouiller	to manage, to get on with something	se mettre à	to begin
		s'occuper	to busy oneself
se demander	to wonder	se peigner	to comb one's hair
se dépêcher	to hurry	se promener	to go for a walk
se déshabiller	to undress	se rappeler	to remember
se disputer avec	to have an argument with	se raser	to shave
s'endormir	to fall asleep	se rendre compte	to realize
s'ennuyer	to be bored	se reposer	to rest

se réveiller	to wake up	se souvenir de	to remember
se sauver	to run away	se taire	to be silent
se sentir	to feel	se tromper	to be mistaken
se servir de	to use	se trouver	to be situated

Verbs not in the above list can be made reflexive to express the idea of 'each other'. They then behave like reflexives in the perfect tense.

Examples: Quand est-ce qu'on va se voir?
(When shall we see each other?)
Quand est-ce que nous nous sommes vu(e)s la dernière fois?
(When did we last see each other?)
Ils se sont rencontrés chez nous
(They met at our house)

Common errors with reflexives

- Failing to recognize that there is a reflexive verb needed
  Example: Je sens triste
  (I feel sad)
  Correct version: Je me sens triste
- Using avoir instead of 'être' or the other way round
- Forgetting to use être in the perfect tense
  Example: Nous nous lavé ce matin
            (We got washed this morning)
  Correct version: Nous nous sommes lavé(e)s ce matin
- Forgetting to make the past participle agree with the subject
  Example: Elles se sont lavé
            (They got washed)
  Correct version: Elles se sont lavées
- Choosing the wrong reflexive pronoun when a reflexive verb is used in the infinitive
  Example: J'ai décidé de se laver
            (I have decided to get washed)
  Correct version: J'ai décidé de me laver
- Using the negative incorrectly

QUESTION FORMS

These are also known as interrogatives. There are five ways of asking a question in French.

1   By tone of voice

A rising tone of voice at the end of a statement turns it into a question.

Example: Ton frère habite à Londres?
          (Does your brother live in London?)
If you are writing, you obviously can't use tone of voice, so if you use it, do not forget the question mark.

2   By beginning with Est-ce que

Add Est-ce que to the beginning of any statement to convert it into a question.

Example: Est-ce que ton frère habite à Londres?
          (Does your brother live in London?)

3   By inverting the subject and verb

Example: Habites-tu à Londres?
          (Do you live in London?)

If the verb ends in a vowel in the third person singular you should add an extra -t- to make it easier to pronounce.

Example: Ton frère, habite-t-il à Londres?
          (Does your brother live in London?)

4   Question words can be used in front of methods 1 and 2 (statement and est-ce que).

Example: Où habite ton frère?
Où est-ce que ton frère habite?
(Where does your brother live?)

5   By adding n'est-ce pas

Add n'est-ce pas to the end of any statement to convert it into a question. It's similar to isn't it?, doesn't he? etc. in English. There is only one French form for all the English ones.

Example: Ton frère habite à Londres, n'est-ce pas?
(Your brother lives in London, doesn't he?)

Here is a list of question words:

Combien?	How much?
Comment?	How? (sometimes: What?)
Où?	Where?
D'où?	Where from?
Lequel . . . ?*	Which one?
Pourquoi?	Why?
Quand?	When?
Qu'est-ce que . . . ?	What . . . ?
Quel . . . ?*	Which, what . . . ?
Qui?	Who?
Quoi?	Pardon? What? (only used on its own)

* Lequel and quel are adjectives and agree with the noun being asked about.

Example: Quelles chaussettes as-tu perdues?
(Which socks have you lost?)

Common errors with questions

■ Attempting to translate the English 'do' in 'Do you live in London?'

Example: Fais tu habiter à Londres
Correct version: Habites-tu à Londres? or Est-ce que tu habites à Londres?

■ Using the wrong question word
It's best to learn such idiomatic questions as:
—Comment t'appelles-tu?   (What's your name?)
—D'où viens-tu?   (Where do you come from?)

■ Replying in the wrong tense. In your reply you should mirror the tense of the question you are asked.

Example: Q   Quand est-ce que tu as quitté l'Angleterre?
A   Je quitte l'Angleterre hier soir
Correct version: J'ai quitté l'Angleterre hier soir

COMMAND FORMS

These are also known as imperatives. French verbs have three command forms, derived from the tu, vous and nous forms of the present tense in most cases.

Use of command forms

The form derived from the tu form is used when talking to one person who is
—a good friend
—a member of the family or a pet
—a young person
The form derived from the vous form is used when talking to two or more people who are
—good friends
—members of the family or pets
—young people
or to one person who is
—an adult who doesn't fit any of the categories above

The form derived from the nous form is used to translate 'Let's do something'.

Formation of commands

-ir and -re verbs

Miss out tu or vous or nous and just use the verb itself.

Examples: Finis ce livre!   Finish that book
            Finissez ce livre!   Finish that book
            Finissons ce livre!   Let's finish that book

            Vends ce livre!   Sell that book
            Vendez ce livre!   Sell that book
            Vendons ce livre!   Let's sell that book

-er verbs

The principle is the same. But miss the -s off the tu form.

Example: Parle!   Talk
            Parlez!   Talk
            Parlons!   Let's talk

Irregular forms

The following verbs have irregular command forms:

avoir: aie   savoir: sache
       ayons   sachons
       ayez   sachez

être: sois   vouloir: veuille
      soyez   veuillez
      soyons   veuillons

Aller has a modified form in the phrase 'Vas-y' (Go to it, On you go).

Reflexive verbs

They have the following command forms:

Example: Réveille-toi!
            Réveillez-vous
            Réveillons-nous

Common errors in command forms

- Incorrect formation
- Adding reflexive pronouns for verbs which are not reflexive
  Example: Viens-toi ici!
  Correct version: Viens ici!
- Failing to realize that 'let's' is a command and not using the -ons command form at all

THE INFINITIVE

In French there are often two verbs in a sentence, the second of which is in the infinitive form. This is often the case in English, too (e.g. 'I prefer to swim').

There are four ways in which French uses two verbs in a sentence. Unfortunately you have to learn which way each verb operates.

1   Verbs followed directly by the infinitive

Some verbs are followed directly by the infinitive.

Example: J'aime jouer au tennis
            (I like playing tennis)

These verbs include:

adorer	to love	désirer	to want, to wish
aimer	to like, to love	détester	to hate
aller	to go	devoir	to have to ('to must')
compter	to intend to	entendre	to hear

espérer	to hope to	préférer	to prefer
faillir	to nearly do something	savoir	to know how to
il faut	you need to	venir	to come (in order to)
monter	to go upstairs (in order to)	voir	to see
penser	to intend to do something	vouloir	to want to
pouvoir	to be able to (to 'can')		

2   Verbs followed by à + infinitive

Some verbs are followed by à and an infinitive.
Example: Il s'est décidé à acheter une Renault
        (He made his mind up to buy a Renault)

These verbs include:

aider quelqu'un à	to help someone to	s'intéresser à	to be interested in
apprendre à	to learn to	inviter quelqu'un à	to invite someone to
commencer à	to begin to	se mettre à	to begin to
consentir à	to agree to	obliger quelqu'un à	to make someone do
continuer à	to continue to		something
se décider à	to make one's mind up to	passer du temps à	to spend time
demander à	to ask to	ressembler à	to look like
hésiter à	to hesitate to	réussir à	to succeed in

3   Verbs followed by de + infinitive

Some verbs are followed by de and an infinitive.
Example: Il a cessé de pleuvoir
        (It stopped raining)

These verbs include:

s'arrêter de	to stop doing something	finir de	to finish doing something
cesser de	to stop doing something	offrir de	to offer to do something
décider de	to decide to	oublier de	to forget to do something
se dépêcher de	to hurry to	permettre de	to allow to
dire de	to tell to	refuser de	to refuse to
essayer de	to try to	regretter de	to be sorry to

4   There are expressions with avoir which are followed by de + the infinitive.

Example: J'ai envie de manger
        (I wish to eat)

These expressions include:

avoir besoin de	to need to	avoir le droit de	to have the right to,
avoir l'intention de	to intend to		to be allowed to
avoir peur de	to be afraid of doing	avoir le temps de	to have time to
	something	avoir envie de	to wish to

5   The preposition pour can also be used to introduce an infinitive.

Examples: Il est allé au café pour boire une bière
        (He went to the café to drink a beer)
        Il est trop jeune pour boire du vin
        (He is too young to drink wine)

6   Similarly, the prepositions sans, avant de and au lieu de can introduce an infinitive.

Examples: Sans hésiter il est parti
        (Without hesitating, he left)
        Avant de partir à la gare il a écrit une lettre
        (Before leaving for the station he wrote a letter)
        Au lieu de travailler, il a joué au flipper
        (Instead of working he played pinball)

7   A perfect infinitive is used after après to express 'after having done something'. The perfect infinitive is formed by using avoir or être as appropriate, plus the verb in question. The usual rules about the agreement of the past participle apply.

Examples: Après être arrivé en France, ils sont allés à Paris
              (After arriving in France they went to Paris)
              Après avoir acheté une pomme, elle l'a mangée
              (After buying an apple she ate it)
              Après s'être rasés, ils se sont habillés
              (After having shaved, they got dressed)

Common errors with infinitives

■   Making the wrong choice of à or de
    Example: Il a fini à lire son journal
    Correct version: Il a fini de lire son journal

■   Mixing up se décider à and décider de. The meaning is the same, but you have to be clear about which one you are using.
    Example: Je me suis décidé de partir
    Correct version: Je me suis décidé à partir

USE OF TENSES WITH DEPUIS

Depuis, meaning since or for, uses different tenses in French than you might expect.

1   If the action is still continuing, the **present** tense is used after depuis.

Example: J'habite à Londres depuis cinq ans
             (I have lived in London for five years (and I still do))

2   If the action lasted for some time, but is now over, the **imperfect** tense is used after depuis.

Example: J'habitais à Londres dupuis cinq ans quand je me suis décidé à quitter la grande
             ville
             (I had been living in London for five years when I decided to leave the big city)

Common error with depuis

■   Using the wrong tenses
    Example: J'ai joué du violon depuis cinq ans
                 (I have played the violin for five years)
    Correct version: Je joue du violon depuis cinq ans

NEGATIVES

There are a number of negatives in French. They have two parts – ne and one other which varies according to meaning.

ne . . . pas	not	ne . . . aucun*	no, not one
ne . . . jamais	never	ne . . . nulle part	nowhere
ne . . . rien	nothing	ne . . . plus	no more, no longer
ne . . . personne	nobody	ne . . . que	only
ne . . . ni . . . ni . . .	neither . . . nor . . . nor . . .		

* Aucun agrees like an adjective

Word order and negatives

1   Generally, the negative forms a 'sandwich' round the verb, the ne going before the verb, with the second part of the negative following it.

Example: Je ne parle pas l'italien
             (I don't speak Italian)

2   In the perfect tense the 'sandwich' is made round the auxiliary verb.

Examples: Je ne suis pas sorti ce matin   Je n'ai pas vu le journal
              (I didn't go out this morning)   (I haven't seen the newspaper)

3   With reflexive verbs the reflexive pronoun is included within the 'sandwich'.

Examples: Je ne me lave pas très souvent   Je ne me suis pas lavé très souvent
              (I don't wash very often)   (I didn't wash very often)

4   If there is a pronoun or pronouns before the verb, they are included inside the 'sandwich'.

Examples: Je ne les regarde pas   Je ne les lui ai pas donnés
              (I don't look at them)   (I didn't give them to him/her)
              Je ne les ai pas regardés
              (I didn't look at them)

Other features of negatives

1   Negatives are usually followed by de, in the same way as 'any' follows negatives in English.

Examples: Je n'ai pas de fromage   Je n'ai pas mangé de fromage
              (I haven't any cheese)   (I haven't eaten any cheese)

2   Aucun, personne and rien can be used as the subject of a sentence. They still require the ne.

Examples: Aucune voiture n'est arrivée   Rien n'est arrivé
              (No car arrived)   (Nothing has happened)
              Personne n'a acheté de gâteau
              (Nobody bought any cake)

3   Jamais, personne and rien can be used on their own in answer to questions.

Examples: Est-ce que tu joues au tennis? Jamais   Qu'est-ce que tu as acheté? Rien
              (Do you play tennis? Never)   (What did you buy? Nothing)
              Qui est là? Personne
              (Who is there? No one)

4   More than one negative can be combined in the following pairs:

— jamais and personne   — plus and personne

Example: Je ne vois jamais personne   *Example*:   Je ne vois plus personne
             (I never see anybody)   (I do not see anybody any more)

— jamais and rien   — plus and rien

Example: Je n'achete jamais rien   *Example*:   Jean ne fait plus rien
             (I never buy anything)   (Jean doesn't do anything

5   All negatives except ne . . . personne come before the infinitive.

Examples: On m'a demandé de **ne plus chanter** au club
              (I have been asked not to sing at the club any more)
              J'ai décidé de **ne jamais acheter** de cigarettes
              (I've decided never to buy any cigarettes)

Ne . . . personne works like this:

Example: J'ai l'intention de **ne voir personne** du collège
             (I do not intend to see anyone from school)

Common errors with negatives

■ Wrong positioning of the two parts of
the negative
   Example: Il n'est venu pas
              (He didn't come)
   Correct version: Il n'est pas venu

■ Missing out the ne. This is understandable,
as it's often skipped over in speech. On
paper, it can't be omitted.
   Example: Il est jamais à l'heure
              (He's never on time)
   Correct version: Il n'est jamais à l'heure

EN + PRESENT PARTICIPLE

The construction en + present participle has two uses:

- to describe two actions which happen more or less at the same time, rendering 'while . . . -ing'.

    Examples: Je me suis cassé la jambe en jouant au hockey
                (I broke my leg (while) playing hockey)
                J'ai lu un roman en traversant la Manche
                (I read a novel while crossing the Channel)

- to explain how something can be done, rendering 'by -ing'.

    Example: En lisant ce livre, vous réussirez à votre examen
                (By reading this book you will pass your exam)

The present participle can only be used when the subject of both verbs is the same. Where it differs, use pendant que + the imperfect tense.

FORMATION OF THE PRESENT PARTICIPLE

For most verbs, take the nous form of the present tense, remove -ons, and add -ant'
Examples: parlons: parlant
             finissons: finissant
             vendons: vendant

There are three exceptions:
    avoir: ayant
    être: étant
    savoir: sachant

COMMON ERRORS WITH EN + PRESENT PARTICIPLE

- Trying to use the construction when there is a change of subject

    Example: Anne-Marie a chanté, Philippe en jouant du piano
    (Anne-Marie sang while Philippe played the piano)
    Correct version: Anne-Marie a chanté pendant que Philippe jouait du piano

- Ignorance of the irregular forms, which are very common

From this point on, verb items are only required at higher level. Check in the Grammar List which are for active, and which for receptive, use.

PLUPERFECT TENSE

USE OF THE PLUPERFECT TENSE

The pluperfect tense is used

- to talk about events in the past which had occurred before other events took place
    Examples: Avant de partir en Amérique, il avait vendu son magasin
                (Before setting off for America he had sold his shop)
                En 1940 le général de Gaulle était venu en Angleterre
                (In 1940 General de Gaulle had come to England)

- in reported (indirect) speech to report things which were originally said in the perfect or imperfect tense
    Examples: 'Il faisait beau ce jour-là' (actual speech)
                ('It was nice that day') (imperfect tense))
                Il a dit qu'il avait fait beau ce jour-là (reported speech)
                (He said (perfect tense) it had been nice that day (pluperfect tense))
                'J'ai acheté des pommes' (actual speech)
                ('I bought some apples') (perfect tense))
                Il a dit qu'il avait acheté des pommes (reported speech)
                (He said (perfect tense) he had bought some apples (pluperfect tense))

FORMATION OF THE PLUPERFECT TENSE

The pluperfect tense is formed in the same way as the perfect tense, except that the **imperfect** tense of the auxiliary verb (avoir or être) is used. The same rules about the agreement of past participles apply, as can be seen in the following examples.

j'avais parlé	nous avions parlé
tu avais parlé	vous aviez parlé
il avait parlé	ils avaient parlé
elle avait parlé	elles avaient parlé
on avait parlé	

j'étais venue(e)	nous étions venu(e)s
tu étais venu(e)	vous étiez venu(e)(s)
il était venu	ils étaient venus
elle était venue	elles étaient venues
on était venu(e)(s)	

je m'étais lavé(e)	nous nous étions lavé(e)s
tu t'étais lavé(e)	vous vous étiez lavé(e)s
il s'était lavé	ils s'étaient lavés
elle s'était lavée	elles s'étaient lavées
on s'était lavé(e)(s)	

If the (e) is in brackets, it is only added if the subject is feminine.

If the (s) is in brackets, it is only added if the subject is plural.

Where an irregular past participle ends in -s, (e.g. assis) no further s is required for the masculine plural agreement.
Example: Les garçons se sont assis

COMMON ERRORS WITH THE PLUPERFECT TENSE

- Using the incorrect form of the past participle, usually caused by not knowing which verbs are irregular. A big help is knowing that

    —all -er verbs except aller are regular
    —no -oir verbs are regular
    —most reflexive verbs are regular

- Using the wrong auxiliary verb
  Example: il avait venu
  Correct version: il était venu

- Failing to make the past participles of verbs which take être agree with the subject. This is particularly common with feminine and/or plural subjects
  Example: Elles étaient allé à Paris
  Correct version: Elles étaient allées à Paris

AGREEMENT OF PAST PARTICIPLE WITH PRECEDING DIRECT OBJECT (PDO)

Verbs which have avoir in the perfect tense do not agree with the subject. (Unlike verbs using être as an auxiliary, which do!) However, where the direct object comes before (precedes) the verb, the past participle of verbs using avoir as an auxiliary **does** agree.

Example 1: J'ai acheté une banane
Comment: no agreement, as no PDO – the direct object comes after the verb.
Example 2: Voici une banane – je l'ai achetée
Comment: 'l' is the direct object, the pronoun for 'une banane'.
            It comes before the verb, so the past participle agrees.
Example 3: Voici les bananes que j'ai achetées
Comment: 'les bananes que' are the direct object and come before the verb, so the past participle has to agree

COMMON ERRORS WITH PDO

■ Failing to notice it and not making the agreement!

VENIR DE + INFINITIVE

This construction renders 'just'. The present tense of venir + de + infinitive is used to mean 'I/you etc. **have** just -ed'.

Examples: Nous venons d'atterrir à l'aéroport de Toulouse
            (We have just landed at Toulouse airport)
            Il vient de partir
            (He has just left)

Similarly, the imperfect tense of venir + de + infinitive is used to mean 'I/you etc. **had** just -ed'.

Examples: Nous venions d'atterrir à l'aéroport de Toulouse
            (We had just landed at Toulouse airport)
            Il venait de partir
            (He had just left)

ETRE EN TRAIN DE + INFINITIVE

This construction renders the English continuous present and continuous past.

Examples: Je suis en train de préparer mon examen
            (I am (in the act of) preparing myself for my exam)
            Vous êtes en train de partir?
            (Are you (in the act of) leaving?)
            J'étais en train de manger
            (I was (in the act of) eating)
            Vous étiez en train de partir?
            (Were you (in the act of) leaving?)

CONDITIONAL

Some forms of the conditional such as je voudrais will be well known to all students of French.

USE OF THE CONDITIONAL

■ as a politer alternative to the present tense when making requests

   Example: Je voudrais une bière, s'il vous plaît
              (I would like a beer, please)
   Contrast: Je veux une bière
              (I want a beer)

■ as a way of expressing what you **would** do **if** something else happened – of expressing conditions

   Example: Si j'étais (imperfect) très riche, je ne travaillerais (conditional) plus
              (If I was very rich, I would not work any more)

FORMATION OF THE CONDITIONAL

The conditional is formed in the same way for all verbs. Take the future stem of the verb and add the imperfect endings. Check the section on the future tense if you are unsure about the future stem. The future and the conditional of the same verb are contrasted below.

Future tense	*Conditional*	*Future tense*	*Conditional*
j'aurai	j'aurais	nous aurons	nous aurions
tu auras	tu aurais	vous aurez	vous auriez
il aura	il aurait	ils auront	ils auraient
elle aura	elle aurait	elles auront	elles auraient
on aura	on aurait		

USE OF TENSES AFTER SI (MEANING 'IF')

The tense used after si are as follows:

1   Si + present tense is followed by the future tense. This is the same as the English.

Example: S'il fait beau, j'irai au parc zoologique
(If the weather's good I'll go to the zoo)

2   Si + imperfect tense is followed by the conditional. This is similar to the English, too.

Example: S'il faisait beau, j'irais au parc zoologique
(If the weather was good I would go to the zoo)

THE PASSIVE

The passive is used in sentences where the subject of the sentence suffers the action of the verb. The French passive is formed by using any tense of être + the past participle. The past participle agrees with the subject.

Examples: Elle a été piquée par une moustique
(She was bitten by a mosquito)
Cette usine a été construite l'année dernière
(The factory was built last year)

Generally, the passive is avoided by

- 'turning the sentence round',
Example: Une moustique l'a piquée
- using 'on' as the subject
Example: On a construit cette usine l'année dernière

English students are strongly recommended not to use the passive – they often get it wrong! (It has been given here for recognition purposes only!)

PRESENT SUBJUNCTIVE

At GCSE level, students will only be required to recognize the subjunctive.

FORMATION OF THE PRESENT SUBJUNCTIVE

The present subjunctive is formed from the ils form of the present tense. Remove the -nt to gain the je form of the subjunctive.

Examples:

parler:	ils parlent	je parle
finir:	ils finissent	je finisse
vendre:	ils vendent	je vende

The endings for the present subjunctive are:

je	-e	nous	-ions
tu	-es	vous	-iez
il	-e	ils	-ent
elle	-e	elles	-ent
on	-e		

Example:

je finisse	nous finissions
tu finisses	vous finissiez
il finisse	ils finissent
elle finisse	elles finissent
on finisse	

IRREGULAR FORMS OF THE SUBJUNCTIVE

The following common verbs have irregular forms:

aller: j'aille, nous allions, ils aillent
avoir: j'aie, il ait, nous ayons, ils aient
être: je sois, il soit, nous soyons, ils soient
faire: je fasse (follows regular pattern)
pouvoir: je puisse (follows regular pattern)
savoir: je sache (follows regular pattern)
vouloir: je veuille, nous voulions, ils veuillent

USE OF THE SUBJUNCTIVE

At GCSE, the following uses may be found in Reading and Listening passages:

1 After il faut que
   Example: Il faut que je vienne
               (I have to come)

2 After: —vouloir que
               —préférer que
               —regretter que
               —il est possible que

   Examples: Tu veux que je fasse la vaisselle?
                (Do you want me to do the washing up?)
                Je préfère que tu y ailles avec lui
                (I prefer you to go there with him)
                Je regrette que ma fille ne soit pas plus forte en anglais
                (I'm sorry my daughter isn't better at English)
                Il est possible qu'ils puissent venir
                (It's possible they are able to come)

PAST HISTORIC

This tense is also known as the passé simple. At GCSE level, students will only be required to recognize the past historic.

USE OF THE PAST HISTORIC

It is an alternative to the perfect tense which is **only** used in formal written French

       —in newspaper articles
       —in stories
       —in novels
       —in history books

It is **not** used in conversation or in letters. The most common form of the past historic is the third person, i.e. il, elle, on, ils and elles.

FORMATION OF THE PAST HISTORIC

-er verbs
Remove the -er from the infinitive and add the following endings:

je	-ai	nous	-âmes
tu	-as	vous	-âtes
il	-a	ils	-èrent
elle	-a	elles	-èrent
on	-a		

Example:

je parlai	nous parlâmes
tu parlas	vous parlâtes
il parla	ils parlèrent
elle parla	elles parlèrent
on parla	

-ir verbs
Remove the -ir from the infinitive and add the following endings:

je	-is	nous	-îmes
tu	-is	vous	-îtes
il	-it	ils	-irent
elle	-it	elles	-irent
on	-it		

Example:

je finis	nous finîmes
tu finis	vous finîtes
il finit	ils finirent
elle finit	elles finirent
on finit	

-re verbs
Remove the -re from the infinitive and add the following endings:

je	-is	nous	-îmes
tu	-is	vous	-îtes
il	-it	ils	-irent
elle	-it	elles	-irent
on	-it		

Example:

je vendis	nous vendîmes
tu vendis	vous vendîtes
il vendit	ils vendirent
elle vendit	elles vendirent
on vendit	

Irregular verbs
Irregular verbs follow two main patterns, and there are some exceptions. There is often a similarity with the past participle, which should help you to spot and understand them.

1   The following group have the same endings as regular -ir and -re verbs, but the first part of the verb is different from the infinitive:

Infinitive	*Past historic*	*Infinitive*	*Past historic*
s'asseoir	il s'assit	mettre	il mit
comprendre	il comprit	naître	il naquit
conduire	il conduisit	prendre	il prit
dire	il dit	rire	il rit
écrire	il écrit	sourire	il sourit
faire	il fit	voir	il vit

Example:

je	vis	nous	vîmes
tu	vis	vous	vîtes
il	vit	ils	virent
elle	vit	elles	virent
on	vit		

2   The second group of verbs, most of which have a past participle ending in -u, take the following endings:

je	-us	nous	-ûmes
tu	-us	vous	-ûtes
il	-ut	ils	-urent
elle	-ut	elles	-urent
on	-ut		

Infinitive	Past historic		Infinitive	Past historic
avoir	il eut		falloir	il fallut
boire	il but		lire	il lut
connaître	il connut		mourir	il mourut
courir	il courut		pouvoir	il put
croire	il crut		recevoir	il reçut
devoir	il dut		savoir	il sut
être	il fut		vivre	il vécut
			vouloir	il voulut

Example:

je fus	nous fûmes
tu fus	vous fûtes
il fut	ils furent
elle fut	elles furent
on fut	

3 Exceptions

Venir and its compounds convenir, devenir, revenir and se souvenir, and tenir and its compounds contenir, obtenir and retenir follow this pattern:

je revins	nous revînmes
tu revins	vous revîntes
il revint	ils revinrent
elle revint	elles revinrent
on revint	

ADJECTIVES

AGREEMENT OF ADJECTIVES

Adjectives change their spelling to agree with the noun they describe. They often have a different spelling for masculine and feminine, and always for the plural. The changes may or may not be heard in speech, but they are always made in writing. Some GCSE Examining Groups have Higher Writing mark schemes which particularly reward good use of adjective agreements.

PATTERNS OF ADJECTIVE AGREEMENT

French adjectives have different patterns for showing agreement.

1 Many adjectives follow this pattern:

Masculine singular	Feminine singular	Masculine plural	Feminine plural
noir	noire	noirs	noires

Others which follow this pattern include: anglais, grand, fort, français, intelligent, interéssant, petit, vert. There are many more. Add them to this list as you come across them.

2 Adjectives which already end in -e (without an accent!) have no different feminine form. They are actually following the same logic as in 1.

Masculine singular	Feminine singular	Masculine plural	Feminine plural
jeune	jeune	jeunes	jeunes

Others which follow this pattern include: bête, célèbre, jaune, mince, orange, propre, rouge, stupide. There are many more. Add them to the list as you come across them.

3 Adjectives which end in -u, -i and -é follow the same logic as in 1, although the extra e in the feminine form does not affect pronunciation.

Masculine singular	Feminine singular	Masculine plural	Feminine plural
bleu	bleue	bleus	bleues
joli	jolie	jolis	jolies
cassé	cassée	cassés	cassées

Others which follow this pattern include: âgé, fatigué, perdu, trouvé. Many of these adjectives are in fact past participles, and they agree like them. There are many more. Add them to the list as you come across them.

4   Adjectives which end in -x follow this pattern:

Masculine singular	Feminine singular	Masculine plural	Feminine plural
joyeux	joyeuse	joyeux	joyeuses

Others which follow this pattern include: délicieux, heureux, malheureux, merveilleux. There are more. Add them to the list as you come across them.

5   Adjectives which end in -er follow this pattern:

Masculine singular	Feminine singular	Masculine plural	Feminine plural
premier	première	premiers	premières

Others which follow this pattern include: cher, dernier, entier.

6   Adjectives which end in -f follow this pattern:

Masculine singular	Feminine singular	Masculine plural	Feminine plural
actif	active	actifs	actives
sportif	sportive	sportifs	sportives
vif	vive	vifs	vives

7   Some adjectives double the last consonant when changing to the feminine form.

Masculine singular	Feminine singular	Masculine plural	Feminine plural
bon	bonne	bons	bonnes

Others which follow this pattern include: ancien, gentil, gras, gros.

8   Many common adjectives are irregular.

Masculine singular	Feminine singular	Masculine plural	Feminine plural
blanc	blanche	blancs	blanches
doux	douce	doux	douces
favori	favorite	favoris	favorites
fou	folle	fous	folles
long	longue	longs	longues
neuf	neuve	neufs	neuves
public	publique	publics	publiques
roux	rousse	roux	rousses
sec	sèche	secs	sèches

9   Three adjectives have extra masculine forms which are used when the adjective is followed by a vowel or a silent h.

Masculine singular	Feminine singular	Masculine plural	Feminine plural
beau or bel	belle	beaux or bels	belles
nouveau or nouvel	nouvelle	nouveaux	nouvelles
vieux or vieil	vieille	vieux or vieils	vieilles

COMMON ERRORS WITH ADJECTIVE AGREEMENT

- Failing to spot the gender of the noun the adjective agrees with and therefore missing the agreement

    Example: J'ai deux pommes énorme
            (I have two enormous apples)
    Correct version: J'ai deux pommes énormes

- Treating an irregular adjective as if it was regular
    Example: J'ai une voiture neufe
            (I have a new car)
    Correct version: J'ai une voiture neuve

POSITION OF ADJECTIVES

1   Adjectives in French, unlike in English, usually follow the noun to which they refer.

   Example: J'ai un pullover noir et un pantalon jaune
                     (I have a black pullover and a yellow pair of trousers)

2   A few common adjectives, however, come before the noun. These are:

beau	haut	mauvais
bon	jeune	petit
gentil	joli	vieux
grand	large	vilain
gros	long	

   Example: C'est un vilain garçon
                     (He's a naughty boy)

3   A few adjectives, including ancien, cher, même, pauvre and propre, change their meaning depending on whether they come before or after the noun.

   Examples: C'est mon ancien professeur   Le pauvre Fred. Il est malade
                       (It's my ex-teacher)   (Poor Fred. He's ill)
                       C'est un professeur ancien   Le Sudan est un pays pauvre
                       (It's an ancient teacher)   (The Sudan is a poor country)

                       C'est ma chère amie   Ma mère a sa propre voiture
                       (It's my dear friend)   (My mother's got her own car)
                       C'est un restaurant cher   Sa voiture est toujours propre
                       (It's an expensive restaurant)   (Her car is always clean)

                       Il porte toujours la même cravate
                       (He always wears the same tie)
                       Il est arrivé le jour même
                       (He arrived that very day)
                       Même mon professeur n'aime pas la grammaire
                       (Even my teacher doesn't like grammar)

COMMON ERRORS WITH THE POSITION OF ADJECTIVES

■ Putting them in the wrong position! It's an easy error to make, as so many common adjectives do come before the noun. However, the list I have given only contains 14 adjectives which always come before the noun, so it ought to be possible to learn them

■ Putting one of those with two meanings in the wrong position and achieving an unintended result
   Example: C'est un pauvre garçon
   Intended meaning: He's a poverty-stricken boy
   Correct version: C'est un garçon pauvre

COMPARATIVE OF ADJECTIVES

To compare one thing with another, add
   —plus (more)
   —moins (less)
   —aussi (as . . . as)
before the adjective, which agrees as usual.

   Examples: Ma mère est plus intelligente que mon père
                       (My mother is more intelligent than my father)
                       Ma mère est moins intelligente que mon père
                       (My mother is less intelligent than my father)
                       Ma mère est aussi intelligente que mon père
                       (My mother is as intelligent as my father)

There are two irregular forms: —bon becomes meilleur
                                                    —mauvais becomes pire

Examples: Cette équipe est meilleure que l'autre
            (This team is better than the other one)
            Cette équipe est pire que l'autre
            (This team is worse than the other one)

COMMON ERRORS WITH COMPARATIVE OF ADJECTIVES

- Failing to make them agree

  Example: Ces garçons sont plus grand que mon frère
            (These boys are taller than my brother)

  Correct version: Ces garçons sont plus grands que mon frère

- Missing the two irregular forms

  Example: Ces vins sont plus bons que les autres
            (These wines are better than the others)

  Correct version: Ces vins sont meilleurs que les autres

SUPERLATIVE OF ADJECTIVES

To say what is the biggest, best, greatest etc., use
  —le plus
  —la plus
  —les plus
+ the adjective.

Examples: Le centre Pompidou est le musée le plus amusant de Paris
            (The Pompidou Centre is the most entertaining museum in Paris)
            La tapisserie à Bayeux est la plus vieille du monde
            (The Bayeux tapestry is the oldest in the world)
            Les Renaults sont les voitures françaises les plus vendues
            (Renaults are the French cars with the highest sales)
The same can be done with le/la/les moins.

Example: Le français est la langue la moins difficile pour moi
           (French is the least difficult language for me)

Once again, there are two irregular forms:

  —bon becomes le meilleur
  —mauvais becomes le pire

Examples: Cette équipe est la meilleure
            (This team is the best)
            Cette équipe est la pire
            (This team is the worst)

ADVERBS

FORMATION OF ADVERBS FROM ADJECTIVES

1 In most cases, -ment is added to the feminine singular form of the adjective, as in the following examples.

Masculine	*Feminine*	*Adverb*
doux	douce	doucement
heureux	heureuse	heureusement
entier	entière	entièrement

2 If the masculine singular form ends in a vowel (usually -e or -i) -ment is added straight onto that, as in the following examples.

Masculine	*Adverb*
vrai	vraiment
difficile	difficilement

3   If the adjective ends in -ant or -ent in the masculine singular form, the adverb follows this pattern:

Masculine   *Adverb*
constant   constamment
évident   évidemment

4   Exceptions which end in -ment

The rules given above have the following common exceptions:

enormément   lentement   profondément
gentiment   precisément

5   Other adverbs are very irregular

Some are adjectives being used as adverbs:
bon   cher   faux   fort

Others are just plain irregular. As these are the most common adverbs, it would be well worth learning this list!

beaucoup   mal   tôt
bien   peu   trop
loin   souvent   vite
longtemps   tard

POSITION OF ADVERBS

The adverb generally goes after the verb (unlike in English – beware!)

Example: Il va souvent au collège
            (He often goes to school)

In the perfect and pluperfect tenses it comes after the auxiliary verb.

Example: Il n'a pas bien dormi
            (He didn't sleep well)

COMMON ERRORS WITH ADVERBS

- Attempting to put a -ment ending on an adverb that doesn't have one

  Example: Il conduisait vitement
              (He was driving quickly)

  Correct version: Il conduisait vite

- Putting the adverb in the wrong place

  Example: Il souvent va au collège
              (He often goes to school)

  Correct version: Il va souvent au collège

COMPARATIVE OF ADVERBS

This operates in much the same way as for adjectives. To compare one thing with another, add
    —plus (more)
    —moins (less)
    —aussi (as . . . as)
before the adverb.

Examples: Ma mère court plus vite que mon père
             (My mother runs faster than my father)
             Ma mère court moins vite que mon père
             (My mother runs less fast than my father)
             Ma mère court aussi vite que mon père
             (My mother runs as fast as my father)

There are two irregular forms:
  —bien becomes mieux
  —mal becomes moins bien

Examples: Cette équipe joue mieux que l'autre
  (This team plays better than the other one)
  Cette équipe joue moins bien que l'autre
  (This team plays worse than the other one)

COMMON ERRORS WITH COMPARATIVE OF ADVERBS

■ Missing the two irregular forms

  Example: Ces garçons chantent plus bien que les autres
    (These boys sing better than the others)
  Correct version: Ces garçons chantent mieux que les autres

■ Confusing mieux and meilleur

  Example: Ces garçons chantent meilleur que les autres)
  Correct version: Ces garçons chantent mieux que les autres

SUPERLATIVE OF ADVERBS

To say what happens the quickest, the least well etc., use le plus + the adverb (regardless of gender)

Example: Annette est arivée le plus vite
  (Annette arrived the quickest)
The same can be done with le moins.

Example: Annette chante le moins bien
  (Annette sings the least well)

Once again, there are two irregular forms:

  —bien becomes le mieux
  —mal becomes le moins bien

Examples: L'équipe galloise a joué le mieux
  (The Welsh team played the best)
  Cette équipe a joué le moins bien
  (This team played worst)

COMMON ERRORS WITH SUPERLATIVES

■ Missing the two irregular forms

  Example: Je vois le plus bien
    (I can see best)
  Correct version: Je vois le mieux

■ Inserting la or les as for an adjective
  Example: L'équipe galloise a joué la mieux
    (The Welsh team played the best)
  Correct version: L'équipe galloise a joué le mieux

NOUNS

GENDER

All nouns in French are either masculine (un, le or l') or feminine (une, la or l'). Knowledge of their gender is particularly well rewarded in GCSE Higher Writing, and it can help with Reading and Listening comprehension, and some aspects of Speaking. With adjective agreements (which depend on a knowledge of the gender of the noun in the first place) and good verb usage, a thorough knowledge of the gender of nouns marks out the very good candidate from the rest.

NUMBER

It is particularly important to take note of whether nouns are singular or plural in order to make sure of adjective agreements and verb forms. Make a habit of it!

PLURALS

Where nouns are plural, most French nouns add an -s, as in English.
Example: une voiture   deux voitures

There are a few groups of nouns which do not do this:

1   Those ending in -s, -x and -z remain unchanged.

    Examples: le fils   les fils
               la voix les voix
               le prix   les prix

2   Those ending in -al change to -aux in the plural.

    Example: le cheval   les chevaux

3   Those ending in -eau, -eu or -ou add an -x in the plural.

    Example: le château les châteaux
              le feu   les feux
              un genou   des genoux

4   Common exceptions include:

le ciel	les cieux	la pomme de terre	les pommes de terre
le mal	les maux	le pneu	les pneus
l'oeil	les yeux	le timbre-poste	les timbres-poste
la petite-fille	les petites-filles	le travail	les travaux
le petit-fils	les petits-fils	le trou	les trous

Note also:

monsieur	messieurs
mademoiselle	mesdemoiselles
madame	mesdames

5   Surnames do not change in the plural in French.

    Example: Nous sommes invités chez les Leclerc
               (We've been invited to the Leclercs)

COMMON ERRORS WITH NOUNS

- Mistakes of gender
   Example: C'est un voiture

   Correct version: C'est une voiture
- Incorrect formation of plurals

   Example: J'ai trois animals à la maison

   Correct version: J'ai trois animaux à la maison

Pronouns take the place of a noun which has been referred to earlier.

PRONOUNS

SUBJECT PRONOUNS

je	I	nous	we
tu	you	vous	you
il	he, it	ils	they
elle	she, it	elles	they
on	one, we, they, you		

USE OF SUBJECT PRONOUNS

Tu is used when talking to **one** person who is
   —a good friend
   —a member of the family or a pet
   —a young person

Vous is used when talking to **two or more** people who are

—good friends
—members of the family or pets
—young people

or to one person who is

—an adult who doesn't fit any of the categories above.

Il and elle can mean 'it' when referring to masculine or feminine nouns.

On has a variety of meanings:

—we
Example: On rentre?
　　　　　　(Shall we go home?)
—one
Example: On est obligé de porter une cravate
　　　　　　(One has to wear a tie)
—you (where the meaning could be rendered more poshly by 'one')
Example: On est obligé de porter une cravate
　　　　　(You have to wear a tie)
—they (where 'they' are unspecified people in authority)
Example: On n'accepte pas de chèques chez Montrichard
　　　　　(They don't accept cheques at Montrichard's)

Ils is used for 'they' where

—all the nouns referred to are masculine
—there is a group of nouns referred to of which one is masculine. (It makes no difference how many feminine ones there are!)

Elles is used for 'they' where all the nouns referred to are feminine.

OBJECT PRONOUNS

DIRECT OBJECT PRONOUNS

me	me	nous	us
te	you	vous	you
le	him, it (masculine)	les	them
la	her, it (feminine)		

INDIRECT OBJECT PRONOUNS

me	to me	nous	to us
te	to you	vous	to you
lui	to him, to her, to it	leur	to them

POSITION OF PRONOUNS

Object pronouns come immediately before the verb or, in the perfect and pluperfect tenses, immediately before the auxiliary.

Example: Je les vois
　　　　　(I see them)
　　　　　Je les ai vus
　　　　　(I have seen them)

In command forms, where the command is straightforward, the object pronouns follow the verb.

Example: Donnez-le-moi!
　　　　　(Give it to me)
　　　　　Note the hyphens!

Where the command is negative, the following pattern applies:

Example: Ne me le donnez pas!
　　　　　(Don't give it to me)

ORDER OF PRONOUNS

The normal order of pronouns can be learned by imagining them as a traditional football or hockey team + a reserve.

Pronouns from each line, starting with the 'forwards', take a position ahead of the line of 'players' below.

Examples: Il nous les a donnés
(He gave them to us)
Vous m'en avez déjà offert
(You have already offered me some)

In straightforward commands, the team is playing a more defensive formation!

Pronouns from each line, starting with the 'forwards', take a position ahead of the line of 'players' below. Note the change of me to moi and te to toi.

Example: Donnez-les-moi!
(Give them to me)
Note the hyphens!

COMMON ERRORS WITH SUBJECT AND OBJECT PRONOUNS

- Failing to recognize that nouns are feminine, and therefore using the wrong subject pronoun for 'it'.

  Example: J'ai acheté une voiture. Il est formidable
  (I have bought a car. It's great)

  Correct version: J'ai acheté une voiture. Elle est formidable

- Getting the pronouns in the wrong order

  Example: Je lui les ai donnés
  (I gave them to him)

  Correct version: Je les lui ai donnés

EMPHATIC PRONOUNS

These are also known as *stressed* or *disjunctive* pronouns.

moi	me, I	nous	us, we
toi	you	vous	you
lui	him, he	eux	them (masculine), they
elle	her, she	elles	them (feminine), they

USE OF EMPHATIC PRONOUNS

1 After prepositions

Examples: chez moi
devant eux
avec nous

2 With c'est and ce sont

Examples: Ah, c'est toi, Maigret!
Ce sont eux

3 To emphasize the subject pronoun

Example: Toi, tu as de la chance
(You are lucky, you are)

4 As a one-word answer to a question

Example: Qui a mangé mon sandwich? – Lui
(Who ate my sandwich? – Him)

5 In comparisons

Example: Napoléon était plus petit que toi
(Napoleon was smaller than you)

6 Combined with -même(s): moi-même (myself), toi-même (yourself) etc. Soi-même (oneself) also exists.

Examples: Vous l'avez vu vous-mêmes
(You saw it yourselves)
On peut faire la lessive soi-même
(One can do the washing oneself)

RELATIVE PRONOUNS

Relative pronouns introduce a clause giving more information about a noun. The correct relative pronoun is determined by its grammatical function within the relative clause.

1 Relative pronoun as the subject of the clause – qui

Examples: La personne qui est arrivée est Canadienne
(The person who has arrived is Canadian)
L'avion qui vole le plus vite s'appelle Concorde
(The plane which flies fastest is called Concorde)

2 Relative pronoun as the object of the clause – que

Clauses of this type will contain a different subject.

Examples: Les personnes que j'aime voir sont importantes pour moi
(The people I like are important to me)
Le travail que je fais est ennuyeux
(The work I am doing is boring)

Note that in the pluperfect and perfect tenses, the past participle will normally agree in this type of clause, as the direct object 'que' precedes the verb (PDO rule).

Example: Les chaussettes que j'ai achetées sont rouges
(The socks that I bought are red)

3 Relative pronoun as the indirect object of the clause – à qui

Example: Voilà l'homme à qui j'ai donné les clés
(There is the man to whom I gave the keys)

4   Relative pronoun expressing 'whose', 'of whom', or 'of which' – dont

Example: Voilà l'homme dont le chien est mort
(There is the man whose dog died)
Regarde la grammaire dont je parle
(Look at the grammar I am talking about)

5   Lequel, laquelle, lesquels and lesquelles are used as relative pronouns after prepositions

Example: Il regardait la voiture derrière laquelle se trouvait le chat
(He was looking at the car behind which was the cat)

COMMON ERRORS WITH RELATIVE PRONOUNS

■ Wrong choice of pronoun, especially between qui and que. This is probably caused by the fact that 'that' can be a relative pronoun in English (either subject or object), and that students don't apply the basic rule that que is only used where there is another subject in the clause.

Example: Voilà la maison qui j'ai vu
(There is the house which I saw)

Correct version: Voilà la maison que j'ai vue

■ Missing out the relative pronoun altogether, as in English.

Example: J'aime la jupe j'ai vue
(I like the skirt I saw)

Correct version: J'aime la jupe que j'ai vue)

INDEFINITE PRONOUNS

There are many of these in French. It's probably best to learn them as vocabulary.

autre
Example: Je n'ai pas vu Jean, mais j'ai vu les autres
(I didn't see John, but I saw the others)

chacun
Example: J'ai beaucoup d'amies. Je les aime chacune
(I've lots of (female) friends. Each one is pleasant)

n'importe can be combined with various other words to mean 'any . . . at all'

Example: n'importe quel(le)   no matter which
n'importe qui   anybody at all
n'importe quoi   anything at all

plusieurs
Example: As-tu des livres d'Astérix? Oui, j'en ai plusieurs
(Have you any Asterix books? Yes, I've got several)

quelqu'un
Example: J'attends quelqu'un
(I am waiting for someone)
Quelques-unes de ces photos sont amusantes
(Some of these photos are entertaining)

tous
Example: Il était aimé de tous
(He was liked by everyone)

tout
Example: Il sait tout
(He knows everything)

tout le monde
Example: Tout le monde est là
(Everyone is here)

Note that tout le monde is singular, despite its meaning!

WORD ORDER

Word order in French is very often similar to that in English. But check the sections on
  —adjectives
  —adverbs
  —negatives
  —pronouns

for various differences.

INVERSION

AFTER DIRECT SPEECH

After direct speech, the subject and verb are inverted. If the verb form ends with a vowel, a -t- is inserted.

Example: 'Je mange' a-t-elle dit
(‘I am eating', she said)
'Nous mangeons' ont-ils dit
(‘We are eating', they said)

AFTER PEUT-ÊTRE

Where peut-être begins a sentence, the subject and verb are inverted.

Example: Peut-être arrivera-t-il ce soir
(Perhaps he'll arrive this evening)

IN CERTAIN SUBORDINATE CLAUSES

In clauses introduced by où the subject and verb are inverted.

Example: Voici le collège où travaille mon cousin
(Here is the school where my cousin works)

NUMBERS AND TIME

CARDINAL NUMBERS

0	zéro	16	seize	70	soixante-dix
¼	un quart	17	dix-sept	71	soixante et onze
⅓	un tiers	18	dix-huit	72	soixante-douze etc.
½	un demi	19	dix-neuf		
⅔	deux tiers	20	vingt	80	quatre-vingts
¾	trois quarts	21	vingt et un	81	quatre-vingt-un
1	un, une	22	vingt-deux etc.	82	quatre-vingt-deux etc.
2	deux				
3	trois	30	trente	90	quatre-vingt-dix
4	quatre	31	trente et un	91	quatre-vingt-onze etc.
5	cinq	32	trente-deux etc.		
6	six			100	cent
7	sept	40	quarante	101	cent un
8	huit	41	quarante et un	102	cent deux etc.
9	neuf	42	quarante-deux etc.		
10	dix			200	deux cents
11	onze	50	cinquante	210	deux cent dix
12	douze	51	cinquante et un		
13	treize	52	cinquante-deux etc.	1,000	mille (mil in dates)
14	quatorze	60	soixante	1,311	mille trois cent onze
15	quinze	61	soixante et un	3,000	trois mille
		62	soixante-deux etc.	1,000,000	un million
				1000,000,000	un milliard

Note the following points:

½ = un demi only in arithmetic. Elsewhere it is une moitié.

(Note, however, that demi can be used as an adjective – e.g. une demi-bouteille, une demi-heure)

For 1, use either un or une, depending on the gender of the object.

There are no hyphens in vingt et un, trente et un etc.

Note the form soixante et onze. Contrast quatre-vingt-onze.

Quatre-vingt-un and quatre-vingt-onze **are** hyphenated.

Mille does not have an *s* in the plural.

Telephone numbers are read out in groups of two or three digits written 546.92.17.

ORDINAL NUMBERS

1st	premier, première (1e)†		12th	douzième (12e)
2nd	deuxième (2e) (second, seconde)*		13th	treizième (13e)
3rd	troisième (3e)		14th	quatorzième (14e)
4th	quatrième (4e)		15th	quinzième (15e)
5th	cinquième (5e)		16th	seizième (16e)
6th	sixième (6e)		17th	dix-septième (17e)
7th	septième (7e)		18th	dix-huitième (18e)
8th	huitième (8e)		19th	dix-neuvième (19e)
9th	neuvième (9e)		20th	vingtième (20e)
10th	dixième (10e)		21st	vingt et unième (21e) etc.
11th	onzième (11e)			

† For 1st use either premier or première, depending on the gender of the object.
* Seconde is used where there is no mention of any other numbers in the same sentence.

Example: Je suis en seconde
          (I am in the '5th year')

TELLING THE TIME

Telling the time may seem an elementary thing to be revising before GCSE. However, it is quite clear that it is over-represented in Listening tests. So you need to be very certain of it.

HOURS

Il est une heure	It's one o'clock
Il est cinq heures	It's five o'clock

QUARTERS AND HALF HOURS

Il est deux heures et quart	It's quarter past two
Il est deux heures et demie	It's half past two
Il est trois heures moins le quart	It's quarter to three

MINUTES PAST AND TO THE HOUR

Il est huit heures dix	It's ten past eight
Il est huit heures moins dix	It's ten to eight

MIDNIGHT AND MIDDAY

Il est minuit	It's midnight
Il est midi	It's midday
Il est midi cinq	It's five past twelve
Il est midi moins dix	It's ten to twelve
Il est midi et demi	It's half past twelve

24-HOUR CLOCK

Il est dix-huit heures	18.00	Il est dix-huit heures quarante-cinq	18.45
Il est dix-huit heures quinze	18.15	Il est dix-huit heures cinquante-neuf	18.59
Il est dix-huit heures trente	18.30	Il est dix-neuf heures deux	19.02

COMMON ERRORS IN TELLING THE TIME

- Confusing et and moins
- Missing out le in moins le quart
- Confusing 12- and 24-hour clocks

DATES

Like times, days and dates are very common in Listening and Reading tests. Make sure you can do them!

DAYS OF THE WEEK

lundi   mardi   mercredi   jeudi   vendredi   samedi   dimanche

Note that they are not written with capital letters!

MONTHS OF THE YEAR

janvier	avril	juillet	octobre
février	mai	août	novembre
mars	juin	septembre	décembre

Note that these don't have capital letters either!

THE YEAR

Given below are possible years of GCSE students' birth and the years in which they sit the exam, for reference.

It will be acceptable to write dates in figures in the Writing tests, so they only need to be known for recognition and for Speaking.

1972	mil neuf cent soixante-douze	1988	mil neuf cent quatre-vingt-huit
	dix-neuf cent soixante-douze		dix-neuf cent quatre-vingt-huit
1973	mil neuf cent soixante-treize	1989	mil neuf cent quatre-vingt-neuf
	dix-neuf cent soixante-treize		dix-neuf cent quatre-vingt-neuf
1974	mil neuf cent soixante-quatorze	1990	mil neuf cent quatre-vingt-dix
	dix-neuf cent soixante-quatorze		dix-neuf cent quatre-vingt-dix
1975	mil neuf cent soixante-quinze	1991	mil neuf cent quatre-vingt-onze
	dix-neuf cent soixante-quinze		dix-neuf cent quatre-vingt-onze
1976	mil neuf cent soixante-seize	1992	mil neuf cent quatre-vingt-douze
	dix-neuf cent soixante-seize		dix-neuf cent quatre-vingt-douze

GIVING THE DATE

Use the following patterns:

Quel jour sommes-nous?	What is the date?
Nous sommes le vingt-neuf février	It's the 29th of February
Quelle est la date?	What is the date?
C'est le vingt-neuf février	It's the 29th of February
le mardi 29 février ⎫	
	Tuesday 29th February
mardi le 29 février ⎭	

CONJUNCTIONS

French has the following common conjunctions which GCSE candidates need to be familiar with:

alors	so, for that reason	mais	but, however
car	for (= because)	ou	or
comme	as	parce que	because
depuis que	since	puisque	since
dès que	as soon as	pendant que	while
donc	therefore, so	quand	when
et	and	si	if
lorsque	when	tandis que	while

Most of these are straightforward in their usage. However, studying the following tips and examples will help to improve your French:

alors   should only be used in the middle of a sentence.

Example: Il avait la grippe, alors il est resté au lit
(He had flu so he stayed in bed)

car	is often confused with pour by non-native speakers. If you could use 'because', then it's OK to use car.

Example: Il était triste car il avait perdu son porte-feuille
(He was sad because he had lost his wallet)

comme	*Example*: Tu peux faire comme tu veux

(You can do as you like)

depuis que	only means 'since' in expressions of time.

Example: Il a commencé à pleuvoir depuis que je suis rentré
(It has begun to rain since I came home)

dès que	*Example*: Dès que je le regarde, il rougit

(As soon as I look at him he reddens)

donc	should only be used in the middle of a sentence.

Example: Il avait la grippe, donc il est resté au lit
(He had flu so he stayed in bed)

et	at the end of a list, there is no comma before the final et.

Example: On nous apporte du cognac, des pipes et du café
(They bring us brandy, pipes and coffee)

lorsque	often refers to the future. When it does, remember that future time requires the future tense in French.

Example: Je t'écrirai lorsque je serai à Londres
(I'll write to you when I am in London)

mais	*Example*: Je suis intelligent, mais il est stupide

(I am intelligent but he is stupid)

ou	*Example*: Je te téléphonerai ou tu me téléphoneras

(I'll phone you or you'll phone me)

parce que	spelt without a hyphen!

Example: Je suis content parce que mon frère m'a donné un cadeau
(I am happy because my brother has given me a present)

puisque	means 'since' as an alternative to because.

Example: Il fait beaucoup de devoirs puisqu'il veut devenir fort en
français
(He does lots of homework because he wishes to be good at
French)

pendant que	means 'while', 'whilst', referring to time.

Example: Pendant qu'il écrivait une lettre, le téléphone a sonné
(While he was writing a letter the telephone rang)

quand	often refers to the future. When it does, remember that future time requires the future tense in French. It's more common than lorsque.

Example: Je t'écrirai quand je serai à Londres.
(I'll write to you when I am in London.)

si	There are special rules governing the tenses after si. Look them up under conditional (page 233).

tandis que	means 'while', 'whilst', contrasting two activities.

Example: Jeanne a fait des économies, tandis que Hélène a tout dépensé
(Jeanne has saved up while Helen has spent everything)

PREPOSITIONS The use of prepositions in French is well rewarded in the accuracy mark scheme used in Higher Writing. This is because there is often no direct, once and for all translation of the English equivalent – the French rendering will vary according to circumstances. In Reading and Listening papers you will have to be aware of the different meanings of various prepositions.

Below are examples of the use of various prepositions, not all of which behave as you might expect. Study and imitation of these will pay dividends!

à	à droite (on the right)
	à bicyclette (by bike)
	au collège (at secondary school)
	à mon avis (in my opinion)
au-dessus de	Ma chambre est au-dessus du salon
	(My bedroom is above the living room)
	Le ballon est passé au-dessus de ma tête
	(The ball passed over my head)
au sujet de	au sujet de la boum (about the party)
avant	avant minuit (before midnight)
	avant d'arriver (before arriving)
dans	dans le placard (in the cupboard)
	On danse dans la rue
	(They dance in the street)
de	la plume de ma tante (my aunt's pen)
	Il était suivi d'un gendarme
	(He was being followed by a policeman)
depuis	J'habite ici depuis deux ans
	(I have been living here for two years)
	En 1985 il habitait là depuis deux ans
	(In 1985 he had been living there for two years)
	Depuis Pâques il n'a rien fait
	(He has done nothing since Easter)
de quoi	De quoi parlez-vous?
	(What are you talking about?
devant	Ils sont devant le café
	(They are in front of the café)
en	Je suis allé à Paris en voiture
	(I went to Paris by car)
entre	Entre nous, c'est un idiot
	(Between you and me, he's a fool)
	Nous sommes entre amis
	(We are among friends)

hors de	hors de danger (out of danger)
jusqu'à	Nous jouerons jusqu'à trois heures
	(We shall play till three o'clock)
le long de	Il courait le long de la rue
	(He was running along the road)
par	J'ai été mordu par un chien
	(I've been bitten by a dog)
	Elles regardaient par la fenêtre
	(They were looking out of the window)
par-dessus	Le chat a sauté par-dessus le mur
	(The cat jumped over the wall)
parmi	Il cherchait quelque chose parmi les rochers
	He was looking for something among the rocks
pendant	J'ai travaillé pendant quatre heures
	(I have worked for four hours)
à peu pres	Je gagne à peu pres cent francs par journée
	(I earn about 100 francs a day)
plus de	J'ai plus de vingt bandes d'Astérix
	(I have over 20 Asterix books)
pour	Nous serons en France pour deux jours
	(We shall be in France for two days)
près de	Assieds-toi près de moi
	(Sit by me)
à propos de	à propos de la boum (about the party)
sous	J'aime me promener sous la neige
	(I like walking when it's snowing)
sur	Le journal était sur le canapé
	(The newspaper was on the sofa)
	Une personne sur cinq porte des lunettes
	(One person in five wears glasses)

INDEX

Accommodation 22
Active use 18
Adjectives 114, 209, 212, 236–9
Adverbs 209, 212, 239–41
Advertisements 140–1, 162–3
Agreement of adjectives 236–8
Agreement 209
Assessment 1–5
Authentic documents 195–8, 201

Basic listening 3, 94–111
Basic reading 3, 126–46
Basic speaking 3, 67–81
Basic writing 3, 168–84
Brochures 141–2, 160–2

Clauses 209
Command forms 225–6
Comparative of adjectives 238–9
Comparative of adverbs 240
Comparatives 209
Conditional 232–3
Conjugation 209
Conjunctions 213, 249–50
Conversation 76–9, 88–90

Days 249
Describing people 29–31
Diary 176–7, 182–3
Documents 195–8, 201

Education and future career 19
Emphatic pronouns 244–5
Examination techniques 6–13

'False friends' 65, 131, 149–50
Food and drink 24–5, 56–60
Form filling 175–6, 182
Formation of adverbs 239
Free time & entertainment 19–20,
    39–41, 73, 78, 90, 129
Friends 79
Future tense 221–2

Gender 241
Geographical surroundings 19, 35–6, 79,
    90
Grades 4–5
Grammar lists 211–3
Grammar 208–51
Guides 141–2, 160–2

Health and welfare 23–4, 51–3
Higher listening 3–4, 112–25
Higher reading 3–4, 147–67
Higher speaking 3–4, 82–93
Higher writing 3–4, 185–207
Holidays 21–2, 45–9, 78
House and home 18, 31–3, 77, 89, 129

IGCSE 5
Imperatives 210
Imperfect tense 219–21
Indefinite pronouns 246
Infinitive 210, 226–8, 232
Instructions 163, 178, 183
Interrogatives 224
Inversion 247
Invitations 143
Irregular verbs 210

Language problems 64–5
Letters 143–4, 155–60, 171–2, 178–80,
    183–4, 188–93, 200
Life at home 19, 33–5
Listening 12–13, 94–125
Lists 172, 180

Magazine articles 144–5, 152–5
Maps 138
Mark schemes 171, 188
Menus 139
Messages 173, 181
Months 249

Narratives 194, 200
Negatives 228–9
Newspaper articles 144–5, 152–5
Notes 173, 181
Nouns 212, 241–2
Number (of nouns) 241
Numbers 213, 247–8

Object pronouns 243
Order of pronouns 244
Ordinal numbers 248
Original, expanding French 194–5, 201

Passive 233
Past historic 234–6
Past participle 210, 231
Perfect tense 217–19
Personal identification, 18, 27–9
Phrases 189–90
Picture composition 200
Pluperfect tense 230–1
Plurals 242
Position of adjectives 238
Position of adverbs 240
Position of pronouns 243
Postcards 173–4, 181–2
Preceding direct object (PDO) 231–2
Prepositions 210, 213, 251
Present participle 210, 230
Present subjunctive 233–4
Pronouns 210–12, 242–6
Public notices 128–31, 136–7

Question forms 224–5

Reading 13, 126–67
Receptive use 18
Reflexive verbs 210, 222–4
'Registers' 114
Relative pronouns 211, 245–6
Reports 194
Rôle plays 69–76, 84–8

School, education and future career 19,
    36–9, 74, 89–90, 129
Services 25, 60–3, 77
Settings 16–66
Shopping 24, 53–6, 71, 74, 130
Social relationships 23, 49–51
Speaking 10–11, 67–93
Stimulus, reply to 177–8, 183
Subject pronouns 242–3
Subjunctive 233–4
Superlative of adjectives 239
Superlative of adverbs 241
Superlatives 211
Syllabus requirements 5

Tenses 165–7, 211
Time 213, 248
Timetables 139–40
Topic areas 16–66
Tourism 21–2, 73, 75
Travel 20–1, 41–5, 130

Verb table 203–7
Verbs 165–7, 203–7, 211–36
Vocabulary 16–66, 97, 114, 128, 149

Weather 26, 63–4
Word order 213, 247
Writing 14, 168–207

Years 249

REVISE GUIDES

G C S E

TO HELP YOU ORGANISE YOUR WORKLOAD

R E V I S I O N

FOR THE COUNTDOWN TO GCSE.

P L A N N E R

LONGMAN

WEEK | DATE | TARGET

4 FOUR

3 THREE

2 TWO

1 ONE

USING THE PLANNER — GET STARTED

▶ Begin on week 12. The reverse side of the planner covers weeks 12 – 5 and this side covers weeks 4 – 1 – the countdown to the exams.

▶ Use a calendar to put dates onto your planner and write in the dates of your exams.

▶ Use the suggestions alongside each week of the planner.

▶ Fill in your targets for each day and try to stick to them. If not, remember to re-schedule for another time.

▶ If you start using the planner less than 12 weeks before your exam try to include the suggestions for those weeks you missed, don't try to catch everything up at once. Spread the tasks fairly evenly over the weeks remaining.

LONGMAN REVISE GUIDES CHECKLIST

Biology
Business Studies
Chemistry
English
English Literature
Mathematics
Physics
World History

Available in August 1988
Art & Design
CDT: Design & Realisation
Economics
German

Also available:
LONGMAN PASS PACKS
(tape and booklet)

Biology
Business Studies
Chemistry
English
English Literature
French
Geography
Home Economics: Food
Mathematics
Physics

✓

GET CONFIDENCE

▶ Have a final read through of all your class notes and coursework.
▶ Read through the summaries you have already made.
▶ Try to reduce these summary notes to a single sheet of A4.
▶ Test yourself to check that you can remember everything on each A4 page.
▶ Go over the practice questions already attempted.
▶ Try to visit the place where the exams are to be held. This will help you to feel more familiar with the setting.

THE DAY BEFORE – GET SET

▶ Read through each A4 summary sheet for your 12 topic areas.
▶ Check that you have all the equipment you need for the exam.
▶ Do something you enjoy in the evening.
▶ Go to bed reasonably early. Tired students rarely give their best.

THE EXAM – GET UP AND GO

▶ Have a good breakfast to give you energy.
▶ Don't panic – everyone else is nervous too.
▶ Remember, the examiners are looking for opportunities to give you marks, not take them away!